38. *Culture, Diaspora, and Modernity in Muslim Writing* edited by Rehana Ahmed, Peter Morey, and Amina Yaqin

Related Titles:
Postcolonial Life-Writing: Culture, Politics, and Self-Representation by Bart Moore-Gilbert

Culture, Diaspora, and Modernity in Muslim Writing

Edited by Rehana Ahmed,
Peter Morey, and Amina Yaqin

 Routledge
Taylor & Francis Group
NEW YORK AND LONDON

First published 2012
by Routledge
711 Third Avenue, New York, NY 10017

Simultaneously published in the UK
by Routledge
2 Park Square, Milton Park, Abingdon, Oxfordshire OX14 4RN

First issued in paperback 2014

Routledge is an imprint of the Taylor & Francis Group, an informa business

Library of Congress Cataloging-in-Publication Data

Culture, diaspora, and modernity in Muslim writing / edited by Rehana Ahmed, Peter Morey, Amina Yaqin.
    p. cm. — (Routledge research in postcolonial literatures ; 38)
    Includes bibliographical references and index.
    1. English fiction—Muslim authors—History and criticism.   2. American fiction—Muslim authors—History and criticism.   3. Islam in literature.   4. Muslims in literature.   5. Muslim authors—Political and social views.   6. Identity (Psychology) in literature.   7. Islam and culture.   8. Muslim diaspora.   9. Islam and literature.   I. Ahmed, Rehana.   II. Morey, Peter.   III. Yaqin, Amina, 1972–
    PR120.M87C85 2012
    823'.9209921297—dc23
    2011033900

ISBN: 978-0-415-89677-1 (hbk)
ISBN: 978-1-138-85158-0 (pbk)

Typeset in Baskerville
by IBT Global.

Contents

PART III
(Mis)reading Muslims

PART IV
Culture, Politics and Religion

Acknowledgments

We would like to thank our respective institutions, Teesside University, University of East London and SOAS, for the various forms of support they have provided for this project. Susheila Nasta, Annabelle Sreberny, Nadje Al-Ali, Tariq Modood, Ziauddin Sardar, Reina Lewis and Emma Tarlo have been good friends to our work at various stages.

The Arts and Humanities Research Council generously provided funding for the Framing Muslims International Research Network and for an Early Career Research Fellowship (Grant Reference: AH/1000577/1). We would like to acknowledge their support, as well as that of the Framing Muslims administrators and technicians, and all the contributors to the many events staged. There are too many names to mention, but we wish to thank in particular the contributors to this volume, whose dedication, flexibility and willingness to meet tight deadlines have made the editorial task much easier.

Thanks should also go to the series editors, Donna Landry and Caroline Rooney, for their initial support for this collection. Likewise, Liz Levine and the editorial team have made the process of compiling and completing the book smooth and painless.

Finally, we would like to thank our families, in particular Sam Hayden, for holding the fort.

Introduction

Rehana Ahmed, Peter Morey
and Amina Yaqin

Muslims and culture are not always seen as synonymous. Muslim communities in modern western societies are often read through the lens of race and politics, filters that frequently cast them as silent objects or a problem to be solved. Literature offers an interesting counterpoint to challenge some of these stereotypical views.

The theme of Muslim writing itself has recently become newsworthy, gaining prominence in the discussions of cultural commentators and in the broadsheets. In early 2009 the *Guardian* published an article on Pakistani fiction in English in their international news section to accompany reports on the political situation in the country. Sitting just above an article on a US missile strike in a tribal area of Pakistan close to the Afghan border, it featured the striking front cover of Mohammed Hanif's debut novel *A Case of Exploding Mangoes* (2008), alongside those of Mohsin Hamid's *The Reluctant Fundamentalist* (2007), Kamila Shamsie's *Burnt Shadows* (2009), Nadeem Aslam's *The Wasted Vigil* (2008) and Daniyal Mueenuddin's collection of short stories *In Other Rooms, Other Wonders* (2009). The article explicitly linked the widespread attention and critical acclaim received by these writers to the turmoil of their country of origin and the global media focus on it, especially in the wake of 9/11 and the 'war on terror'. Compared to their more famous Indian counterparts such as Arundhati Roy and Vikram Seth, they were 'perceived to be producing a grittier and more engaged style of work' which an international readership 'hungry for books about Pakistan' has embraced.[1] *Granta*, a mainstream magazine devoted to publishing new writing with a global outreach, brought out a special issue on Pakistan in 2010 which stands out alongside its provocatively titled publications on 'The F Word', 'Sex', 'Work'. The broader canvas of Muslim writing, indicative of a diversity of ethnic transnational affiliations, has also been given a platform of its own in the form of prizes such as the Muslim Writers Awards—the product of a partnership between Penguin Books, Puffin Books and the Institute of English Studies. Founded in 2006, it has a remit to introduce promising writers from within the Muslim community. The Man Booker Prize has since 2000 shortlisted three Muslim writers, the British Asian Monica Ali in

2003, the Libyan Hisham Matar in 2006 and the Pakistani Mohsin Hamid in 2007. In 2011 the non-Muslim Lebanese novelist Amin Maalouf, whose work engages with Islamic history and culture, was shortlisted for the Man Booker International Prize.[2] In the North American context, Muslim writers have found a platform for their work through associations such as the Islamic Writers Alliance, which nurtures Muslim talent by sponsoring faith-based writing and enabling networking. The success of writers such as Mohsin Hamid and Daniyal Mueenuddin in winning or reaching the shortlists of prestigious American prizes and the establishment of the Arab American Book Award in 2006 indicate a growing responsiveness to Muslim writing. Along with Hamid, writers like Mohja Kahf and Khaled Hosseini are contributing to a new landscape of Muslim American literature.

* * *

The title of this collection, *Culture, Diaspora and Modernity in Muslim Writing*, is partly a necessary staking out of marker posts, an establishment of parameters within which a meaningful unity can be imposed on the works of writers from a host of backgrounds and with a diversity of political and religious perspectives. However, it also identifies some of the key considerations behind the production, consumption and critical analysis of their texts. Culture, diaspora and modernity are themes that many of the writers address—either explicitly or implicitly—but the terms simultaneously describe our contemporary moment and its shaping concerns.

To write of 'culture' in relation to Muslims at the present time is, inevitably, to invoke their silent but nonetheless defining Others, non-Muslims. It is also to enter a debate that can be characterized by a sense of creeping paralysis. Discussion atrophies around the notion that there must be such a thing as *a* singular Muslim culture, something which is often seen as in aggressive competition with other cultures. We would argue that this is wrong on three counts. First, the historical spread of Islam has ensured that localized customs and practices are very different, have deep roots and yet travel (being at the same time crucially transformed) with the spread of Muslim populations around the world—a process that has gone on since the establishment of the religion in the seventh century of the Christian era, but which has received added impetus from colonization and, subsequently, decolonization. Second, this discourse also contains the veiled imputation that the same homogeneous 'Muslim culture' challenges the internal coherence of an equally monolithic 'West', something which is nothing more than ahistorical wish-fulfilment on the part of purists and ideologues on both 'sides'.[3] Third, there is the danger of understanding culture as something fixed and static, thereafter looking for nugatory examples that are characteristic or 'authentic'. In a sense, this is the most insidious danger of all as the search for authenticity can seduce even the most well-meaning liberals and Islamophiles. Culture becomes fit only for the museum or the laboratory, rather than the logic of practices and the result of evolving lived experience that it must inevitably be in reality. Static modes of understanding culture owe much to European nationalism and the colonial project. Since 9/11 the idea of Islamic civilization and culture has been stripped of its complexities, with debates over everything from foreign policy to the politics of dress becoming infected by the notion that the antithetical formations of Islam and the West are involved in a civilizational zero sum game in which no quarter can be given. Yet it is less the case that pristine cultures—in the sense of shared values, as embodied in language, religion, custom and ethnicity—have been challenged by postcolonial population movements around the world, more that the longer history of global interconnectedness has resurfaced again in the modern age. The writers considered in our volume map the results of such connections while also exploring the tensions, compromises, acceptance and rejection that colour experience from a Muslim perspective. It goes without saying that, just as their own relationship to Islam and Muslim identity is complicated, frequently uneasy and occasionally downright antagonistic, the work discussed here is similarly conflicted and marked by the striations of voice, character and context.

When it comes to the notion of 'Muslim writing' a similar semantic ambiguity presents itself. Is Muslim writing to be understood as the preserve of those authors self-identifying as Muslim, or those for whom the rituals and inner-promptings of faith are at the heart of their sense of identity? The current collection certainly presents examples of novelistic characters for whom religion, or its rediscovery, is at the core of their being—one thinks of the female protagonists in Leila Aboulela's fiction, or of Ali's *Brick Lane* (2003) where Islam is, for the protagonist Nazneen, a quiet source of guidance and sustenance. In her contribution to this volume, Lindsey Moore explores two very different Bildungsromane by Arab Muslim women writers: Adhaf Soueif's 1992 *In the Eye of the Sun*, situated between Egypt and Britain, and Leila Aboulela's 2005 *Minaret*, based in Sudan and Britain. In doing so, the essay elucidates the various ways that Islam signifies for Arab women both in their countries of origin and as migrants in Britain, and how religion interacts with gender as well as national and transnational identifications in constructions of the self. Crucially it explores the extent to which these Arab Muslim coming-of-age narratives articulate feminist perspectives, and highlights the complexity of defining feminism in the postcolonial spaces that they bring into focus. The lack of teleological progression in these fragmented narratives—which move backwards and forwards in time as well as across different spaces—is further suggestive of the complexity of Arab Muslim women's self-production and more generally of the conflictual relationship between gender, place and cultural politics. By bringing into dialogue two novels published thirteen years apart, which together span almost four decades, Moore is also able to chart a more general shift in modes of identification from Arab to Muslim. As she indicates, especially in the wake of 9/11 Muslim women across the globe are increasingly finding ways of empowering themselves through their faith.

Gender has historically been at the forefront of Muslim identification in the West and Muslim women writers often articulate both the anthropology of gender positions in the societies they have grown up in and an individual politics of representation. In this volume, Ruvani Ranasinha analyses the fiction and non-fiction of the cosmopolitan Pakistani writer Kamila Shamsie. She argues that Shamsie's writing presents a liberal view of gender which incorporates 'a belief in the superiority of western secular gender norms' but shies away from a narrative of 'western intervention in non-western cultures on the grounds of gender equality'. Shamsie's novel *Broken Verses* offers comparative representations of Islam in Pakistan as both 'inherently patriarchal' and as a 'misogynist deployment' of religion by the state to control its women. Ranasinha suggests that there is a blurring of the normative boundaries between the secular and the sacred through the representation of a pioneering secular Pakistani feminism that has to subsequently contend with a younger generation who look for comfort in the rituals of the religious and cultural practices of Islam. She concludes that Shamsie's writing can be understood in the context of wider debates surrounding Muslim women, affiliating itself to the work of Muslim feminists such as Sara Ahmed and Leila Ahmed and disavowing the notion that 'repressive roles are inherent to Islamic culture and Islam' with nuanced characterizations and a spiritual understanding of Islam.

Yet, equally, cannot Muslim writing be understood also as being produced by authors hailing from a Muslim cultural background, for whom God and faith may have receded entirely from their sense of themselves and their affiliations in the world? Hanif Kureishi and Salman Rushdie are perhaps the most famous exemplars of this latter type. Yet between them and Aboulela lie a range of positions combining faith and doubt, materialism and spirituality, individualism and community, in ways that undermine the distinct binaries into which those terms usually resolve themselves. In her essay, Claire Chambers examines a novel charting one such example of complex identity formation: Robin Yassin-Kassab's *The Road from Damascus* (2008). Chambers explores the overlaps and interplay between what otherwise seem antithetical positions through the main character, Sami. The novel reveals identity to be something negotiated and constantly 'in process', and where the secular and the sacred are always already mixed. Its intertextuality embraces ironic sideswipes at contemporary celebrity writers who have a troubled relationship with Islam, like Salman Rushdie. Yet it also notes those ancient texts that 'cross-fertilize' the Islamic and Judeo-Christian traditions, such as the *Epic of Gilgamesh* and the Noah/Nur stories found in both Bible and Quran. Sami must navigate his way through these traditions and worldviews arriving, in the end, at what Chambers calls a 'conditional, inclusive spirituality'—an appropriate if provisional conclusion to his own critical journey through the range of available positions.

Given this sense that Muslim and non-Muslim texts are mutually shaping and cannot be sealed off from one another, we have chosen to include writing *about* Muslims from an external perspective in our volume. This is also because, in recent years, the 'view from outside', whether sympathetic or hostile, has served to fix and establish a way of seeing—one might almost call it a structure of feeling about—Muslims in the West, that other depictions have been forced to answer. Such representations can be seen to serve certain ideological agendas, as do those well-meaning exposés of the repressions enacted by nominally Muslim nation-states on their citizens that appeared after 9/11. Taken together they too define the territory for much Muslim-identified writing and so have earned their place in the story.

* * *

The diversity of worldviews embodied in writing from Muslim cultural backgrounds belies those suggestions of a narrow monoculture uncomfortable with personal expression or questioning, which have circulated over the last few years. The authors and texts studied by contributors to this book represent a vast array of experiences and geographical locations. As might be expected, they reveal a rich inheritance that the writers constantly interrogate, sometimes coming to an acceptance of their Muslim legacy, and sometimes rejecting it. The modern world decisively shapes these contemporary fictions, even when they are set in the past or claim a historical sweep. One thinks, too, of authors and texts not included here, from Tariq Ali, with his *Islam Quintet* (1992–2010), or Naguib Mahfouz, whose dissections of Cairo society marry existential concerns with reflections on the co-presence of modernity and religion, to Abdulrazak Gurnah with his novels exploring identity which also map the presence of Islam on the eastern seaboard of Africa.

The upsurge of forms of politicized Islam is, of course, what has caused most of the disquiet in the West over the past decade or so. One might not expect politicians and the media to be particularly subtle or culturally informed when responding to fast-moving global crises—although one might hope they would take time to educate themselves more effectively before making far-reaching public pronouncements. The schism between those two supposed monoliths, 'Islam' and 'The West', diagnosed by many after the 9/11 terror attacks, came to be shaped by such utterances, performatively creating a so-called 'clash of civilizations' between parts of the world, and populations, whose interaction has been mutually shaping for centuries. It was common to find political leaders pronouncing on Islam's backwardness and its need to enter 'the modern world'.[4] Of course, the simplification involved in such rhetoric quickly runs up against the reality of diverse populations within the major cities of the modern multicultural western world, and the spotlight is turned on allegedly recalcitrant Muslim communities 'at home'.

Anshuman Mondal's essay in this volume explores some of the consequences of splitting Muslim culture and thinking from what is perceived as an always-secular modernity. In his account of Ed Husain's hugely successful memoir of the roads to and from radicalization, *The Islamist* (2007), Mondal picks up on the monolithic and static depiction of almost all Muslim political organizations as a threat to secular western societies. The essay pays particular attention to the book's distinctive narrative structure, use of repeated tropes and phrases, conflations and simplifications in the treatment of political Islam. Being a retrospective narrative, told by an older, wiser Husain, *The Islamist* purports to give a more synoptic and informed perspective. Nevertheless, a whole variety of, in fact, very different Muslim political bodies are tarred with the brush of extremism, or at the very least extremist sympathies. At the same time, Mondal shows how, rather than being a pre-modern throwback, 'Islamisms (in the plural) are decisively shaped by their encounter with the modern state', something Husain downplays.

As a literary critic, Mondal is interested in the way the narrative holds its authority for us, as readers. Indeed, throughout his piece attention is paid to the distinctive formal qualities of *The Islamist* as a tripartite narrative shaped by a highly significant fall-redemption model. This insight explains much: not least, perhaps, the ease with which it was assimilated into the canon of intercultural confession. *The Islamist* persuades the western reader in part because it can be 'placed'; it has the familiar shape of a literary confessional, as well as offering insights into the strange world of radical Islam. In view of this, the gap that is identified between the narrating and experiencing selves is central to the truth claims made by and for the text: the sense that the 'first-hand experience' of Husain, as narrated in the book, somehow also guarantees its objectivity and therefore truth. (Perhaps this tells us something about the British press and public's *desire* to have 'one true book' to open up the phenomenon of radicalization. There certainly seems to have been much projection of this kind in the book's reception.)

So perhaps it is not too fanciful to identify a distinct strain of exoticism colouring western readings of the Muslim Other: a frisson of fear caused by difference, but also comfort in the idea that 'they' can be made more like 'us'. This neo-Orientalist perspective strives for the establishment of a corpus of images, standing for true knowledge, which will both legitimize repressive legislation and surveillance of Muslims 'at home', and facilitate interventionist military projects overseas. In the months after 9/11, literature became one conduit for the production and reception of such images, through the publication of several texts—some of them claiming non-fictional status—'exposing' life under repressive Islamic regimes in those parts of the world from which a renewed threat was felt to emanate. 2003, in particular, was a vintage year for such Muslim misery memoirs with the appearance of Azar Nafisi's *Reading Lolita in Tehran*, Åsne Seierstad's *The Bookseller of Kabul* and Khaled Hosseini's *The Kite Runner*. In her reading of the latter novel, Kristy Butler focuses on the text itself, and on its reception and subsequent pedagogical use. She shows the ideological interpellation of many American readers, as evidenced in reviews posted on the Amazon website, providing an interesting snapshot of how a certain totalizing post-9/11 view of Muslims becomes framed. Muslims are a problem and Muslim nations are perennially crisis-ridden and in need of our help. Butler is alert to the way in which Afghanistan is conjured through the familiar terms and tropes of the West. This tendency is prevalent even in the classrooms of notionally liberal educators who used the novel to promote a more informed understanding of topical issues among their students. A meaningful engagement with the Other culture is diminished by an approach via the paradigms of the already-read: catharsis, militarism, valour and the extinction of an extremist enemy who looks very like those other enemies—the Nazis—over whom liberal democracy has triumphed on its way to global hegemony.

The production and reception of works like *The Kite Runner* point to a broader trend. In recent years the literary landscape has been marked by a number of efforts to assimilate and familiarize the supposed alien culture and practices of Islam and Muslims. In this context, several of the writers examined in this book have taken on—or had thrust upon them—the mantle of spokesperson for parts of the Muslim world. In Britain, authors such as Salman Rushdie, Kamila Shamsie and Mohsin Hamid regularly find themselves invited to contribute to newspaper opinion columns and media discussion programmes, in part to bring their Muslim cultural capital to bear, refuting stereotypes and contextualizing debates. (This takes place even in those cases, such as that of Rushdie, where the author has either deliberately distanced himself from, or is openly hostile to, Islam in its collective political guises.) Shamsie, for example, took it upon herself to refute the shrill Islamophobic pronouncements of Martin Amis, while also asking why more members of the western literary establishment did not take the trouble to refute his outburst. In her brief commentary piece she rejected the insistence on Muslims positioning themselves in opposition to acts of terrorism, as if failure to do so indicated complicity. Her own reluctant intervention is marked by an awareness of the inevitable danger of being pigeonholed as a representative Muslim spokesperson.[5] Such 'Muslim representatives' sometimes run the risk of being employed in tokenistic ways by a predominantly non-Muslim media in search of 'authentic' voices who will nevertheless find themselves locked into predetermined agendas in which Muslims are always being forced to respond to the charge of disloyalty or threat.[6] Even so, when the chasm of cross-cultural misunderstanding is as wide as it undoubtedly still is, all efforts to bridge it might be welcome, even if the results are questionable or artistically compromised.

One instance of a flawed attempt to imagine across cultures comes in John Updike's *Terrorist*, published in 2006. Anna Hartnell's analysis here concentrates on the construction of the Muslim subject—in the form of the young would-be suicide bomber Ahmad—in a high-profile novel that attempts to 'deal' with the issue of Islamist terrorism. Hartnell notes Updike's attempts to domesticate aspects of Ahmad's unfamiliar religious motivations, such as the turn to violent jihad. She identifies an implicit prioritizing of Christian models of religiosity and the separation of sacred and secular spheres in post-Enlightenment society. While attempting to situate Ahmad's political acts within religious ideology, Updike fails to consider the communal aspects of religion—especially Islam—that actually make it resistant to the kind of critique he is undertaking. Hartnell points out how Ahmad's radicalization takes place in isolation, with little reference to the politics of the Islamic world, cited as a decisive factor by most commentators and by jihadist militants themselves. Perhaps this is another example of Updike's preference for the isolatable individualism of the Protestant mind. Ultimately, Updike's *Terrorist* works within Orientalist representational conventions even while sympathizing with parts of Ahmad's critique of a soulless, materialistic and sex-obsessed contemporary America. Updike's 'view from the outside', as far as Muslim writing is concerned, offers an important snapshot of some of the besetting tendencies in modern representation of cultural difference around Muslims.

Updike's vision is one that separates the private sphere of religious faith from the public realm of collective activity in ways that mimic the wider prejudices of the society of which he is a part. That a self-declaredly transnational author such as Salman Rushdie essentially shares this view might set us thinking about whether the divide between cultures—or at least between the mindsets of their educated elites—is actually as stark as is sometimes claimed. Rushdie was, famously, once the poster boy of postcolonial literature, in the days when a distinctive sensibility, political orientation and set of aesthetic strategies were being carved out of the experiences of post-Independence migration and metropolitan racism respectively. Yet one might claim that his class position, education at Rugby and Oxford, 'freak fair skin'[7] and secular leanings always made him a somewhat unlikely spokesperson for Britain's predominantly working-class and—in some cases—devout immigrant population. His fall from this rather precarious height came with the publication of his novel, *The Satanic Verses*, in 1988 and the resulting fatwa by Iran's Ayatollah Khomeini. Looking at a Rushdie novel from almost twenty years later, *Shalimar the Clown* (2005), Peter Morey identifies an intensified aversion to public religion in the novel's pastoral idyll of a tolerant Kashmir ruined and appropriated by the forces of nationalist and fundamentalist aggression. The rise of communalist tension is played out in a tale of doomed Hindu-Muslim love, betrayal and the quest for revenge. However, Morey claims that the political dimensions of the struggle these characters are allegorically supposed to represent are, to a large extent, eclipsed by an emphasis on personal relations and experiences of loss which take on an almost pathological insistence. He suggests that the book becomes increasingly characterized by melancholic tropes which bleed across from the world of the characters and their relationships, in the end saturating the narrative as a whole and preventing any effective working through of the political causes of loss. This is of a piece with the book's take on politicized religion, whose representatives are depicted as fanatical and irredeemable caricatures: a portrayal in keeping with Rushdie's increasingly hostile and dismissive attitude to religious identity politics.

* * *

Such well-travelled writers as Rushdie, Shamsie, Hamid and others indicate the importance of the spread of postcolonial networks throughout the world. If there is an important difference to be observed between those much-feted (and reviled) cosmopolitan intellectuals jetting around the world to their conferences and book launches, and the grounded quotidian experiences of economic migrants, refugees and others, their respective experiences are nonetheless conditioned by the possibility of a Muslim diaspora. This is a concept which lies at the heart of Muslim writing whatever intellectual perspective it comes from, cultural, faith-based or secular. The notion of exile common to most diasporas is historically a formative experience in shaping Muslim identity. In the Islamic context, the Prophet Muhammad's migration from Mecca to Medina that marks the beginning of the Hegiran calendar is a period during which the model of Islamic citizenship is laid down with specific guidelines for migrants and their host community. Ziauddin Sardar argues that in the Quran migration is seen as a 'beneficial exercise'.[8] It is not something to be understood purely as an escape from oppression but is also necessary for the pursuit of knowledge. More generally migrants and refugees are looked at favourably as those who add to the economy and intellectual capital of the new home. Thus travel and exile have been, from the start, essential components of the Muslim sense of self.

Diasporas, as they have been studied in the humanities and social sciences, incorporate refugees, migrants, guest workers, expatriates, the exiled and self-exiled. When diasporas come together, they tend to do so less out of a natural affiliation than by force of circumstance. These groupings can be transnational, or as James Clifford has suggested, a political means to define a distinctive local community 'in historical contexts of displacement'.[9] Diasporas have specific histories of arrival and settlement which if ignored can lead to a simplistic understanding of differences based on geographical isolation.[10] For Muslim diasporas, whether in the US or the UK, there is a complexity in the formation of identities which can be seen to structure themselves in distinctive ways. Haideh Moghissi, Saeed Rahnema and Mark Goodman define the key factors in diasporic formations to be inclusive of an 'internal configuration' that incorporates 'ethnicity, nationalism, culture, language, sectarian and class diversities' as well as the significant 'external characteristics' of the host society such as 'immigration and settlement policies, political system, social, economic and cultural development'.[11] They suggest that when these internal and external factors come into play they can lead to a polarization of positions resulting in an 'us' and 'them' divide between the western and the Muslim worlds. This in turns leads to a heightened sense of separate Muslim identity in the diaspora, which need not always be a reflection of an increasing turn to fundamentalist religious belief, but instead is part of a reaction toward a negative scapegoating of Muslim individuals and societies. Commenting on the current situation, Olivier Roy speaks of a new globalized Islam in which the Muslim believers' relationship to Islam is 'reshaped by globalisation, westernisation and the impact of living as a minority'.[12] In short, the Muslim diaspora is recognized as articulating a minority discourse underwritten by the historical experience of an Islamic civilization and defined around ethnic identities.

While a substantial Muslim diaspora in Britain began to form in the second half of the twentieth century, especially with the post-Independence flow of migrants from the Indian subcontinent, Muslims from all walks of life had been arriving in Britain from its former colonies and protected territories for centuries. Humayun Ansari cites the mid-nineteenth century as the point when Muslims began to establish more settled communities in parts of Britain, including east London, Liverpool, Manchester, South Shields and Cardiff.[13] Many came as seamen, working on the ships that traded across the expanding British Empire, but others, from more privileged backgrounds, came as merchants, students or professionals. The communities they formed were diverse: in South Shields the majority were Yemeni and Somali sailors, whereas South Asians were more numerous in London, and West Africans in Liverpool.[14] These early migrants worked hard to establish their religious practices and sustain their cultural identities in Britain, with the foundation of places of worship in Cardiff in 1860, Woking in 1889 and Liverpool in 1891.[15] In the years following the Second World War and decolonization, Britain's Muslim community expanded and became increasingly visible through its continued establishment of communities, especially in industrial centres such as London, Birmingham, Leeds and Bradford, Oldham, Cardiff and Glasgow. News of the 1962 Commonwealth Immigrants Act, which was to remove the right of entry into Britain for Commonwealth citizens, saw an influx of migrants from the Indian subcontinent, many of them Muslim. The predominantly male population began to diversify as their wives and families joined them. While the majority are South Asians, Britain's Muslim population today traces its origins to a wide range of nations in Europe, Africa and the Middle East. Since 9/11 a more self-conscious British Muslim identity has emerged, eclipsing broader British Asian categorizations.

The earliest Muslim settlers in North America were brought as slaves in the eighteenth and nineteenth centuries from those parts of western and central Africa with existing Muslim populations—although a paucity of records makes it hard to establish what portion of the estimated ten million Africans uprooted during the era of slavery may have been Muslim. It is with the arrival of significant numbers of Muslim migrants from Syria, Yemen and other Arab countries to work in industrial cities such as Chicago, that one can talk of the beginning of a Muslim American identity. In particular, a large

Arab community gathered in the inter-war years in Dearborn, Michigan, to take advantage of employment opportunities in the automobile industry that was developing around Detroit.[16] Around the same time, Elijah Muhammad was developing the fledgling Nation of Islam, with its colour-conscious local adaptation of Islam, which was to play such a significant role in the Civil Rights era. The rise of interest in Islam in the 1960s can be seen as part of that spirit of social and cultural pluralism that marked the decade, as well as being intimately linked to African American self-assertion. Charismatic figures such as Malcolm X and Muhammad Ali gave glamour and a political edge to Islam in the United States, long before it came to be associated with anti-Americanism and terror. The pressure under which the Muslim communities in America have come since 9/11 ought not to be underestimated, with harassment and deportations being followed by controversies over the so-called Ground Zero Mosque and the Congressional hearings on radicalization.[17] Nonetheless, a new generation of Muslim Americans are asserting the right, in culture and the arts as well as politics, to have their voices heard.

In this volume, Salah D. Hassan argues that for all Muslims migration is an infinite phenomenon involving different cultural contexts and geographical locations. Hassan traces the shift in American attitudes toward Islam from a liberal nineteenth-century valuation of a cosmopolitan Andalusian model, through twentieth-century political formations such as the Nation of Islam, to the twenty-first-century election to the Presidency of Barack Hussein Obama. Hassan argues that despite being a small minority, Muslims in the US have, since 9/11, been at the centre of media attention and securitizing policies. According to Hassan, Muslim American is used as a category to encompass the dual ethnicities of Arab American, Iranian American, Pakistani American. It is also inclusive of those who have converted to Islam but do not have an ethnic connection to it. Hassan offers a close reading of the Muslim convert Michael Mohammad Knight's *The Taqwacores*, a novel about Muslim punk rock that exemplifies the formation of a new sub-culture which is not stereotypical and offers fresh identifications for young Muslim Americans, white or non-white. Knight thus complicates the ethno-racial picture of the Muslim American and adds a new voice to the recorded history of Muslim migrations in the US.

Michael Mohammad Knight's work suggests a combative reassertion of Muslim youth identity in the face of antagonism and caricature. Of course, in the years since 2001 the principle spectre lurking behind the representation of Muslim cultural narratives is that of terrorism. Stephen Morton's essay examines how post-9/11 Muslim writing has grappled with the 'pernicious stereotypes' from a global war on terrorism that has exclusively targeted Muslims. Morton brings together both Muslim and non-Muslim writers, to offer a critique of an aesthetics of liberalism which tends to pathologize the Muslim subject, as found in Martin Amis's short story 'The Last Days of Muhammad Atta' and Ian McEwan's *Saturday* (2005). On the other hand,

Philip Roth's *The Plot Against America* (2004) complicates this picture with an allegorical critique of the Bush administration's authoritarian interventions and curtailment of civil liberties for Muslim citizens. From a Muslim perspective Kamila Shamsie's *Burnt Shadows* is seen to provide an 'important historical counterpoint' to longstanding Orientalist tropes, while Morton sees neoliberal globalization as being at the heart of Mohsin Hamid's *The Reluctant Fundamentalist* and Salman Rushdie's *Shalimar the Clown*. Morton concludes with a forceful reading of Moazzam Begg's 2006 retelling of his imprisonments in Kandahar and Guantánamo Bay.

* * *

Begg's text, like that of Ed Husain, is an example of how Muslim writers have used the autobiography form to give shape to their sense of personal development in troubled political times. As they give voice and subjectivity to a minority group that is frequently objectified and marginalized, such 'insider' accounts of 'Muslimness' will inevitably be received as representative. Freighted with this burden, they have a powerful potential both to challenge the stereotyping perceptions of Muslims that pervade twenty-first-century British culture and, conversely, to reinforce them. Rehana Ahmed offers a reading of two recent examples of these memoirs by British journalists of Pakistani heritage: Sarfraz Manzoor's 2007 *Greetings from Bury Park: Race, Religion, Rock 'n' Roll* and Yasmin Hai's 2008 *The Making of Mr Hai's Daughter: Becoming British*. Her analysis investigates the ways in which the tensions between an individual subjectivity and a communitarian adherence to culture and faith manifest themselves in these coming-of-age narratives, as they negotiate between the pull of a liberal individualist lifestyle and that of family, community and mosque, between speaking as an 'I' and on behalf of a collective. The autobiographical subjects, who straddle categories of class as well as culture and religion, productively complicate homogenizing constructions of the 'British Muslim'. Yet their conformity to a model of the 'good', secular British Muslim, who has, to an extent, broken free from the prescriptions of his or her cultural background, makes these memoirs susceptible to co-option into discourses which valorize secular modes of being Muslim while stigmatizing other, more assertive Islamic identities.

The politics of representation can also affect the way in which Muslim fiction is received, as has been evident in the case of Monica Ali's *Brick Lane*. Sara Upstone extricates this highly successful yet controversial novel from a web of criticisms that has cast it as an inauthentic or 'failed' representation of the Tower Hamlets Bangladeshi Muslim community. While literary criticism long ago rejected a static correlation between realism and reality, this notion was nevertheless applied to *Brick Lane* by reviewers and literary critics as well as by local Bangladeshi protestors in their reception of the novel. Whereas the latter demonstrated against the novel for its perceived 'misrepresentation' of their community, the former criticized it especially for its overly optimistic, unrealistic ending that fails to convey accurately the experiences of the minority community it represents. Upstone counters such criticisms, not by attempting to detach the novel from the social context with which it clearly engages, but by rethinking its relationship to multicultural politics. She argues that *Brick Lane* in fact articulates a 'utopian realism' that engages with existing, post-9/11 social realities for British Muslims but simultaneously gestures beyond these to a renewed and expanded multiculturalism that can crucially encompass religiosity as well as secularism. Thus, Upstone highlights the powerful 'resistive potential' of realist fiction to enable us to think outside norms and prescriptions to a future where British Muslims can experience a full and equal citizenship.

The protest against Ali's novel, led by the Greater Sylhet Development and Welfare Council, differed from its best known antecedent, the 1989 Bradford-based demonstrations against Rushdie's *The Satanic Verses*, in so far as it focused not on the denigration of a religion but rather on the perceived distortion and stereotyping of a community.[18] Yet both protests were grounded in the marginalization and vulnerabilities of the communities in question; while Rushdie's detractors were mobilizing in the context of decades of racism and unemployment,[19] Ali's were speaking from one of the most disadvantaged communities in Britain against the background of the increased Islamophobia that followed the 9/11 attacks. To highlight this material context is not to advocate censorship but to deconstruct reductive representations of literary controversies involving minority groups in terms of a clash between religious or cultural dogma and censorship, on the one hand, and secular creative freedom on the other. Writers of Muslim heritage, such as Kureishi and Rushdie, have been understandably vociferous in their defence of the freedom of expression and their refusal to assume a burden of representation—one that has only become more pressing as Muslims have been put increasingly in the spotlight.[20] Yet a liberal construction of these issues in term of a censorship–free speech dichotomy is premised on a highly problematic perception of the right to free speech as absolute and inviolable, regardless of the social consequences, and obscures the asymmetries of the public domain in which some people are more free and able to speak and be heard than others. The political effect, moreover, is an entrenchment of stereotypes of Muslim (and more broadly Asian) minorities as retrogressive, intolerant and fundamentalist.

The hostile political and media response to the protests in Britain against Rushdie's novel was not just to do with a liberal objection to the obstruction of freedom of expression, but was also rooted in a deep discomfort with the assertion of a collective religious identity. Current and recent political discourses of multiculturalism have often marginalized British Muslims by privileging a liberal notion of equality as 'individualism and cultural assimilation' rather than as the recognition and support of difference, especially religious difference, in the public sphere.[21] Consequently, practices such as the wearing of the hijab, the building of mosques, the maintenance of tightknit communities of Muslims, requests for more Muslim state schools, as well as protests against creative works, have come under attack from across much of the political spectrum, and demands for Islam to be confined to the private domain are commonplace. In the wake of events and controversies centring on British Muslims, a reluctant tolerance for assertive Muslim cultural identities and practices has waned further, even among the centre-left whose anti-racist credentials have been eroded by an inability to fully accommodate a faith-identified minority group. Tariq Modood cites 2001 as a 'turning point' in this respect, with the summer race riots in the north of England closely followed by the 9/11 attacks in the US.[22] The official reports commissioned in the wake of the riots linked the outbreaks of violence to the so-called separatism of the Muslim communities involved, occluding the various social factors that lead to the formation and maintenance of more discrete communities such as 'white flight' and racism.[23] The then Home Secretary David Blunkett's response was to call for a 'test of allegiance' and to claim that Britain was suffering from an 'excess of cultural diversity', while Kenan Malik, an erstwhile anti-racist spokesperson, claimed that 'multiculturalism has helped to segregate communities far more effectively than racism'.[24]

Multiculturalism is also blamed for social practices that appear to have been imported along with the Muslim migrant community in Britain. They are often seen as a hangover from the claustrophobic and parochial communal structures developed in the country of origin, and are considered to be at odds with normative British culture. In recent years, forced marriage—not always easily distinguished from the non-coercive tradition of arranged marriage—and domestic violence and murder in the name of honour, have joined political radicalization as focal points of media interest and opprobrium. A lack of integration is often blamed for the continuation of certain criminal practices: their perpetuation sometimes being used to imply an ontological difference between Muslim immigrant communities and the wider society around them. In her essay on Nadeem Aslam's 2004 novel *Maps for Lost Lovers*, Amina Yaqin contextualizes the phenomenon of honour killing, which lies at the heart of the novel. She outlines the national and international discourses by which the idea of an almost pathological investment in honour has been pinned onto Muslim societies in particular, and how politicians and the press have used this as ammunition in a more general assault on multiculturalism in Britain. Yaqin reads Aslam's somewhat controversial story of doomed love in a segregated community somewhere in the north of England as a brave attempt to explore the often hidden and mythologized practice of honour-based crime, yet one that is hamstrung both by its own didactic and almost anthropological impulses, and by the contending desire to valorize individual romantic choice against the collective will of a community seen as inherently oppressive. This unresolved tension gives the book its distinctive quality of unsettling ambiguity; it has been read both as an indictment of Muslim backwardness and as pandering to western metropolitan stereotypes.

The rise of what might be called a Muslim identity politics is also explored in Bart Moore-Gilbert's piece on Hanif Kureishi and Mohsin Hamid. This essay suggests that identity and recognition are 'policed' in Kureishi's *The Black Album* (1995) and Hamid's *The Reluctant Fundamentalist*. It sets the novels in an ongoing context within which 9/11 marks a sea change, but where existing trends are essentially accelerated. Moore-Gilbert shows how contemporary social critiques often take insufficient notice of Islam as a form of politicized identity that might arise to challenge the hegemony of liberal capitalism. He also makes the important distinction between an idea of recognition as being conferred and the Frantz Fanon-inspired notion that it must be forcibly taken. In Kureishi's *The Black Album*, these themes appear in the ambiguous playing out of recognition for characters such as Shahid, and form part of the novel's critique of authenticity more generally. Moore-Gilbert identifies a tension between the requirements of group and individual recognition and suggests that Shahid is 'martyred' by the existing dynamics of recognition that vie to position and 'speak for' him. In Hamid's *The Reluctant Fundamentalist*, the protagonist Changez ceases to be an embodiment of Francis Fukuyama's globalized capitalist world order after 9/11 as the demands of racial essentialism and national loyalty take hold. Hamid's text deliberately sidesteps the matter of the 'representability' of Islamic fundamentalism through an implication that, at least for now, the phenomenon may be 'unwriteable' because unrecognizable in western representational terms which still rely heavily on the stereotyping of Muslim subjects.

* * *

As Amin Malak has noted, 'While postcolonialism involves numerous heterogeneous discourses, making it impossible to view the field as uniform, there is a discernible common denominator that indicates a resistance to engage with religion as a key category pertinent to the debate about contemporary neo-colonial reality.'[25] This volume seeks to contribute to developing a critical framework for incorporating religious identity formation into postcolonial literary studies. While our focus here is limited to writing in English, the diverse languages of those Muslim cultures to which the authors are affiliated nevertheless give shape to the form and content of their narratives. The constantly evolving nature of Islam as faith, as a way of life and as a global presence, means that Muslim writing will continue to chart and inform intellectual debates on modernity and culture into the future.

Notes

1. Saeed Shah, 'As Their Country Descends Into Chaos, Pakistani Writers Are Winning Acclaim', *Guardian*, 17 February 2009, 23.

2. Beyond the world of commercial publishing, the Pakistani writer Aamer Hussein, best known for his carefully crafted short stories that deal with themes of nostalgia, exile and loss, has also seen success through an independent publisher specializing in Middle Eastern writing. In 2004, he was elected a Fellow of the Royal Society of Literature.
3. Mahmood Mamdani cites Marshall Hodgson's account of how the notion of 'the West' itself as a category changed throughout history as the boundaries of European power shifted. See Mahmood Mamdani, *Good Muslim, Bad Muslim: America, the Cold War and the Roots of Terror* (New York: Three Leaves Press/ Doubleday, 2005), 29.
4. Matthew Tempest, 'Blair Sees Iraq as "Clash about Civilization"', *Guardian*, 21 March 2006. See also Samuel Huntington, *The Clash of Civilizations and the Remaking of World Order* (New York: Simon and Schuster, 1996).
5. Kamila Shamsie, 'Martin Amis' Views Demand a Response', *Guardian*, 19 November 2007; see also 'Martin Amis interviewed by Ginny Dougary', *Times Magazine*, 9 September 2006.
6. See Peter Morey and Amina Yaqin, *Framing Muslims: Stereotyping and Representation after 9/11* (Cambridge, MA: Harvard University Press, 2011), 79–112.
7. Salman Rushdie, *Imaginary Homelands: Essays and Criticism, 1981–1991* (London: Granta, 1991), 18.
8. Ziauddin Sardar, *Reading the Qur'an: The Contemporary Relevance of the Sacred Text of Islam* (London: Hurst, 2011), 159.
9. James Clifford, 'Diasporas', *Cultural Anthropology* 9.3 (1994): 302–338 (308).
10. Avtar Brah, *Cartographies of Diaspora: Contesting Identities* (London: Routledge, 1996).
11. Haideh Moghissi, Saeed Rahnema and Mark Goodman, *Diaspora by Design: Muslim Immigrants in Canada and Beyond* (University of Toronto Press, 2009), 8.
12. Olivier Roy, *Globalised Islam: The Search for a New Ummah* (London: Hurst, 2002), 1.
13. Humayun Ansari, *'The Infidel Within': Muslims in Britain since 1800* (London: Hurst, 2004), 24–25.
14. Ibid., 135.
15. 'From Scholarships, Sailors and Sects to the Mills and the Mosques', *Guardian* online, 18 June 2002, http://www.guardian.co.uk/uk/2002/jun/18/september11. religion (accessed 24 July 2011).
16. Iftikhar Malik, *Islam and Modernity: Muslims in Europe and the United States* (London: Pluto Press, 2004), 156–180.
17. For stories of the harassment of Muslims in the US after 9/11 see Moustafa Bayoumi, *How Does It Feel to Be a Problem?: Being Young and Arab in America* (New York and London: Penguin, 2009).
18. Rehana Ahmed, *'Brick Lane*: A Materialist Reading of the Novel and its Reception', *Race & Class* 52.2 (October 2010): 25–42.
19. Yunus Samad, 'Book Burning and Race Relations: Political Mobilisation of Bradford Muslims', *New Community* 18.4 (1992): 507–519.
20. See, for example, Colin McCabe, 'Interview: Hanif Kureishi on London', *Critical Quarterly* 41.3 (1999): 37–56 (53); Salman Rushdie, *Step Across this Line: Collected Non-Fiction 1992–2002* (London: Vintage, 2002), 62, 345.

21. Tariq Modood, 'Muslims, Religious Equality and Secularism', in Geoffrey Brahm-Levey and Tariq Modood, eds, *Secularism, Religion and Multicultural Citizenship* (Cambridge: Cambridge University Press, 2009), 168–169.
22. Tariq Modood, *Multiculturalism: A Civic Idea* (Cambridge: Polity Press, 2007), 10.
23. Paul Bagguley and Yasmin Hussain, 'Flying the Flag for England? Citizenship, Religion and Cultural Identity among British Pakistani Muslims', in Tahir Abbas, ed., *Muslim Britain: Communities Under Pressure* (London: Zed Books, 2005), 208–221 (210–212).
24. Tahir Abbas, 'British South Asian Muslims: Before and After September 11', in Tahir Abbas, ed., *Muslim Britain: Communities Under Pressure* (London: Zed Books, 2005), 3–17 (12); Modood, *Multiculturalism*, 10–11.
25. Amin Malak, *Muslim Narratives and the Discourse of English* (New York: State University of New York Press, 2004), 17.

1 Writing Muslims and the Global State of Exception

Stephen Morton

The writer and political activist A. Sivanandan has argued that 'the war on asylum and the war on terror . . . have converged to produce a racism which cannot tell a settler from an immigrant, an immigrant from an asylum seeker, an asylum seeker from a Muslim, a Muslim from a terrorist'.[1] If, as Sivanandan suggests, predominant stereotypes of Islam have tended to frame Muslims as dangerous individuals in the global 'war on terrorism', how have contemporary Muslim writers tried to counter these pernicious fictions of Muslims? Beginning with a brief discussion of the neo-Orientalist rhetoric about 'Muslim terrorists', a form of rhetoric that reinforced the case for the detention and torture of 'enemy combatants' at prison camps such as Abu Ghraib and Guantánamo Bay, this chapter tries to address this question by considering how the 'war on terrorism' has also been waged as a war against Muslims. Specifically, I consider how tropes and narratives of militant Islam have been used to frame the justification of emergency measures in the global 'war on terror', and to produce new regimes of knowledge that survey, regulate and criminalize particular Muslim populations and Islam more generally. Developments in the 'post-9/11 novel' have tended to contribute to these pernicious stereotypes of Muslims by suggesting that Islam is the cause of political violence, rather than examining the ways in which different Muslim populations have been the victims of a violent western foreign policy in Palestine, Afghanistan and Iraq. Against such dominant representations of Muslims, the chapter attempts to survey and analyse the ways in which contemporary Muslim writers have attempted to challenge and contest the framing of Muslims as violent extremists. In particular, the chapter will suggest that contemporary fiction by writers of Muslim background not only highlights the imperialist provenance of contemporary British and American foreign policy, but also offers a space for reimagining the historical legacies of anti-colonialism as a countervailing narrative to the 'war on terror', a war which Giorgio Agamben has aptly called a global state of exception.

* * *

Over the last decade, the western media has been replete with Islamophobic stereotypes that associate Muslims with terrorism, Sharia law, the practice of veiling, and the preaching of global jihad. From the notorious cartoon illustrations of the Prophet Muhammad as a terrorist in the Danish newspaper *Jyllands-Posten* and the depiction of the Muslim cleric Abu Hamza al-Masri as a synecdoche for the British Muslim population to the television images of Palestinians cheering in response to the attacks of September 11, 2001, the representation of Muslims in the western media reconfigures an Orientalist conceit. As Edward W. Said emphasized in *Covering Islam* (1981), the dominant, western-based global media and government experts tend to reproduce damaging verbal and visual images of the Muslim world in order to justify western economic and foreign policies towards Iran, Iraq, Palestine, Pakistan or Afghanistan. In Said's words:

> For the general public in America and Europe today, Islam is 'news' of a particularly unpleasant sort. The media, the government, the geopolitical strategists, and—although they are marginal to the culture at large—the academic experts on Islam are all in concert: Islam is a threat to western civilization. Now this is by no means the same as saying that only derogatory or racist caricatures are to be found in the West. I do not say that, nor would I agree with anyone who did. What I am saying is that negative images of Islam continue to be very much more prevalent than others, and that such images correspond not to what Islam 'is' . . . but to what prominent sectors of a particular society take it to be. Those sectors have the power and the will to propagate that particular image of Islam, and this image therefore becomes more prevalent, more present, than all the others.[2]

The prevalent 'image' that Said refers to here describes certain verbal and visual stereotypes that are reproduced by the western media and foreign policy to stand in for the Muslim world. Such stereotypes include, for example, the belief that 'Muslims live in a make-believe world, that the family is repressive, that most leaders are psychopathological, that the societies are immature'.[3] In the aftermath of the global 'war on terror', Said's reflections seem strikingly prescient. For Peter Morey and Amina Yaqin,

> Said succinctly captures what we would call the frame governing representations of Muslims and the resulting attenuation of real knowledge about what is in fact a heterogeneous set of cultural systems, when he suggests that there is an 'incitement to discourse' about Islam, which 'canonizes certain notions, texts and authorities' confirming its 'medieval', 'dangerous' and 'hostile' nature.[4]

Following Maxwell McCombs's analysis of the media frame, Morey and Yaqin further claim that in the global discourse of terrorism, Muslims are framed in the terms of 'belonging, "Otherness" and threat'.[5] In mainstream popular cultural narratives such as Fox's US thriller series, *24*, for instance, the figure of the 'Muslim terrorist' is framed as a dangerous enemy within: a westernized Muslim, who is marked as a threatening 'Other' even though that figure also performs the rituals associated with the Protestant work ethic and the heteronormative nuclear family.[6]

The framing of Muslims in the dominant discourse of terrorism has also provided the justification for political techniques such as the suspension of human rights for Muslims in the diaspora, the 'rendition' of Muslims suspected of terrorism to locations beyond the jurisdictions that guarantee the rights of such prisoners, and the indefinite detention of so-called 'enemy combatants' at global war prisons such as Camp Delta, Guantánamo Bay. Judith Butler has shown how the 'racial and ethnic frames by which the human is currently constituted' are also crucial to the techniques of US imperial sovereignty employed during the 'war on terror'.[7] Citing the Bush administration's argument that 'the involuntary hospitalization of mentally ill people who pose a danger to themselves and others' provides a 'legal precedent' for the detention of suspected terrorists without criminal charge, Butler argues that such an analogy has broad and significant implications:

> We have to hesitate at this analogy for the moment, I think, not only because, in a proto-Foucaultian vein, it explicitly models the prison on the mental institution, but also because it sets up an analogy between the suspected terrorist or the soldier and the mentally ill . . . The terrorists are *like* the mentally ill because their mind-set is unfathomable, because they are outside of reason, because they are outside of 'civilization', if we understand the term to be the catchword of a self-defined Western perspective that considers itself bound to certain versions of rationality and the claims that arise from them . . . Indeed, one has to wonder whether it is not simply selected acts undertaken by Muslims extremists that are considered outside the bounds of rationality as established by a civilizational discourse of the West, but rather any and all beliefs and practices pertaining to Islam that become, effectively, tokens of mental illness to the extent that they depart from the hegemonic norms of Western rationality.[8]

What Butler implies without explicitly stating here is that the imagery and rhetoric framing the stereotype of the 'Muslim terrorist' as an irrational and dangerous Other is as important to the techniques of 'extraordinary rendition', indefinite detention, and torture employed during the 'war on terror' as those techniques of counter-insurgency themselves. For this reason, it is crucial that we consider the extent to which literary and cultural representations of Muslims have participated—either directly or indirectly—in the techniques of US imperial sovereignty during the 'war on terror'.

One might assume that developments in the so-called 'post-9/11 novel' would offer a more subtle and nuanced representation of Muslims than that which is offered in American popular cultural narratives such as *24*. It may thus strike some readers as surprising to find that the very analogy between the 'Muslim terrorist' and the mentally ill, which Judith Butler critiques in *Precarious Life* (2004), is reiterated in Ian McEwan's novel *Saturday* (2005). Focalized through the consciousness of Henry Perowne, a neurosurgeon living in a large house on London's Fitzrovia Square, the novel details Perowne's ambivalence about the demonstration against the Iraq war in March 2003 and documents his encounter with Baxter, a criminal figure suffering with Huntingdon's disease, who forcibly enters Perowne's home and attempts to sexually assault his daughter, Daisy, after Perowne and Baxter collide in a car accident. In this novel, it is McEwan's use of Mathew Arnold's poem 'Dover Beach' that provides the civilizational frame of reference for the novel's codified representation of Muslims. As a staunch advocate of the ideological role of culture at a time of religious crisis, Arnold functions as a metonym for a timeless view of the literary artwork that can counter the anarchy associated with the 'war on terror'. As some critics have noted, it is precisely Daisy's performance of Mathew Arnold's poem 'Dover Beach' that prevents her from being sexually assaulted by the deranged and degenerate working-class figure of Baxter in front of her family at their London home in Fitzrovia. Elaine Hadley, for example, states that 'at the climactic crisis in Ian McEwan's recent novel, *Saturday* (2005), set in the days before the United States declares war on Iraq, Matthew Arnold's "Dover Beach" (1867) saves the day'.[9] It is by reciting part of Arnold's poem that Daisy manages to magically 'tranquilize the savage pathology of a home intruder'.[10] It is moments such as these which lead Arthur Bradley and Andrew Tate to suggest that '*Saturday* is a fragile profession of faith in the supernatural power of literature itself'.[11] McEwan's use of Matthew Arnold in the novel thus raises broader questions about the novel's relationship to the ideology of liberal humanism (with which Arnold's writing and criticism are associated) prior to the start of the war in Iraq in March 2003. Such questions are played out in the third-person narrator's reflections on the war, which are focalized through the eyes of Perowne. In a heated exchange with his daughter about the war and the anti-war demonstration in London, Perowne accuses Daisy of being a member of the iPod generation which ignores Saddam's military dictatorship: 'The genocide and torture, the mass graves, the security apparatus, the criminal totalitarian state'.[12] He also points out that the Bali bombings were an attack on western liberal lifestyles: 'What do you think the Bali bombing was about? The clubbers clubbed. Radical Islam hates your freedom' (191). Perowne's supposedly liberal defence of the war and his critique of Islam with Daisy may seem to reinforce the Blair government's case for the war in Iraq, and it is this political stance—however ambivalent or plural it might be—that has prompted one reviewer to suggest that the novel might have been the product of a Tony Blair appointed committee.[13] Such a reading may overlook those moments in the novel wherein the third-person narrator encourages us to think critically about Perowne's liberal beliefs and values. For the narrator says at one point in the novel that Perowne recognizes that he has become a 'docile citizen' who has 'lost the habits of scepticism . . . [and] isn't thinking independently' (181). Yet McEwan's narrator not only foregrounds the contradictions and problems with Perowne's liberal view of contemporary geopolitics and Islam; he also draws attention to his attempt to discipline and control Baxter's very body and life. For after Perowne and his son successfully overpower Baxter by knocking him down the staircase and rendering him unconscious, Perowne proceeds to surgically remove a blood clot from Baxter's brain in a local hospital. This act of care towards a violent criminal suffering from mental illness may seem to be unusual, but I would suggest that it is consistent with the novel's critical engagement with the ideology of liberalism. For Perowne's clinical treatment of Baxter mirrors the liberal British state's regime of biopolitical control: the attempt to control and regulate the life of the population, and those individuals and groups who transgress its norms and values. What I am suggesting, in short, is that the novel's representation of Baxter as a dangerous individual parallels the British state's attempt to control its Muslim population.

In *The Biopolitics of the War on Terror* (2007), Julian Reid has argued that the 'war on terror' highlights the ways in which modern liberal societies have always waged wars on human populations by subordinating the human life of the population to what he calls logistical life. What Reid means by logistical life is

> the life lived under the duress of the command to be efficient, to communicate one's purposes transparently in relation to others, to be positioned where one is required, to use time economically, to be able to move when one is told to, and crucially, to be able to extol these capacities as the values which one would willingly, if called upon, kill and die for.[14]

Reid draws heavily on Michel Foucault's account of war, biopolitics and disciplinary societies throughout the book in order to make the argument that the post-Kantian claim that liberal societies are founded on an ethos of peace is an ideological fiction and to examine which 'forms of life have been and are deemed capable of peaceful living under liberal conditions, and, conversely, which forms are associated with the threat of war'.[15] Specifically, Reid invokes Foucault's account of the origins of modern forms of disciplinary and biopolitical power in the military sciences of organization in *Discipline and Punish* (1977) in order to 'demonstrate how liberal regimes of governance emerged during the eighteenth century in response to the challenge of how to overcome the problem of war within society'.[16] One of the more provocative arguments that Reid presents in his book is his suggestion that Terror is the name of the form of life that is resistant to biopolitical regimes of control because it refuses the demands of a logistical life. In this way, he seems to attribute a radical political agency to terrorism, which resides in its resistance to biopolitical control.

In the Foucauldian terms of Reid's argument, Baxter's act of terror could be understood as an attempt to assert his sovereign power over his own life in response to Perowne's attempt to control the life and death of subjects who are deemed to threaten the values of the liberal state. And by framing Baxter in this way, McEwan encourages readers to think about the parallels between Baxter's degeneracy and what Perowne calls 'Radical Islam' (191). For if Perowne's attempt to diagnose Baxter's violent actions against his family are understood as an attempt to reform and civilize Baxter, this narrative could be read as an allegory for the British state's attempt to define and produce a 'good British Muslim' subject in the aftermath of 9/11 and 7/7.

Yet for all the self-consciousness of *Saturday*, there are clearly limitations to McEwan's critical engagement with British liberalism. Significantly, in an interview published in the *Telegraph* magazine, McEwan has spoken against the charge that criticizing Islam is racist. As he puts it: 'Chunks of left-of-centre opinion have tried to close down the debate by saying that if you were to criticize Islam as a thought system you are a de facto racist. That is a poisonous argument'.[17] In making this claim, McEwan—like his fellow writer Martin Amis—seems to overlook how the criticism of Islam has been linked to the framing of Muslims in the current global 'war on terror'. Such a racist discourse has allowed western nation-states to define Muslims as a threat to the secular, democratic values of liberal societies. Yet in contemporary fiction, this racist discourse is often codified. In 'The Last Days of Muhammad Atta', Martin Amis attempts to forensically reconstruct the thoughts and bodily ablutions of Muhammad Atta on 10 September 2001.[18] Drawing on *The 9/11 Commission Report* and the instruction manual given to each of the men involved in the attacks on America of September 11, 2001, the story proceeds to suggest that Muhammad Atta was a misogynist and a cold-blooded killer. At one point in the story, the narrator describes how Atta had been given 'a four page booklet in Arabic, put together by the Information Office in Kandahar (and bound by a grimy tassel)' (100), but he had chosen not to read this until the day before their deadly mission. By fictionalizing Muhammad Atta's last day, Amis suggests that Atta is unable to separate his mind and his body, or to achieve 'sublimation by means of jihadi ardour' (101). Instead, Amis suggests that Atta was motivated by what he calls the 'core reason':

> The core reason was of course all the killing—all the putting to death. Not the crew, not the passengers, not the office workers in the Twin Towers, not the cleaners and the caterers, not the men of the NYPD and FDNY. He was thinking of the war, the wars, the war cycles that would flow from this day. (122)

Amis's suggestion that Atta's reason for participating in this attack was to provoke more death might seem to question the religious rhetoric that was invoked in the instruction manual to frame the attack. In this respect, Amis's fictionalization of Atta could be seen to interrogate the causal relationship that has been drawn between religion and violence. The anthropologist Talal Asad, for instance, has suggested that what has been described in the western media as 'the Islamic roots of violence' is very misleading because it assumes a necessary correlation between religion and violence, where there is no such correlation. The crucial point for Asad is that religion is supplementary to an act of terrorism: it can under certain circumstances provide a transcendental structure that justifies acts of violence in retrospect, but a scriptural precedent is not in itself essential for a violent act to be carried out.[19] Yet in 'The Last Days of Muhammad Atta' there are clear limits to Amis's interrogation of the equation of violence and religion. Specifically, Amis's attempt to evoke the interior consciousness of Muhammad Atta can be read as a criminal psychological profile that encourages readers to equate Muslims with terrorism, even if the protagonist of Amis's story is an apostate who seems to be more motivated by nihilism and a fear of endless existence than by a commitment to religious extremism.[20] In doing so, Amis provides further justification for the racialization and criminalization of Muslims in the 'war on terror'. Such a view is further reinforced by Amis's argument in an interview published in *The Times Magazine* that

> The Muslim community will have to suffer until it gets its house in order. What sort of suffering? Not letting them travel. Deportation—further down the road. Curtailing of freedoms. Strip-searching people who look like they're from the Middle East or from Pakistan . . . Discriminatory stuff, until it hurts the whole community and they start getting tough with their children.[21]

If McEwan and Amis contribute to the framing of Muslims as a threat to the values of the British liberal state, Philip Roth's novel *The Plot Against America* (2004) uses a counter-factual historical narrative to explore the ways in which the executive powers of the US presidency could be used to suspend the normal rule of law and to strip certain ethnic groups of the rights associated with citizenship.[22] Speculating on the possibility that the anti-semitic American aviator, Charles Lindbergh, could have become the American president, Roth invents a dystopian world in which American Jews are scapegoated for supporting the war against Nazi Germany. Here, the parallels with the Bush administration and the emergency measures passed during the 'war on terror' are striking. Just as Lindbergh passes a law preventing Jews from participating in public life, places the Jewish community under police surveillance and delivers speeches that spread anti-semitic feeling, so the former US President George W. Bush used his executive powers to suspend the normal rule of law and to authorize the indefinite detention of people suspected of involvement with terrorist activities. In so doing, Roth offers a powerful—if indirect—critique of the Bush administration's framing of Muslims in the 'war on terror'.

* * *

Whereas Roth uses a counter-factual historical narrative of 1930s America to explore the wider implications of the 'war on terror', Kamila Shamsie's novel *Burnt Shadows* (2009) draws explicit attention to the parallels between the prose of counter-insurgency in late colonial India and the contemporary discourse on terrorism after September 11, 2001 through a critical dialogue with E. M. Forster's novel *A Passage to India* (1924). Just as Dr Aziz is framed in *A Passage to India* by a colonial state that projects its anxiety of losing political authority in the aftermath of the 1857 Indian rebellion onto a racist fantasy of a hyper-sexualized Muslim man, so Sajjad Ashraf in *Burnt Shadows* is framed by his employer's wife, Elizabeth Burton, for improper sexual conduct with their Japanese house guest and survivor of the Nagasaki A-bomb, Hiroko Tanaka. Significantly, Hiroko subsequently compares Elizabeth's misrecognition of the emergent and mutual sexual desire between Hiroko and Sajjad as an act of rape to Elizabeth's granddaughter Kim's irrational fear of Muslim men, such as Abdullah, an illegal immigrant from Afghanistan and former member of the *mujahideen* who works as a taxi driver in New York City. As Hiroko puts it in a heated exchange with Kim: "'Ilse once accused Sajjad of being a rapist. She told me afterwards, those were two minutes in which she was lost. And look at you now, Ilse's granddaughter. You don't even know you're lost . . . You condemn a man based on five minutes of conversation'".[23] This ontological condition of 'being lost' can be read as a symptom of mourning: a mourning of the loss of colonial power signified by India's Independence and a mourning of the loss of Kim's father Harry during the war in Afghanistan. Such a reading recalls Judith Butler's account of the political dimension of mourning in *Precarious Life*. Against President George W. Bush's assertion on 21 September 2001 that 'we have finished grieving and that *now* it is time for resolute action to take the place of grief',[24] Butler argues that grief can be a 'resource for politics' if it leads to 'a consideration of the vulnerability of others'[25] and a questioning of the political norms that determine why the lives of Americans are grievable and the lives of Iraqis, Palestinians and Afghanis are not.[26] Furthermore, by arguing that 'the world itself as a sovereign entitlement of the United States must be given up, lost and mourned',[27] Butler offers a radical democratic vision of global power relations in the twenty-first century.

Shamsie further interrogates the political dimension of grief by decentring the 9/11 attacks on America and situating them in relation to a broader history of western imperialism that includes the nuclear bombing of Nagasaki, the Partition of India after Independence, and the Soviet invasion of Afghanistan. Hiroko's traumatic experiences of Nagasaki are not only inscribed in the scars on her back, but also shape and determine her fears about whether she will be able to have children following a miscarriage. When Harry Burton suggests that she has heroically 'overcome' the trauma of the bomb, Hiroko questions whether she is physically and psychically able to overcome this trauma, considering the '"not right" foetus which her body had rejected' (181). In this way, Hiroko struggles to contest the dominant medical-legal discourse that frames the bodies and subjectivity of nuclear survivors as *hibakusha*, or 'those subjected to the bomb and/or radiation'.[28] As well as being marked by the discourse of the bomb, Hiroko's narrative is haunted by the image of her dead fiancée, Konrad Weiss. As she explains to Sajjad:

> Those nearest the blast were eradicated completely, only the fat from their bodies sticking to the walls and rocks around them like shadows . . . I looked for Konrad's shadow. I found it. Or I found something that I believed was it. On a rock. Such a lanky shadow. I sent a message to Yoshi Watanabe and together we rolled the rock to the International Cemetery . . . And buried it. (76–77)

Like Hiroko, Sajjad is haunted by loss and melancholia for a home that he left behind. To escape from the violence in Delhi that followed the Partition of India, Sajjad and Hiroko honeymoon in Istanbul, and when they return to Delhi, Sajjad learns that his oldest brother, Altamash, was killed in the Partition riots, and his sister-in-law and her daughter were killed on the trains that crossed the border in Punjab between India and Pakistan. In a passing reference to Partition's violence, Hannah Arendt in *The Origins of Totalitarianism* (1987) links the creation of a population of twelve million refugees at Partition to a broader failure of the nation-state to 'treat stateless people as legal persons'.[29] The routine, systematic and organized violence against refugee populations in the Punjab certainly gave the lie to the political discourse of rights and citizenship. The historian Yasmin Khan notes how

> Political safeguards for minorities proved paper tigers . . . in the face of the Punjabi tragedy and they offered too little and too late for those who had lost faith in the state's ability to protect them; the speed of events on the ground outstripped deliberations about the rights of citizenship in the constitutional arenas of India and Pakistan.[30]

The permit system devised in 1948 that subsequently developed into passport legislation in 1951 further served to police the boundary line between India and Pakistan.[31] The trauma produced by such laws is articulated in Sajjad's diasporic narrative in *Burnt Shadows*. On attempting to return to Delhi after his honeymoon and the Partition violence, Sajjad is refused entry by the Indian consulate on the grounds that he is 'one of those Muslims who chose to leave India'. This decision, he explains to Hiroko, 'can't be unchosen' (125).

In the wake of this loss and suffering, and following the suspension of his political rights as an Indian citizen after Partition, Sajjad resigns himself to a life as a *muhajir* in Karachi. In this respect, Sajjad's diasporic narrative parallels that of Hiroko. For just as Hiroko struggles against being defined by the dominant medical and legal discourse that frames the subjectivity of nuclear survivors as *hibakusha*, so Sajjad tries to resist the shame attached to the label of *muhajir*, an Urdu term denoting a migrant who came to Karachi from India after Partition. Yet despite Hiroko and Sajjad's historical experiences as refugees who are haunted by memories of the homes to which they are unable to return, Shamsie also suggests that the experience of being a refugee is inherently cosmopolitan, in so far as it involves inhabiting different worlds and different languages, and crossing borders in the process.

It is tempting to read Konrad Weiss's words that 'barriers were made of metal that could turn fluid when touched simultaneously by people either side' (82) as a metafictional commentary on Shamsie's cosmopolitan vision of a borderless world after September 11, 2001. Yet such a reading is complicated by Raza Ashraf's narrative. Like Hiroko and Sajjad, their multilingual son, Raza Ashraf, becomes an errant translator who befriends a young Afghan arms smuggler in Karachi and subsequently infiltrates a *mujahideen* training camp in Afghanistan during the war against the Soviets under the pseudonym of Raza Hazara. Following the tragic death of his father Sajjad, Raza is recruited as a professional translator by a private American security contractor based in Afghanistan and is implicated in the murder of his friend and colleague, Harry Burton, by an Afghani gunman. Significantly, Raza is framed for this crime by Steve, an American CIA paramilitary operative who suspects Raza of being an Islamic fundamentalist partly because he 'saw him prostrating himself in front of a mosque' but also because of his 'skill at deception' (281), which is demonstrated in Raza's ability to pass as an Afghan. Steve's framing of Raza for the murder of Harry Burton not only foregrounds the discourse of Islamophobia that underpins the 'war on terror'; it also highlights the way in which the deterritorializing potential of private military contractors and security firms to circumvent the international rule of law are ultimately reterritorialized by the sovereign power of the United States, which Steve embodies. When Raza questions whether Steve has legal jurisdiction over A and G, the private security firm for which Raza works, Steve replies by asserting that 'I employ your employers . . . They've given me operational control until they fly in a replacement' (303). Before he begins his transatlantic escape from Afghanistan to Canada via Iran, Raza tosses out 'his passport and green card and watched the wind sift fine particles of sand on to the documents that made him legal' (308). By throwing out the documents that identify his citizenship and ethnicity, Raza may resist the reterritorializing regimes of US imperial sovereignty. But in doing so, he also experiences the 'terror of unbecoming' that is associated with being a refugee (308). In this respect Raza may appear to exemplify the condition of bare life that Giorgio Agamben attributes to the refugee. In a commentary on Hannah Arendt's chapter 'The Decline of the Nation-State and the End of the Rights of Man', Agamben argues that 'the refugee is the sole category in which it is possible today to perceive the forms and limits of a political community to come'.[32] For Agamben, the figure of the refugee calls into question the universal claims of human rights declarations by 'breaking up' the assumption that the 1789 Declaration of the Rights of Man and the Citizen includes human subjects who are not citizens. What is more, the refugee highlights the fiction that national belonging is guaranteed by nativity or birth, and thereby 'throws into crisis the original fiction of sovereignty'.[33] For Agamben as for Arendt, it is the Nazi holocaust of the European Jews that clearly exemplifies the failure of universal human rights declarations to protect the rights of human populations. Yet Agamben's argument also has important implications for understanding the contemporary framing of refugees as terrorists or enemy combatants that is fictionalized in Shamsie's novel. The analeptic structure of *Burnt Shadows* seems to demand a recursive reading in response to the question posed in the novel's prologue by an as yet unnamed protagonist as he waits to be clothed in an orange jumpsuit: '*How did it come to this?*' (1). If we take this masculine figure to be Raza, and the orange jumpsuit to be an iconic metonym of contemporary global war prisons such as those at Guantánamo Bay, then the question and the context in which it is posed can be read as a rhetorical statement about the way in which Muslims have been framed in the 'war on terror'. But if we reread the prologue in light of the multiple narratives that follow, the question can also be read as a reflection on the way in which the so-called 'war on terror' is overdetermined by the violent legacies of western imperialism in the twentieth century such as the atomic bombing of Nagasaki and Hiroshima, India's Partition, the CIA's covert war against the Soviet military in Afghanistan and the proliferation of nuclear weapons in India and Pakistan. In this reading, *Burnt Shadows* offers an important historical counterpoint to dominant narratives of the 'war on terror', which ignore the historical role of the United States in the training of militant groups during the Cold War.[34]

If the contemporary discourse of terrorism is based in part on Orientalist tropes and stereotypes of a barbaric and violent Islam, Mohsin Hamid's novel *The Reluctant Fundamentalist* (2007) may seem to question such stereotypes through its representation of Pakistan from the perspective of Changez, a migrant who returns to Lahore after receiving an elite education at Princeton, and working for the American valuation company, Underwood Samson. *The Reluctant Fundamentalist* borrows a narrative strategy from Albert Camus' 1956 novella *The Fall*, in which the protagonist addresses a silent male interlocutor in a single, uninterrupted monologue. Yet whereas Camus's narrator-protagonist, Jean-Baptiste Clamence, addresses philosophical questions about death, judgement, friendship and religion, Hamid's first person narrator-protagonist relays his disaffection with the global expansion of America's economic and military influence to an American visitor to Lahore, whom he suspects of being an undercover CIA agent. As a highly educated migrant, Changez performs the role of a native informant who advises the unnamed and silent American visitor about different aspects of Pakistani culture, including the food and drink on the café menu, the informal practice of drinking alcohol, the young women from the National College of Arts wearing paint speckled jeans and the city planning of Lahore. This representation of Pakistani culture seeks to contest the West's framing of Pakistan as a rogue state of terrorists and Islamic fundamentalists. As Changez puts it:

> Four thousand years ago, we, the people of the Indus River basin, had cities that were laid out on grids and boasted underground sewers, while the ancestors of those who would invade and colonize America were illiterate barbarians. Now our cities were largely unplanned, unsanitary affairs, and America had universities with individual endowments greater than our national budget for education. To be reminded of this vast disparity was, for me, to be ashamed.[35]

Changez's sense of shame is compounded by his recognition that after working for Underwood Samson for a few months, he begins to see the rest of the world through American eyes. During an assignment in Chile, for instance, where he is required to value a book publishing company that is not profit making, the owner of the company, Juan-Bautista, compares him to the Christian boys who were captured by the Ottoman Empire and trained to be Muslim soldiers. These boys, who were known as 'janissaries', 'were ferocious and utterly loyal: they had fought to erase their civilizations, so they had nothing else to turn to' (151). Juan-Bautista's comparison prompts Changez to reflect on how he had become 'a modern-day janissary, a servant of the American empire at a time when it was invading a country with a kinship similar to mine and was perhaps even colluding to ensure that my own country faced the threat of war' (152). Changez's reflections on his own complicity in the US-led 'war on terror', and his realization that 'finance was a primary means by which the American empire exercised its power', can be seen to parallel Ugo Mattei's contention that a 'state of emergency is a stabilizing political category, a true foundation for predatory capitalism'.[36] And by refusing to play the role of modern janissary to the West, Changez brings the economic agenda of the US-led 'war on terror' to the fore. Yet in doing so, he also runs the risk of being subjected to the discursive frame of counter-insurgency, symbolized in the novel by the gaze of the mysterious American. Towards the end of the novel, Changez offers a series of reflections on the justification for the wars in Iraq and Afghanistan. He observes how:

> a common strand seemed to unite these conflicts, and that was the advancement of a small coterie's concept of American interests in the guise of a fight against terrorism, which was defined to refer only to the organized and politically motivated killing of civilians by *killers* not wearing the uniforms of killers. (178)

Here, Changez not only offers an insightful criticism of the way in which the meaning of terrorism is defined by narratives of counter-terrorism to justify the state's use of military force. He also demonstrates that the word itself masks the ways in which the 'war on terror' serves American economic and geopolitical interests at the expense of human lives in Iraq, Pakistan and Afghanistan. He observes: 'the lives of those of us who lived in lands in which such killers also lived had no meaning except as collateral damage' (178). The precarious lives of civilians in Pakistan during the US war in Afghanistan is further borne out by Changez's story of a boy who was allegedly involved in a plot to assassinate an American development worker. This boy, as Changez explains, 'had disappeared—whisked away to a secret detention facility, no doubt, in some lawless limbo between [America and Pakistan]' (182). The framing of this boy mirrors Changez's own experiences of Islamophobia, which are manifested in the responses of other people to the beard he grew as a sign of solidarity with Muslims in Pakistan and Afghanistan after the attacks of September 11, 2001. We have already seen how Martin Amis called for the racial profiling of Muslims 'who look like they're from the Middle East or from Pakistan'. It is precisely such techniques that *The Reluctant Fundamentalist* subjects to critical scrutiny. By staging the production of the racialized Muslim body through the visual trope of Changez's beard, Hamid encourages readers to question the use of such racialized stereotypes in the discourse of terrorism.

If, as Hamid suggests, the 'war on terrorism' masked an imperialist agenda, this imperialist agenda is inextricably entwined with the history of neoliberal globalization. Yet this history of neoliberalism can also work to erase the cultural and historical singularity of violence and terror in South Asia, as Salman Rushdie has suggested in his 2005 novel *Shalimar the Clown*. *Shalimar the Clown* embeds a story about the militarization of Kashmir in a broader narrative of neoliberal globalization and US foreign policy in South Asia from the Bretton Woods Agreement to the US-led war in Afghanistan following the attacks on America of September 11, 2001. In so doing, Rushdie attempts to find a literary form appropriate to describe the transnational social and political relations that underpin globalization. As the narrator puts it, 'Everywhere was a part of everywhere else. Russia, America, London, Kashmir. Our lives, our stories, flowed into one another's, were no longer our own, individual, discrete. This unsettled people'.[37] And yet at the same time, Rushdie's narrator seems to insist on the historical singularity of the conflict in Kashmir. Against the history of American foreign policy in South Asia, Rushdie offers a similar vision of the global political future to that outlined by Judith Butler in *Precarious Life*. By framing Shalimar's murder of the US ambassador Max Ophuls as a 'Kashmir story' rather than an 'American story', Rushdie's narrator Kashmira grieves for Kashmir against the political norms and 'alien cadences of American speech' (372) which define Shalimar's murder of Ophuls as a 'terrorist action' against America's global political sovereignty. In so doing, Rushdie offers a political elegy for Kashmir that highlights the limitations of American foreign policy in post-colonial South Asia from the Truman administration to the Bush administration, and mourns the lives of many Kashmiris, whose deaths have been overshadowed by the Cold War and the US-led 'war on terrorism'.

* * *

In a first-hand account of his detention at the Baghram air base, Kandahar and at the US Military Detention Camps at Guantánamo Bay, Moazzam Begg describes his experience of negotiating with the official military language and procedures that were used by his interrogators to justify his detention as Kafkaesque.[38] Such a parallel seems particularly apposite when one considers that Begg's detention without trial was founded in part on a signed confession that was obtained under the threat of torture. In a reading of Kafka's *The Trial* (1925) and 'In the Penal Colony' (1919), Giorgio Agamben has argued that confession and torture are bound together. For Agamben, Josef K.'s self-slandering exemplifies the way in which the law depends on the baseless self-accusation of the human subject, which Agamben distinguishes from a confession.[39] Whereas the baseless self-accusation is a 'strategy that seeks to deactivate and render inoperative the accusation, the indictment that the law addresses toward Being', the 'one who has confessed is already judged'.[40] Yet if a confession is obtained under torture, how is this different from a baseless self-accusation? By emphasizing the falsity of his signed confession, and the use of torture to obtain this confession, Moazzam Begg suggests that his confession to interrogators is nothing more than a baseless self-accusation obtained through the use of force. In so doing, Begg also questions the demonization and dehumanization of detainees at Guantánamo Bay, many of whom are Muslims. Against the sovereign power of the US military, which sought to define him as an enemy combatant who should be stripped of the legal rights defined by the terms of the Geneva Convention and international law, Begg constructs a writerly self that persistently questions the authority of his captors, and affirms his cultural identity as a British Muslim. Like Shamsie's reflections on the wars in Afghanistan, Hamid's account of the intensification of violence between Pakistan and India, and Rushdie's imaginative reframing of the conflict in Kashmir, Begg's autobiographical account of his detention at Guantánamo Bay allows for a more nuanced and critical interrogation of the colonial genealogies of violence, which underpin the framing of Muslims in the global 'war on terror'. Indeed, taken together, such narratives can be seen to create a space for reimagining the historical legacies of anti-colonial resistance and struggle as a counterpoint to the wars in Afghanistan and Iraq, and the narratives that justify them.

Notes

1. A. Sivanandan, 'Race, Terror and Civil Society', *Race and Class* 47.3 (January 2006): 1–8 (2).
2. Edward W. Said, *Covering Islam: How the Media and the Experts Determine how We See the Rest of the World* (London: Vintage, 1997), 144.
3. Ibid., 147.
4. Peter Morey and Amina Yaqin, 'Muslims in the Frame', *Interventions* 12.2 (2010): 145–156 (146).
5. Ibid., 147.
6. See Peter Morey, 'Terrorvision', *Interventions* 12.2 (2010): 251–264.
7. Judith Butler, *Precarious Life: The Powers of Mourning and Violence* (London: Verso, 2006), 90.
8. Ibid., 72.
9. Elaine Hadley, 'On a Darkling Plain: Victorian Liberalism and the Fantasy of Agency', *Victorian Studies* 48.1 (Autumn 2005): 92–102 (92).
10. Ibid.
11. Arthur Bradley and Andrew Tate, *The New Atheist Novel: Fiction, Philosophy and Polemic after 9/11* (London: Continuum, 2010), 34.
12. Ian McEwan, *Saturday* (London: Vintage, 2006), 191. Citations will hereafter be inserted in the text.
13. John Banville, 'A Day in the Life', *New York Review of Books*, 26 May 2005.
14. Julian Reid, *The Biopolitics of the War on Terror: Life Struggles, Liberal Modernity and the Defence of Logistical Societies* (Manchester: Manchester University Press, 2007), 13.
15. Ibid., 5.
16. Ibid., 12.
17. Stephen Adams, 'Ian McEwan: Criticising Islam is not Racist', *Telegraph Magazine*, 13 March 2010.
18. Martin Amis, 'The Last Days of Muhammad Atta', in *The Second Plane: September 11: 2001–2007* (London: Vintage, 2008), 95–121. Citations will hereafter be inserted in the text.
19. See Talal Asad, *Formations of the Secular: Christianity, Islam, Modernity* (Stanford: Stanford University Press, 2003) and *On Suicide Bombing* (Stanford: Stanford University Press, 2007).
20. See Bradley and Tate, *The New Atheist*, 53–55.
21. 'Martin Amis interviewed by Ginny Dougary', *Times Magazine*, 9 September 2006.
22. Philip Roth, *The Plot Against America* (London: Jonathan Cape, 2004).

23. Kamila Shamsie, *Burnt Shadows* (London: Bloomsbury, 2009), 361. Citations will hereafter be inserted in the text.

24. Cited in Butler, *Precarious Life*, 29.

25. Butler, *Precarious Life*, 30.

26. Ibid., 34.

27. Ibid., 40.

28. Lisa Yoneyama, *Hiroshima Traces: Time, Space, and the Dialectics of Memory* (Berkeley: University of California Press, 1999), 85.

29. Hannah Arendt, *The Origins of Totalitarianism* (London: Andre Deutsch, 1987), 290.

30. Yasmin Khan, *The Great Partition: The Making of India and Pakistan* (Yale University Press, 2008), 157.

31. Ibid., 195.

32. Giorgio Agamben, 'We Refugees', trans. Michael Rocke, http://www.egs.edu/faculty/agamben/agamben-we-refugees.html (accessed 8 April 2009).

33. Ibid.

34. For more on the historical role of the United States in the training of militant Islamic groups during the Cold War, see Giovanna Borradori, *Philosophy in a Time of Terror: Dialogues with Jürgen Habermas and Jacques Derrida* (Chicago: University of Chicago Press, 2003), 95–96; Jason Burke, *The 9/11 Wars* (London: Allen Lane, 2011); Jason Burke, *Al-Qaeda: The True Story of Radical Islam* (London: Penguin, 2004); John L. Esposito, *Unholy War: Terror in the Name of Islam* (Oxford: Oxford University Press, 2002); and Steve Coll, *Ghost Wars: The Second History of the CIA, Afghanistan, and Bin Laden, from the Soviet Invasion to September 10, 2001* (London: Penguin, 2004).

35. Mohsin Hamid, *The Reluctant Fundamentalist* (London: Hamish Hamilton, 2007), 34. Citations will hereafter be inserted in the text.

36. Ugo Mattei, 'Emergency-Based Predatory Capitalism: The Rule of Law, Alternative Dispute Resolution and Development', in Didier Fassin and Mariella Pandolfi, eds, *Contemporary States of Emergency* (New York: Zone Books, 2010), 89.

37. Salman Rushdie, *Shalimar the Clown* (London: Jonathan Cape, 2005), 37. Citations will hereafter be inserted in the text.

38. Moazzam Begg, *Enemy Combatant: A British Muslim's Journey to Guantánamo and Back* (London: Free Press, 2006), 155.

39. Giorgio Agamben, 'K.', in *Nudities*, trans. David Kishik and Stefan Pedatella (Stanford: Stanford University Press, 2011), 20–36.

40. Ibid., 24–25.

Part I
Writing the Self

2 Bad Faith

The Construction of Muslim Extremism in Ed Husain's *The Islamist*[1]

Anshuman A. Mondal

The function of a memoir is to reflect on the past but its purpose—sometimes explicitly stated but otherwise implicit in the form—is to draw lessons for the present. Moreover, as a published account of personal experience, it is a document that is at once both social and private. Its lessons are not just for the benefit of the individual who wrote it but are also directed towards its readers as being of general interest and concern. It was for precisely these reasons that Ed Husain's *The Islamist* became one of the publishing sensations of 2007, selling over 50,000 copies in its first year. The paperback edition is garlanded with praise from some of the foremost opinion-formers in contemporary Britain; Simon Jenkins urges people to 'read this articulate and impassioned book' whilst Martin Amis found it 'persuasive and stimulating'. The reviewers in the national press were equally impressed. Many reviews echoed *The Observer*'s description of the text as 'captivating and terrifyingly honest' whilst some went further: *The Daily Mail* said it was 'far more than just an arresting testimony of a mind freeing itself from the shackles of extremism' whilst *The Daily Telegraph* felt the book should be 'prescribed like medicine'.[2]

Furthermore, the book's influence extends well beyond the commentariat; there are clear signs that it has had a profound impact on government thinking and policy *vis-à-vis* Muslim political radicalism. The BBC reported in 2008 that 'one government official e-mailed scores of colleagues inside Whitehall late last year, effectively instructing them to read it', and the announcement in April of that year by the then Home Secretary, Jacqui Smith, that moderate foreign imams had been invited to tackle extremism displayed the hallmarks of Husain's championing of the subcontinent's tradition of Sufi political quietism.[3]

Clearly, this public reaction was due in large part to the conviction that general lessons for our times could be drawn from this personal account of one young man's experience of certain radical 'Islamist' movements. What, however, are the lessons that can be drawn from such a text? To the extent that Husain's own experience is taken to be instructive to the wider community, it is because that experience is seen to be illuminating aspects of British *public* life that had hitherto remained beyond scrutiny. To answer the question thus requires a careful examination of the way in which the personal experience is framed within a public narrative about 'Islamism'. It is not my intention to impugn Husain's account of his own personal experiences but, in so far as his subjective experience is taken to validate the text's representation of a social phenomenon (Islamism)—that is, in so far as his representation of what he calls 'the Islamist movement' in Britain is taken to be 'true' because he speaks of it from 'first-hand' experience—there is also an 'objective' dimension to his text which does indeed deserve critical examination.

That objective dimension—its representation of social 'facts'—is in turn determined by yet another dichotomy that is inherent to the genre of memoir. All memoirs consist of at least *two* subjectivities. There is a 'narrating' self which is looking back from the vantage point of the present on an 'experiencing' self. Some memoirs delineate a continuity between these two selves (I came to be how I am because of who I was) whilst others operate on the basis of a discontinuity—the self looking back is radically *different* from the self that experienced the events being narrated. *The Islamist* falls into the latter category but, as we shall see, there is a consistent blurring of the distinction between the two selves that creates a representational uncertainty which is of critical importance in determining the ideological position of the text.

From the retrospective point of view of the narrating self the narrative arc of the book is redemptive: an innocent but vulnerable younger self falls into bad ways (tempted, if you like), becomes disillusioned and eventually recovers by turning his back on a wayward past (one can hardly imagine the book receiving such acclaim had it not been so). It is particularly this middle period, the period of Husain's active involvement in Islamism, that concerns us here. This seems to have commenced at some point in 1990 and encompassed roughly a decade and a half although his turning point seems to have occurred about halfway through this period, in 1996 or 1997. The three part narrative arc is thus roughly bisected into two halves, the threshold being some point in the middle of the 'fall' period. If the first half chronicles the descent into the Islamist 'underworld' the second half documents the slow and agonizing ascent back to enlightenment and a particular understanding of the Islamic faith that is radically at odds with those being advocated by the Islamists he encountered.

Prior to his initial encounters with Islamism, Husain recalls his attachment to an elderly Bengali Sufi mystic called Shaikh Abdal-Latif whom his family venerated as a *pir* or spiritual master. Husain seems to have devoted himself to this Sufi (whom he calls 'Grandpa') as thoroughly as he later devoted himself to the Islamist cause (a recurring trope throughout the narrative is his tendency to throw himself wholeheartedly—and often uncritically, at first—into whatever enterprise has taken hold of him at any given moment). He writes that he was eager to learn more about Islam because of Grandpa's influence and he requested extra out-of-hours Religious Education classes from the head of department at Stepney Green School, a Mrs Rainey. He was joined by another student, Abdullah Falik, whose influence would eventually lead Husain into Islamist circles.

Ironically, it was within the secular institution of the school and under the guidance of a Christian that he would become exposed to Islamist ideas for the first time. He writes, 'The first book I read about Islam in English was *Islam: Beliefs and Teachings* by Gulam Sarwar . . . At school, Sarwar's was the main textbook for those studying RE'. He goes on to say,

> Grandpa had never spoken about an 'Islamic state' . . . he never raised a subject known as 'Islamic politics'. Yet, in Sarwar's book, there was a chapter on 'The Political System of Islam' . . . In concluding his introductory chapter Sarwar . . . commended the efforts of several organizations that were dedicated to the creation of 'truly Islamic states' and mentioned several groups by name, including the Muslim Brotherhood in the Middle East and Jamat-e-Islami in the Indian subcontinent . . . Today, in British schools, Sarwar's book continues to be used in RE classrooms.[4]

It is at this point that Husain introduces one of the major tropes in his narrative, one that increases in significance as his narrative develops. Sarwar was

> the brains behind the separation of Muslim children from school assemblies into what we called 'Muslim assembly', managed by the Muslim Educational Trust (MET). What seemed like an innocuous body was, in fact, an organization with an agenda . . . Ostensibly it all seemed harmless but the personnel all belonged to Jamat-e-Islami front organizations in Britain. (21–22)

Whilst these facts may well be true it is the metaphor Husain uses to describe his exposure to Islamism through 'front organizations' that is of interest. As the narrative progresses, Islamism is increasingly portrayed as a virus that infects the social body of Britain's Muslim communities. The covert and underhand nature of its transmission is particularly insidious—a threat that is invisible is greater than one out in the open.

Husain then catalogues other examples of Islamist dissimulation, which collectively amount to what might be termed the trope of 'crypto-Islamism'. Virtually every Muslim organization is noted as being a 'front' for Islamism: Islamic societies on college and university campuses; Young Muslims Organization UK (YMOUK); the Islamic Society of Britain (ISB) and the Muslim Association of Britain (MAB); the Muslim Council of Britain (MCB); East London Mosque; The Islamic Foundation; and even the Respect Party. At times, Husain is very explicit about this. 'Nearly every Muslim representative body, mosque, and publishing house was under Islamist control' (208), he states, 'and they [the Islamists] began to be seen as "mainstream" Islam'

(214). This panders to fears that the Islamist 'takeover' has already—or is about to—come to pass, and is all the more malign because of its covert and insidious nature.

There is no doubt that front organizations continue to be used by militant Islamist groups to elude surveillance, but the problem with Husain's representation is that he presents deception as a systematic political strategy on the one hand (he speaks of organizations making deliberate efforts to 'conceal their extremist connections'), and, on the other, he extends this to cover all Muslim organizations such that it seems impossible to conceive of mainstream Muslim organizations that are *not* crypto-Islamist.

He is clearly scarred by Hizb-ut-Tahrir, the Islamist organization he joined in his youth and subsequently left: it 'had given me a particular dislike for *all* organizational forms of Islam' (168). But this dislike—and mistrust—of Islamic organizations of all kinds extends to a blanket suspicion of all Muslim efforts to organize politically and, in fact, implicates 'moderate' as well as 'radical' Muslims: how are we to distinguish the 'genuine' moderate groups from the front organizations? His response is to equate 'moderate' Islam with a non-political pietism that is radically antithetical to Islamism. This moderate Islam, to which 'the majority of the world's Muslims still adhere', is, he says, 'deeply personal, highly spiritual, and Sufi-influenced' (237).

According to Husain, this is the stark choice facing today's Muslims: either Islamism (equated with 'extremism') or non-political, individual pietism. According to the Quilliam Foundation's website, Muslims should become politically engaged and integrated as 'citizens, not as a faith community' or 'ideologues with a Muslim-centric approach'.[5] It is little wonder that his ideas have resonated with a secular political establishment that is deeply suspicious of any form of religious politics. But, in presenting the matter in such a way, Husain misses a crucial distinction that scholars of politics in Islam have long upheld between 'Islamism' and 'Muslim politics'.

In his excellent survey of global political Islam, Peter Mandaville says that Islamism is a form of 'Muslim politics' that is concerned with establishing a 'normative' sense of social and political behaviour embedded in Islamic principles, and is usually—in its 'classic' formulation—oriented towards the capture of state power and the establishment of an Islamic state in order to guarantee and instigate Islamic social 'normativity'—usually through the application of Sharia law. 'Muslim politics', on the other hand, is 'a more inclusive formulation that allows us to examine political actors who define their motivations and goals, at least in part, as related to Islam, but who do not pursue anything like the establishment of formal Islamic political systems'.[6] As such, Islamism is not the sum of all Muslim political possibilities in the way that Husain suggests.

By these definitions, all 'mainstream' organizations in Britain—including those that may have been 'Islamist' in the past—have long since abandoned Islamism but continue to pursue forms of Muslim politics because that is what many, if not most, Muslims in the United Kingdom actually want—a politics informed in some way by the values and ethics of Islam (such as a strong emphasis on social justice, for instance, or what can best be described as 'neighbourliness', that is, a strong sense of social responsibility towards others). This politics is pragmatic, content to work within established systems of parliamentary democracy, is keen on establishing political partnerships with like-minded organizations from other faith and secular groups (for instance, the Respect Party or the Stop the War coalition) and eschews not only violence but also other Islamist shibboleths such as Sharia law or the idea of an Islamic state.[7] From this perspective, the MCB, for example, is certainly pursuing a Muslim politics but it would be absurd to argue that it is still Islamist—even if it is acknowledged that it once was. Husain, however, suggests that any form of Muslim politics must, *ipso facto*, be Islamist or crypto-Islamist. He therefore finds it difficult to identify a form of 'moderate' Islam that might be different to his own conception of it; seeing crypto-Islamists behind every façade, in every dark corner, he exhibits a mindset that is, ironically, a mirror-image of those Muslims who see Jewish conspiracies everywhere.

* * *

Husain's analysis of Islamism itself is even more problematic. The fundamental rhetorical strategy in *The Islamist* is to present Islamism as a highly unified, global movement; even when the text acknowledges the fractures, factionalism and the in-fighting between Islamist groups, Husain nevertheless is at great pains to point out that there is still an underlying unity to 'the Islamist movement'. Thus, despite saying that 'the East London Mosque had been the site of rival factions of the Jamat-e-Islami in Britain' (24), he nevertheless says that, 'we were attached to the YMO, and so to Jamat-e-Islami, part of the worldwide Islamist movement' (61); despite being told that Hizb-ut-Tahrir was considered by Wahhabis and other Islamists as 'deviant in creedal matters' (83) and that Sunnis believed them to be 'infidels', we are still meant to believe that Islamists 'were *all* at one with Wahhabis in creed' (234, original emphasis).

For Husain, there are two sides to the global Islamist movement, which are inseparable. On the one hand, there is an ideological unity underpinning all Islamisms everywhere; on the other, there are organizational links, continuities, partnerships and affiliations that bind all Islamist groups to each other such that, taken together, we can speak of *an* Islamist movement. He suggests that since there are many overlaps in the thought of key Islamist thinkers from different parts of the Muslim world, their ideas can be taken to be equivalent to each other. Thus, he links the ideas of the Egyptian Sayyid Qutb, writing in the 1950s and 1960s, to those of Abu A'la Mawdudi, who founded the Jamaat i-Islami (JI) in Northern India in the 1930s, and Hasan al-Banna, who founded the Muslim Brotherhood (MB) in Egypt in 1928.

Above all these stands Taqi Nabhani, the founder of Hizb-ut-Tahrir, to whom Husain gives unwarranted importance; most scholars of Islamism agree that Nabhani's was a minor current in the larger ecology of Islamist thought.[8] Beyond that, there is the austere Islam preached by the eighteenth-century Arabian cleric Muhammad Ibn Abd al-Wahhab, known as Wahhabism.

Husain's attempts to reconcile such disparate ideological strands lead him to make several injudicious statements that have no basis in historical fact, nor do they stand up to the merest scrutiny. When he declares that Islamists 'were *all* at one with Wahhabis in creed' (234), he is, quite simply, wrong. There are overlaps, of course, but Husain argues that Islamism and Wahhabism are the *same* because they are both 'literalist'. This is not true; most Islamists are literalists in some aspects of their interpretation but in others they exercise free interpretation (*ijtihad*), especially in political matters. The most influential Islamist thinkers—Mawdudi, al-Banna, Qutb—all advocated an interpretative, rather than literalist approach to the sources, and they did so because Islamisms are decisively shaped by their encounter with the modern state. They are thus fundamentally modernist, and their ways of thinking derive from the Islamic modernism of pioneer reformers such as Muhammad Abduh, appointed by Lord Cromer as the *mufti* of Egypt and greatly admired by him.[9]

Islamism represents one current of Islamic modernism, alongside other more 'progressive' ones. Wahhabism, on the other hand, developed long before the modern state and its habits of thought appeared in the Muslim world. It is a backward-looking, revivalist movement that sought to arrest the decline of the Muslims of Arabia by escaping history; Islamists, on the other hand, take as axiomatic the modern belief in historical progress (as Husain tacitly admits when he speaks of how Hegelian their thought is).

Husain also makes a great deal out of the idea of 'influence'. The fact that Qutb openly acknowledged Mawdudi as an influence is taken by Husain to mean that Mawdudi's Islamism is basically the same as Qutb's. Although Qutb borrowed some of Mawdudi's ideas, he developed them in ways that were very different, and which reflected the very different circumstances in which they wrote. In particular, by the time Qutb wrote his infamous book *Signposts on the Road* (1964) in an Egyptian jail, his circumstances were such that his earlier attempts to reconcile the individual (derived from his immersion in western liberalism) with the ethical obligations to the community (which he took to be Islam's imperative) had given way to a totalitarian vision of the primacy of the community above all else. Accordingly, an earlier openness to democracy diminished and was replaced by vanguardist militancy.[10]

By contrast, Mawdudi's principal concern was with the Islamization of society such that it would be ready to accept an Islamic state if and when it actually materialized. Firmly rooted within the Indian Muslim political establishment, Mawdudi could afford to take the long view, and his gradualism is accompanied by a much stronger emphasis on democratic transformation of the existing order. Moreover, having matured in a political arena in which competition between different groups was taken for granted, and in a country that had several different Muslim traditions, Mawdudi understood that the Islamic state could not just be imposed from above. This commitment to social transformation through the democratic political process is in marked contrast to groups such as Hizb-ut-Tahrir who see democracy as *haram* in Islam.

Mawdudi's emphasis on the bottom-up Islamization of society as a necessary step prior to the establishment of the Islamic state meant that he simply could not countenance the use of violence for such purposes, unlike Qutb. More importantly, by the time he wrote *Signposts*, Qutb advocated a *takfiri* position; as he saw it, the majority of Egypt's so-called Muslims acquiesced in the tyranny of the Nasserite state and were thus implicated in its *jahiliyya* (the term used to refer to the pre-Islamic period of 'ignorance' in Arabia, recast by Qutb to refer to the godlessness of the modern world) and therefore should be considered 'the enemy'. Needless to say, *takfirism* would have rendered Mawdudi's entire strategy null and void. The ideological chasm between Mawdudi and Qutb is as wide as that between Fabianism and Bolshevism.

These and other ideological differences are significant enough to warrant speaking of Islamisms, in the plural, but Husain's elision of them in favour of an all-embracing ideology of Islamism is, in fact, necessary in order for him to be able to string together all 'Islamist' groups into a singular global movement that encompasses political parties such as Pakistan's Jamaat-i-Islami and its offshoots (e.g. Young Muslims Organization UK), the Muslim Brotherhood and its affiliates (HAMAS, Muslim Association of Britain), Hizb-ut-Tahrir and al-Muhajiroun, the Taliban and beyond them, the militant jihadist organizations such as al-Qaeda. The basic architecture of Islamism as presented by Husain is simple: Muslim politics = Islamism = extremism = terrorism. Just as they are all bound together by a singular ideology, so too are they presented as being organizationally linked by what might be heuristically conceptualized as an 'escalator' whereby any sort of Muslim politics is Islamism which is, in turn, 'extremist' and is thus a 'waypoint' into terrorism. There are continual slippages in the text between 'Islamist', 'extremist' and 'jihadis' (the first occurs before the book itself begins, in the Preface) which signal these connections.

To illustrate how the 'escalator' works, Husain cites some individuals whose trajectories testify to the links that, in Husain's opinion, indubitably join Islamists from the bottom of the 'escalator' to the jihadists at the top. For instance, we are told of Babar Ahmed, 'who had once been a member of the youth wing of ISB [Islamic Society of Britain]', and is now 'set to be extradited to the US on terrorism charges' (280). Similarly, the MCB is linked to 'extremism' by Dr Abdul Bari, its current chairman, because he once had links to Jamaat-i-Islami in Bangladesh. It is not, however, apparent that we can necessarily infer the characteristics of a particular group from the kinds of individuals that might have, at some point, come into contact with it or are members of it for the simple reason that organizations cannot be held responsible for the opinions or behaviour of individual members unless they explicitly endorse or incite them. To do otherwise leads to logical implications that are absurd when analogously applied to other groups and political communities; it would suggest, for example, that the Royal Society for the Protection and Care of Animals (RSPCA) is a militant 'front' organization just because a few animal rights militants might once have been members. It is also by no means clear that the trajectories of particular individuals who move from group to group can, in fact, demonstrate that links exist between them. Would we then conclude that there are 'links' between the RSPCA and militant animal rights groups because a few have moved from one to the other? Or between the Catholic Church and violent anti-abortionists? Yet Husain's 'escalator' model prompts the reader to make such connections with respect to Muslim political organizations.

* * *

Much of the value of Husain's memoir lies in the fact that it is an insider's account. There are, however, limitations to this approach. The view from inside 'the goldfish bowl' might tell us many interesting things about the internal operations of an organization, but it also risks distorting the picture of the world outside it. In particular, it risks inflating the view from inside whilst, conversely, minimizing developments outside. For instance, it is clear that Husain exaggerates the importance of Hizb-ut-Tahrir. According to him, it had 'a powerful presence in several British universities' (104), and 'dominated Muslim groupings on campuses up and down the country' (116). 'Our ideas were being discussed behind closed doors by every single Muslim group in Britain', he says, and 'so previously moderate Islamist organizations began to adopt our radical stance'. With a flourish, Husain suggests that 'in political discussions our Muslim opponents were never able to defeat us' (99–100).

Hizb-ut-Tahrir clearly sees itself as a vanguardist party, as do most Islamist organizations. Husain's account clearly reflects how that vanguardist mentality shaped the behaviour and worldview of Islamists. '[W]e felt as though we were the pioneers, at the cutting edge of this new global development', he says (73–74); they 'provided direction and leadership' to 'ordinary Muslims' who were 'not Islamists' (62). This was so successful that 'our arguments spread like wildfire amongst the students' (141) and the students were 'almost without exception, under our control' (66). Like all vanguardist groups, the Islamists saw the Muslim 'masses' as pliant and easily led—like 'unthinking sheep', according to Husain (140).

It is not clear whether this is just what he thought at the time or is what he still thinks now—that is, whether this is presented as the subjective perspective of the 'experiencing' self of the time, or the presumably more 'objective' vision of the 'narrating' self looking back. There is certainly counter-evidence in the text itself, which shows that Hizb-ut-Tahrir's reach amongst 'ordinary' Muslims was not what they thought it was, nor was their self-importance justified. Despite the 'widespread euphoria' they had apparently generated in Tower Hamlets, Husain admits that a meeting they organized at Whitechapel to call for jihad in Bosnia 'had not been as successful' as they had hoped. Undaunted, they pushed ahead with plans for a national conference to discuss Hizb-ut-Tahrir's call for a caliphate. Again, this was a 'shambolic failure, though at the time very few of us were prepared to admit the fact . . . The possibility that Muslims were simply not interested in our conference did not dawn on us' (137–138).

And yet, whilst Husain's narrating self seems prepared to acknowledge—at times—that the reality outside 'the goldfish bowl' was not how it seemed from the inside, in a more profound sense his narrative continues to represent reality from the inside. It is surprising that the book has virtually no 'ordinary' Muslim voices in it, apart from those of 'Grandpa' and his father. Non-Islamist young Muslims simply do not figure; everything revolves around 'the movement', and the perspectives of those who never subscribed to Islamism—the overwhelming majority, as Husain concedes—are simply unavailable. This is an unwitting testimony to the book's narrowness of perspective—and the insularity of Islamists.

It also results in an equivocation that blurs the distinction between the 'inside' perspective of the experiencing self and the 'outside' perspective of the narrating self, which in turn blurs the distinction between Islamists and 'ordinary' Muslims. On the one hand, Husain writes 'At that time, being a young Muslim could only mean being an Islamist' (178), but on the other hand he says, 'Most of the young students were ordinary Muslims not Islamists' (62). The distinction between the narrating self, looking in from the outside, and the experiencing self, looking outwards from the inside, is not clear. The latter clearly signals a more 'objective' view when placed alongside such comments as 'the student population, almost without exception, [was] under our control' (66), but the 'At that time' in the former example clearly signals a narrative distance between past and present which suggests that it too is being articulated from the 'outside' perspective. However, far from challenging the 'inside' perspective of the experiencing self it corroborates that point of view.

This equivocation is repeated in the final chapter, when the narrative arc has reached the redemptive point at which Husain feels confident enough to admit that any lingering Islamist sentiments within him have been thoroughly banished—and thus the narrating self is firmly in control. Within the space of a few paragraphs he writes, 'The ideology . . . that led to the successful suicide bombings of 7 July 2005 and many similar though thwarted attempts since then is still alive and *firmly rooted among Britain's young Muslims*'

(283, emphasis added), and, in contrast, 'Most Muslims are already upright Britons, contributing to their country as much as any other British citizen' (284). Both of these statements are clearly articulated by the more 'objective' narrating self, but one endorses the perspective of the Islamist experiencing self, whereas one contests it.

Clearly the product of a lingering vanguardist mentality oscillating between the inside perspective of an experiencing self that truly did believe that Islamists were representative of the wider Muslim population, and the outside perspective of a narrating self that is aware that they were not, these contradictions and ambivalences throw into doubt the veracity of Husain's portrayal of Muslim life in Britain and of the place of Islamism within it. Which of the two statements above should the reader take to be true? Consequently, *The Islamist* is at least complicit in, if not directly contributing to, the reinforcement of those stereotypes common in public discourse that similarly blur the distinction between *some* Muslims (i.e. Islamists, terrorists, extremists) and *all* Muslims.[11] The lessons one can draw from such an account are comforting to political agendas that are hostile to Muslims in general and/or seek to uphold prevailing assumptions and prejudices against contemporary Muslims rather than challenge them.

* * *

One of the weaknesses of vanguardism is that it believes that the 'masses' are 'unthinking sheep', and so the vanguard need not take any interest in what they are thinking, in what they are making of the concepts that are being 'passed on' to them. Those in the vanguard are therefore not prepared when they turn round and find that the masses have turned away from them (if, indeed, they were ever behind them in the first place). This makes it very difficult for such people to come to terms with the fact that change could occur without them. The final chapter, entitled 'Return to England', suggests that absolutely nothing has changed within Muslim communities in the decade and a half since Husain began his Islamist career. He returns to the East London mosque 'to see if the management had moved away from Islamism . . . Sadly, I was disappointed' (279). Islamist ideas about global jihad, the Islamic state and the primacy of the *ummah* are still 'accepted as normal and legitimate' (277). It is as if British Muslims are stuck in the 1990s.

This allows Husain to maintain a vanguardist position. If nothing has changed 'outside', all that has *really* changed is that Husain has switched sides. He is now simply in the anti-Islamist vanguard as opposed to the Islamist one. This is perhaps why the launch of the Quilliam Foundation was met with such frenzied excitement; because of *The Islamist*, many have come to believe that Quilliam is at the cutting edge of 'moderate' Muslim efforts to tackle Muslim radicalism.

But Husain, by his own account, has experienced the processes of change and transformation within British Muslim communities that have been underway for some time now. He recounts his experiences within the Islamic Society of Britain, after he left Hizb-ut-Tahrir, and notes that it was comprised of two factions, one that sought to establish links with the Muslim Brotherhood, and another committed to developing a British Islam that 'wanted to sever ties with Islamic movements' (172). The only thing that bound them together was their antipathy to Hizb-ut-Tahrir, which was the reason it was formed in the first place. It duly split in 1997 and one (the British faction) remained the Islamic Society of Britain, whilst the other became the Muslim Association of Britain.

Husain's time with the Islamic Society of Britain was confusing for him, principally because the organization was going through an identity crisis. 'What were the ISB?' Husain asks, 'were they Islamists or British Muslims looking to lead an ordinary life? Or both?' (177). He is unable to give any satisfactory answers, not least because his account of the period is itself, frankly, confusing. On the one hand, he characterizes it as an Islamist organization, but on the other hand, we are told it is the vehicle through which Husain encounters 'moderate' Muslim scholars like Nur Keller and Hamza Yusuf, whom he now upholds as role models (he was introduced to them by Inayat Bunglawala, who became the spokesperson for the Muslim Council of Britain, yet Husain continues to characterize Bunglawala and the MCB as Islamists and 'extremists'). He then takes the confusion of the Islamic Society of Britain to be an indication of its inability 'to sever Islamist ties' because of the 'inherent Islamist desire . . . lurking' within it (172). It does not seem to occur to him that the confusion was part of the *process* of struggling to establish a new, British form of Islam rather than a symptom of an 'inherent Islamist desire'.

In fact, the Islamic Society of Britain is one of a large number of organizations, individuals and processes that, for the best part of a decade, have been contesting older Islamist ideas, to varying degrees. Young Muslims Organization UK, for instance, is one of the groups that participated in the Radical Middle Way, an initiative sponsored by the then Labour government that challenged 'extremist' ideologies, and provided a forum for 'ordinary' Muslims to contribute to that process.[12] However, anyone unfamiliar with the contemporary Muslim scene in Britain, and who has read *The Islamist*, might be forgiven for thinking that it is still an 'extremist' Islamist organization. Another participant in the Radical Middle Way is *emel* magazine, which is edited by Sarah Joseph, a former member of the Islamic Society of Britain. *emel* is a lifestyle magazine for socially mobile Muslims that takes Muslim integration in Britain for granted. As for Inayat Bunglawala, his departure from Islamism has been well-documented in many articles and interviews. He has publicly acknowledged, for instance, that Muslims were wrong to demand the banning of Rushdie's *The Satanic Verses*.[13]

Even an organization like the City Circle (which is considered an exemplar of 'moderate' Islam) has changed a great deal over the years. Asim

Siddiqui, its chair, has observed that many young Muslims who had come across the organization in its early days were surprised by the direction it has since taken. He said,

> I recently met a girl who said to me, 'Is this the same City Circle which was set up in '99? Because that was really religious, really conservative and you guys don't seem conservative now.' It *is* the same City Circle, but even I would almost not recognize it. It would have been a different meeting then: segregated, fairly religious topic—we have *really* changed. Everyone has been on a journey.[14]

All these transformations represent the visible tip of deeper, grassroots shifts in perception and attitude that signal what Asef Bayat, the director of the International Institute for the Study of Islam in the Modern World (ISIM), calls 'post-Islamism'. He characterizes it as

> an endeavour to fuse religiosity and rights, faith and freedom, Islam and liberty. It is an attempt to turn the underlying principles of Islamism on its head by emphasizing rights instead of duties, plurality in place of a single, authoritative voice, historicity rather than fixed scriptures, and the future instead of the past.[15]

He acknowledges, however, that it is a nascent phenomenon that is still quite fragile, and that there are contradictions and confusions in the ways that Muslims are relating to it. For example, some young Muslims are openly disavowing the notion of the Islamic state or the desirability of Sharia law, whilst others are still residually attracted to Sharia law as a concept (even though they admit to the difficulties in implementing it in countries where Muslims are in a minority) but have very little interest in an Islamic state or the global *ummah*.[16] The permutations are myriad, suggesting an acute ideological flux.

Post-Islamism also encompasses what the French sociologist Amel Boubekeur calls 'cool Islam'. She has documented changes in the way young European Muslims relate to Islam after the 'failure of political Islamism'. A 'new Muslim elite', she argues, 'is bringing with them a new urban Muslim culture from within the Occident' through the embedding of Islam in patterns of consumption and capitalist markets.[17] 'Islamic goods and services promote an ethical point of view resulting from an Islamic faith' instead of the 'utopian' Islamist project of state-formation.[18] The 'ethislamic', as she calls it, of 'cool Islam' is reflected in products such as the Dawah Wear jogging suit, or The Capsters, a Velcro hijab that allows the sporty Muslim woman to adjust it according to the needs of her chosen sport. These patterns of production and consumption have, as their counterpart, a micro-politics that is local, invites partnerships with non-Muslims, is network-based and eschews traditional Islamist politics, which is grandiose, hierarchical and centralized.[19]

The Islamist does not register any of these developments, which are testimony to a dynamism within Muslim communities that is at odds with the rather patronizing stereotype that *The Islamist* often upholds, namely that Muslims are uncritical and unable to refashion themselves. Its underlying argument would suggest that Husain does not believe these changes are either genuine or, indeed, possible. 'Once an Islamist, always an Islamist' is the message conveyed by the 'crypto-Islamist' motif. Notwithstanding Husain's genuine confusion about Islamism itself, and all the other flaws in his argument, the effect (if not intent) is disingenuous at the very least.

This may be due to the generic demands of memoir; after all, if its appeal is based on some general lessons it can offer for understanding contemporary affairs, it would not be wise to admit that the picture presented is out of date. I am not suggesting that radical and militant Muslim groups no longer exist because that is clearly not the case. What I am suggesting is that the manner in which Husain represents contemporary scenarios is flawed. It offers a very narrow and limited sketch of Muslim communities and it occludes a great deal. It thereby misrepresents the ecology of thought within contemporary Muslim communities in Britain.

Its perspective is further distorted by the focus on organizations as the prime site of interest. This emphasis overlooks just how much activity is taking place outside them, amongst individuals and unorganized groups who are trying to reinterpret their faith in relation to the unprecedented challenges these 'western' Muslims now face. This is not to suggest that organizations are not significant, merely that the organization-led perspective—whether from the inside, or the outside (the British government's approach)—risks overlooking the contributions of that mass of 'ordinary' Muslims who are beginning to undertake the slow process of reform in earnest. For new forms of grassroots thinking are percolating in the disorganized fluidity of social life, in bedrooms and sitting rooms, on the streets and in meeting places, which pulse with the beat of thoughts not yet spoken, with ideas not yet thought. These are the spaces where the genuinely 'new' emerges, not in the more disciplined and regulated spaces of established Muslim organizations. In any case, forward thinking Muslim organizations are beginning to register and foster these developments. These include groups as diverse as City Circle, the Islamic Society of Britain, the Quilliam Foundation and British Muslims for Secular Democracy, as well as participants in the Radical Middle Way, such as Young Muslims Organization UK, and newspapers and magazines like *Q-News* and *emel*. In time some of these will, perhaps, articulate these ideas effectively and coherently in the public arena.

Unfortunately, *The Islamist* presents a very monochromatic, dualist picture of Muslim life in Britain (which is ironic given that Husain correctly and consistently critiques Islamists for their Manichean view of the world). Its success was predicated on its affirmation of a series of assumptions and prejudices held by the secular political establishment and a state security apparatus primed to pursue a 'war on terror' in which the principal antagonists are Muslims of a certain kind, namely militant Islamists. To gain this endorsement, however, a heavy price has been paid for *The Islamist* does not do justice to the polychrome, multivalent, contradictory and dynamic texture of Muslim communities in Britain and Europe as they struggle to come to terms with the Islamist legacy and all it has bequeathed them.

Notes

1. An abridged version of this essay appeared in *Prospect* (July 2008): 34–37.
2. Anushka Asthana, 'A True Islamic Voice', *The Observer*, 6 May 2007; the *Mail on Sunday* passage is quoted inside the book's front cover, as is the one from *The Daily Telegraph*.
3. On the Home Office's change of strategy see http://www.guardian.co.uk/world/2008/apr/17/islam.religion (accessed 29 April 2011).
4. Ed Husain, *The Islamist* (London: Penguin, 2007), 20–21. Citations will hereafter be inserted in the text.
5. Husain founded the Quilliam Foundation along with another ex-Islamist, Majid Nawaz, as the 'world's first counter-extremism think tank'. It has become an extremely influential organization and is well funded by the British political establishment. See www.quilliamfoundation.org (accessed 29 April 2011).
6. Peter Mandaville, *Global Political Islam* (London: Routledge, 2007), 20–21.
7. See, for instance, Anshuman A. Mondal, *Young British Muslim Voices* (Oxford: Greenwood, 2008). See also my essay 'British Islam after Rushdie', *Prospect* online, 26 April 2009, http://www.prospect-magazine.co.uk/article_details.php?id=10737 (accessed 29 April 2011).
8. Mandaville, *Global Political Islam*, 266.
9. See Anshuman A. Mondal, 'Liberal Islam?' *Prospect* (January 2003): 28–33.
10. Charles Tripp, 'Sayid Qutb: The Political Vision', in Ali Rahnema, ed., *Pioneers of Islamic Revival*, 2nd edn. (London: Zed Books, 2005), 154–183.
11. See the report by the Commission on British Muslims and Islamophobia, *Islamophobia: Issues, Challenges and Action* (Stoke-on-Trent: Trentham Books, 2004). See also Elizabeth Poole, *Reporting Islam: Media Representations of British Muslims* (London: I. B. Tauris, 2004); and Julian Petley and Robin Richardson, eds, *Pointing the Finger: Islam and Muslims in the British Media* (Oxford: Oneworld, 2011).
12. See Phillip Lewis, *Young, British and Muslim* (London: Continuum, 2007), 145.
13. Inayat Bunglawala's many blogs and articles on *The Guardian's* 'Comment is Free' website, document this journey away from Islamism. The specific reference here is to 'I used to be a book burner', 'Comment is Free', 19 June 2007, http://www.guardian.co.uk/commentisfree/2007/jun/19/notsurprisinglytheawarding; and 'Words can never hurt us', 'Comment is Free', 26 September 2008, http://www.guardian.co.uk/commentisfree/2008/sep/26/islam.religion (both accessed 2 May 2011).
14. Mondal, *Young British Muslim Voices*, 154–155.
15. Asef Bayat, 'What is Post-Islamism?' *ISIM Review* 16 (Autumn 2005): 5.
16. Mondal, *Young British Muslim Voices*, ch. 7. See also Lewis, *Young, British and Muslim*, chs 3, 4 and 5.

17. Amel Boubekeur, 'Cool and Competitive: Muslim Culture in the West', *ISIM Review* 16 (Autumn 2005): 12.
18. Ibid.
19. Ibid., 13. See also Emma Tarlo, *Visibly Muslim: Fashion, Politics, Faith* (Oxford: Berg, 2010).

3   Reason to Believe?

Two 'British Muslim' Memoirs

Rehana Ahmed

As issues and controversies centring on Muslims have become increasingly prominent in the media and in political debate, the 'British Muslim' has become an object of curiosity and at times fearful fascination for a mainstream British reading public. The demands of the market are evidenced in the proliferation of autobiographical memoirs by young British writers of Muslim heritage in the wake of 9/11 and the July 2005 bombings on London transport. Ranging from Guantánamo Bay veteran Moazzam Begg's account of his three-year incarceration in the US military base (*Enemy Combatant*, 2006) and former 'Islamic radical' Ed Husain's memoir (*The Islamist*, 2007) to Shelina Zahra Janmahomed's light-hearted tale of finding 'Mr Right' (*Love in a Headscarf*, 2009) and journalist Zaiba Malik's narrative of growing up as a British Muslim in Bradford (*We Are A Muslim Please*, 2010), these autobiographical works are important examples of British Muslims 'transform[ing] themselves from objects of representation to Subjects of representation', asserting their subjectivities in the context of the homogenizing neo-colonial discourses that surround Muslims.[1] They also inevitably carry a weighty 'burden of representation' in a climate of fear and perceived threat— a burden that they shoulder knowingly and by choice, in order to make an intervention in representations that circulate about British Muslims.[2] Their designated status as 'insider' accounts that are 'representative' of 'Muslim experience' endows them with a particular potency to challenge but also, alternatively, to reproduce and confirm such discourses.

This essay focuses on two recent examples of autobiographical memoir, both by British journalists of Pakistani Muslim origin: Sarfraz Manzoor's 2007 *Greetings from Bury Park: Race, Religion, Rock 'n' Roll*, and Yasmin Hai's 2008 *The Making of Mr Hai's Daughter: Becoming British*.[3] The memoirs chart the authors' personal histories—from their parents' arrival in England through their school and university years to their establishment of successful careers in journalism—in the context of wider social and cultural issues relating to race, faith and class, and punctuated by political events that have placed Muslims in the spotlight: the 1989 'Rushdie Affair', the 2001 attacks on the World Trade Center and Pentagon, and the 2005 London transport bombings. Each narrative considers the role of religious faith and culture in the life of a young British Pakistani; the rise in 'Islamic fundamentalism' among British Muslim youth; the place of politics in religion; the competing demands of secular modernity, *mahalla* and mosque; and the complex relationship between individual, family, community and nation. The essay probes in particular the tensions between a liberal notion of individual subjectivity and an adherence to community, culture and faith in these articulations of 'British Muslim' selfhoods, and the ways in which the autobiographical form shapes and is (re)shaped by these tensions. It further traces the ideological ambivalences of the narratives to their authors' positions on the borders of categories of class, culture and religion, and considers what these textual contradictions reveal about the position of Islam in Britain today.

* * *

I take as the title for this essay that of the penultimate chapter of Sarfraz Manzoor's *Greetings from Bury Park*: 'Reason to Believe'. The phrase is the title of a song by Bruce Springsteen, whose lyrics underpin the narrative throughout, providing chapter titles and epigraphs, as well as the title of the book itself (an allusion to Springsteen's first studio album, *Greetings from Asbury Park, NJ*, released in 1973, shortly before two-year-old Manzoor's arrival in Bury Park, Luton). The song 'Reason to Believe' suggests the tenacious faith of humankind in the face of adversity, a 'universal' story that transcends 'geography, race [and] religion' (102). In Manzoor's memoir, it is also used to denote the narrator's own conflicted relationship with his inherited religion, Islam; his unsuccessful struggle to find a 'reason to believe'. Thus, the phrase, with its dual meaning, encapsulates the layering of and tension between a universalizing and individualizing narrative that could relate to 'anyone', and a culturally specific memoir that is rooted in and conveys the experience of being a Pakistani Muslim Briton. This duality in turn maps on to the intersection of the private and the public evident throughout both memoirs. Each is punctuated by the same key events, the first private (but with universal resonance) and the other two public (but with particular significance for Muslims), which impact profoundly on the autobiographical subject: the death of their fathers and the 9/11 and 7/7 attacks. Indeed, each memoir can be read in both private/universal and public/culturally specific terms: they are narratives of the loss of a beloved father *as well as* of an originary, stable sense of home and self through migration; of marginalization through adolescent anxiety *as well as* through racial and cultural difference; and of conflict between youthful rebellion and parental expectation *as well as* between the competing demands of secular individualism and religious community.

This duality, integral to much postcolonial autobiography, underlines the powerful potential of these personal, and at times highly emotive, narratives to enable but also, conversely, to circumscribe a critical engagement with public discourses about Islam. Gillian Whitlock describes the ability of autobiography, or 'life narrative', to elicit empathy from a reader. It is the personal nature of the genre, its reference to 'lived experience', as well as its 'gestures of sincerity, authenticity, and trust', which facilitate identification with the autobiographical subject.[4] The 'I' is the universal subject. In the context of 'Muslim life narratives' marketed to and consumed by non-Muslim western readers, this can potentially work to 'personalize and humanize categories of people whose experiences are frequently unseen and unheard' and facilitate crucial cross-cultural dialogue.[5] However, as Whitlock points out, it is the rhetorical power of the genre that simultaneously makes it particularly amenable to co-option as a subtly manipulating form of propaganda. Whitlock discusses in particular Afghan women's life narratives and their uses by different interest groups, including to legitimize US military intervention in Afghanistan, but her point remains applicable, in a less direct sense, to the kind of British Muslim memoir that this essay takes as its focus.[6] In post-9/11 Britain, Islam and its practitioners are frequently constructed as antithetical to a normative liberal multiculturalism and aligned with retrogression, intolerance and oppression.[7] How readily can these memoirs be co-opted into such a construction? Both memoirs have been received by critics with epithets that suggest their ability to elicit empathy: 'tender', 'sad and lyrical' and 'richly humane' (*Greetings from Bury Park*), and 'affectionate, sometimes sad' and 'touching' (*The Making of Mr Hai's Daughter*).[8] Both of the autobiographical 'I's, moreover, exist on the privileged peripheries of the family and community life they sketch. Do they thereby align themselves with and interpellate an 'outsider' liberal western reader who can, in turn, identify Manzoor and Hai as enlightened 'escapees' from the perceived constraints of Muslim culture and valorize his or her own preconceptions in the process?[9] Or do these narratives, rather, deconstruct and resist such constructions, in the vein of the 'autoethnographic' or counter-ethnographic accounts that Mary Louise Pratt explores, appropriating the 'idioms' of hegemonic discourses surrounding Muslims in order to challenge them?[10] Are these more nuanced narratives that facilitate a critical and counter-hegemonic cross-cultural engagement with a frequently subordinated and denigrated minority group?

In more general terms, the phrase 'reason to believe' evokes the secularist dichotomy of Enlightenment reason versus blind faith. Manzoor gestures towards this dichotomy in his account of the role of Islam in his life: he alludes to Islam as indecipherable, inaccessible and remote, as rituals to be followed blindly and unquestioningly, while also acknowledging that this interpretation of Islam is shaped by his parents' adherence to certain cultural, as opposed to doctrinal, rules (215–217, 226–227). In Hai's narrative, too, Islam is at times identified with rules and an abnegation of individuality (201, 273, 333). And yet the phrase 'reason to believe' also hints at a possibility of bridging, and therefore deconstructing, that dichotomy; the word 'to' is a linking word, a bridge rather than a barrier. It posits 'belief' as potentially stemming from 'reason' and so having some basis in the material and historical. It also sketches a connection between belief and individual choice, again destabilizing normative associations of Islam with the suppression of individuation and free will. In my reading of the two memoirs, I will explore how far they deconstruct the binary of 'reason' versus 'belief' that so frequently fixes Muslims as liberal Britain's cultural 'Other'.

The borderline position between 'reason' and 'belief' occupied by Manzoor and Hai themselves is shaped by their ambivalent class position as well as by their hybrid subjectivities as Britons of Pakistani Muslim heritage. While Hai is from a more privileged background than Manzoor, whose memoir is particularly moving in its evocation of the impoverishment of his family's early years in Britain and the impact this had on their futures, both exist between social categories and both are socially mobile, ultimately moving away from their class as well as cultural backgrounds. Whitlock draws a distinction between 'memoir' which for her is 'the prerogative of the literate elite', and 'testimony' as 'the means by which the disempowered experience enters the record . . . not necessarily under conditions of their choosing'.[11] In this essay I privilege the term 'memoir' (and indeed the second subtitle of the hardback edition of *The Making of Mr Hai's Daughter* is 'A Memoir'). Yet as successful British Muslim journalists, Manzoor and Hai can be located on the borderline between these two categories. They are certainly 'authorized and accredited witnesses' of the British Muslim communities and cultures they represent, their class status arguably delimiting their ability to identify with the latter; but they are also 'marginal' and potentially 'resistant' subjects who are affiliated to those same communities.[12]

Their intermediary class and cultural status prevents an exoticization and easy consumption of these narratives of cultural difference. Graham Huggan describes how the 'authentic' culturally 'other' object is produced by removing that object from its historical situation, or by decontextualizing it, so that it becomes metonymic of the culture from which it originates.[13] Thus it is rendered non-threatening to the metropolitan consumer, who can access the 'Other' without being implicated in the power relations which shape the relationship between 'Self' and 'Other'. Both Manzoor's and Hai's memoirs cross between inside and outside, community and context, problematizing the idea of a singular authentic Muslim subject and locating the varied subjectivities and practices they sketch in contemporary Britain. However, Manzoor's and Hai's peripheral position in relation to the Muslim communities that they portray also has the potential to entrench divisions between the 'good' Muslim, who has largely 'escaped' his or her cultural and religious background or for whom faith remains uniquely personal and spiritual;[14] and the 'bad' Muslim, who is immersed within culture and community and asserts his or her 'Muslimness' and right to being a Muslim in the public sphere. Again, Huggan is useful here, specifically his appraisal of the tensions between the oppositional potential of 'ethnic autobiography' and the constraints placed upon it by the expectations of a white liberal readership.[15] In the case of British Muslim autobiography, in order to cater to those expectations the autobiographical 'I' might distance itself from the aspects of Muslim culture that do not fit so easily with the central tenets of a liberal multiculturalism, and, in so doing, testify to the good character of some, assimilated British Muslims. A close reading of the two memoirs will illuminate how they negotiate the conflicting pulls of market demands and oppositionality, reason and belief, individualism and communitarianism. My aim in analysing these personal narratives is not to dispute their sincerity or validity but rather to explore and elucidate the political conditions, implications and potential effects of two texts that engage with and enter into the public domain with considerable rhetorical power.

* * *

The paratextual elements of a book shape the reader's expectations of what is to come and thus their approach to the text. Already evident on the cover of *Greetings from Bury Park* is a tension between 'universality' and cultural specificity. It comprises juxtaposed images of prayer beads, sunglasses, a Bruce Springsteen record and concert ticket, and childhood photographs of the author with his younger sister and father. The beads, when placed alongside a pair of sunglasses, could also be read as a sub-cultural fashion accessory, especially by the uninitiated western reader, leaving the photographs, displaying brown faces, as the only clear visual signifier of 'Muslimness' or Asianness'. As snapshots of the 'real', these last in particular add 'authenticity' to the narrative, confirming its status as a 'true story'. The main paragraphs of the back-cover 'blurb', which describe the content of the narrative in broad brushstrokes, mapping its trajectory from 'Lahore to Luton to Ladbroke Grove' and clearly alluding to the protagonist's race and religion, are sandwiched between two summative comments which, echoing the title itself, emphasize its 'universal' themes, marginalizing race and religion. So reviewer Andrew Collins says of *Greetings* that 'you don't have to be a Muslim . . . to get into [it]', and just below it is described as 'an inspiring tribute to the power of music to transcend race and religion' and 'a touching salute of thanks from one working-class Pakistani Muslim boy to the father who died too soon for his son to make him proud'. This last comment simultaneously particularizes (with the words 'Pakistani Muslim') and universalizes (through emphasis on the father–son relationship and the overcoming of hardship). While the singularity of the word 'one' contests the racializing reduction of 'Pakistani Muslim boys' to a homogeneous collective, the individualization it implies also connotes a distancing of the author from the group identity to which he is affiliated. Thus it suggests a refutation on the part of the singular autobiographical subject of both the homogenizing tendencies of mainstream representations of Muslims and the collectivist demands of a minority Pakistani Muslim family and community.[16] And while the cover legitimization of Manzoor's memoir by a British Asian writer who is *not* of Muslim heritage (Hari Kunzru) and two white British journalists suggest a desire on the part of the publisher to reach a mainstream British readership, it also mirrors and anticipates Manzoor's own self-detachment from the Pakistani Muslim culture he describes.

Greetings is in many ways a 'triumph-over-adversity' narrative,[17] about overcoming barriers—of class and poverty, traceable in part to the author's family's migration from Pakistan and their minority status in Britain, but also of (religious) culture and community which are often configured as constraining. In his exploration of the marriage practices of his Pakistani family and community, the arranged marriage emerges as the antithesis to individual love (178–211). When, under maternal pressure, he agrees to be open to approaches from potential brides, Manzoor's verdict is that 'everyone seemed a little too into religion; none sounded like they might actually be a laugh'. And on discovery that one of them wears a hijab, he immediately runs scared (208–209). The 'God-fearing, super-Muslim' anonymous *hijabi* contrasts with the rebellious, foul-mouthed, dyed-haired Laila, the first focus of Manzoor's 'suppressed yearnings' (194–198). Whereas Laila liberates him from his own sense of cultural responsibility and comes to represent individual freedom, the *hijabi*, with her indifference to Springsteen and British pop music and her disapproval of swearing, suggests conformity and obedience.[18] Traceable here is a dichotomy between religious observance or communal cultural practices and Enlightenment values such as autonomous subjectivity and freedom. It is, as is typical of *Greetings*, elliptical rather than overt, emerging here and there in glimpses, which suggests an uneasiness with an assertive Islamic identity on the part of Manzoor. As Reina Lewis has shown, it is in fact especially in contemporary British Muslim veiling practices that the binary of individual subjectivity versus religio-cultural prescription can be deconstructed. The rhetoric British Muslim women use to explain their decision to veil, Lewis demonstrates, frequently

> combines the secular-Enlightenment-derived notion of conscious choice with an allegiance to a universalizing revivalist politics that decrees veiling to be a divine requirement . . . The exponent of veiling is presented as a self-directed sovereign subject—a riposte to the presumption of many . . . that veiling is always and only a sign of female subordination and lack of individuation.[19]

Moreover, the co-existence of religious communitarianism with subjectivity, agency and argumentation becomes particularly evident if we consider the relationship between Muslim practices, such as veiling, and the unequal and frequently hostile context in which they are enacted. Especially for British Muslim youth, such practices can work as a form of agential self-empowerment within a predominantly secular liberal public sphere, as well as against the patriarchal authority of their parents.[20]

Indeed, Manzoor does show an awareness of the possibility of a more critical Islam which does not prescribe obedience and the surrender of doubt, drawing a distinction between religion and the 'cultural values' of his parents' generation.[21] And yet his stated awareness remains truncated, failing to develop into a consideration of the forms this version of Islam might take. In a revealingly elliptical passage where he contemplates his religion of heritage, Manzoor asserts:

> The biggest lie that I was told when I was growing up was that there was only one way to be a Muslim. That way was to be obedient, deferential and unquestioning; it was to reject pleasure and embrace duty, to renounce sensuality and to never ever ask why . . . I kept believing in an Islam which was more tolerant, which did not take itself so seriously that it burnt the books of those it did not approve of. I wanted to be a Muslim like Philip Roth was a Jew or Bruce Springsteen was Catholic. When I was young, that did not seem possible, and so I ran away from my religion. But, eventually, it caught up with me. I still hope to find my reason to believe. (238–239)

The certainty of the word 'lie' is not contrasted with any correction or enlightenment; on the contrary, as the narrative past cedes to the narrative present, where one might expect some illumination of the discovered 'truth', we learn that Manzoor has still not found an alternative mode of being Muslim. Indeed, the assertion that his religion has now 'caught up with' him repeats a claim just a few pages earlier that 'on 9/11 my religion caught up with me', thereby substituting the bafflement that dominates his response to the attacks of 9/11 for the greater understanding of Islam that the reader is set up to expect (235). Manzoor's bafflement at 9/11 and 7/7—and at the much earlier protests by Bradford-based Muslims against Salman Rushdie's *The Satanic Verses*—echoes the limits of understanding articulated in the responses of a range of liberal Anglo-American writers and commentators to the attacks on the Twin Towers.[22] Manzoor's reaction is one of 'alienation', 'confusion' and fear; he cannot 'understand their anger' or, in the case of the 7/7 bombers, 'why they hate[d] this country so much?' (228, 264). His bafflement forecloses explanation and engagement, severing these events from history, economics and politics.[23]

Revealingly, a more tolerant, open and enabling version of Islam emerges in the narrative only where it remains firmly in the private sphere and associated with an older generation. It is as a consequence of renewed interest in his faith, evidenced by frequent visits to the local mosque and plans to visit Mecca, that Manzoor's father takes his younger, fashion-crazy sister Uzma to purchase a pair of knee-high boots (43). Normatively counterposed, religiosity and an overtly sexy fashion item associated with secular permissiveness are brought together. In another incident, Manzoor's mother's religious blessing before an important job interview that will give him independence from his family and cultural expectations, is portrayed, in emotive terms, as profoundly enabling (174–175). It is in this individual, private and purely spiritual relationship with religious faith that the dichotomy between religious strictures and western freedoms breaks down. When religion is private, it is potentially enabling and breeds tolerance; conversely, when it asserts itself in the public domain, it is at best humourless and at worst murderous. That the hijab remains virtual in Manzoor's narrative, its wearer just a voice on the end of the telephone, is suggestive of a general invisibility or absence of an assertive political Muslim identity that is not extremist or violent. The binary of political Islamism versus private faith leaves little room for the activism of British Muslims as a minority group, their mobilization for the right to participate in civic life *as Muslims*, which is impelled in part by the subordinate social position and exclusion experienced by many.[24] If the hijab-clad women is reduced to a virtual cipher for piety and humourlessness, the working-class men who protested against Rushdie's novel in the context of decades of social deprivation and an increasingly hostile attitude towards local Pakistani communities, become implicitly linked with the perpetrators of violent attacks such as those of 9/11 and 7/7: 'If they were prepared to get this upset about a book what else might they get angry about? What else might they be prepared to do?' Manzoor asks (228).[25]

The only other mention of the hijab in Manzoor's memoir occurs in passing in a discussion of the 7/7 bombings. Here, Manzoor contrasts the legal right to wear the hijab enjoyed by a younger generation of British Muslim students with his elder sister Navela's pioneering battle to wear trousers instead of the stipulated skirt to her local Luton school (267). This contrast immediately follows one between the 'extremism' of the bombers, which is construed as a form of ungrateful rejection of the secure Britishness that *they* enjoyed, and Manzoor's own, earlier struggle for acceptance as British (ibid.). Through this juxtaposition, the contemporary integration of Muslim practices into Britishness, exemplified by the hijab, is implicitly aligned with a rejection of Britishness, or with separatism. There is an uncomfortable hint in this somewhat disjointed passage of a continuum from assertive Muslimness to separatism to extremism. In stark contrast to the uneasy presence of the hijab in Manzoor's narrative, other forms of clothing (whether Uzma's boots, his elder brother Sohail's stonewashed jacket and jeans, or the unique *shalwaar kameez* his mother and sisters design when they are not making dresses for British Home Stores) are constructed as a means of asserting an individual identity, against the constraints of cultural conformity and poverty—the latter signified by the family's women's exploited labour sewing clothes (174–175, 62, 66–67). The hijab is, then, an uncomfortable fit in the individualist 'struggle-against-adversity' narrative that dominates Manzoor's memoir.

Manzoor's reversion to his own and his sister's youth when attempting to consider twenty-first-century 'Islamic' extremism can also be seen as a sort of narrative evasion or ellipsis. A more pronounced immersion in the past comes to dominate the final pages of the memoir. Curiously, in place of any considered engagement with the London transport bombings on the part of the narrating autobiographical subject, we are offered the responses of each of his parents—imagined in the case of his deceased father whose reaction is clearly rooted in his generational difference:

> 'And if we had known that they would spit in the face of our labour and our dreams, bring shame to the community, blacken the name of Pakistan . . . and all for what? And they say they're Muslims, and they say it's about politics.' . . . 'Politics is what you talk about before you have families, isn't that right Manzoor sahib' one of the others might say. (268)

It is as if the autobiographical subject is hiding behind the previous generation to compensate for his own lack of answers—for the breakdown of his narration of the place of Islam in his own life and in contemporary multi-cultural Britain. Manzoor's father's friends' absorption of the political in the personal (or 'families') in the above quotation is redolent of the pragmatism of the Muslim men Manzoor contrasts with Rushdie's dissenters—'Muslims who believed in their religion enough to pray and fast but were too busy fiddling the social security to have time to demonstrate against a book they would never read' (228). Whereas Manzoor's father's imagined reaction is to perceive the bombers as ungrateful for a previous generation's labour, Manzoor's mother sees 'the human tragedy rather than the political context' of the bombings, immediately contemplating the emotional fallout for the families of the perpetrators (267). Again, in her response—and so, effectively, in Manzoor's—the personal obscures or privatizes the political, and Manzoor's narrative takes refuge in an earlier generational perspective. The split timeframe of the autobiographical form enables a further degree of ellipsis: while we are told what the narrated subject thinks and feels at various points in his life, the narrating subject frequently remains silent. *Greetings*, then, through its expression of bafflement and strategies of evasion, could be said to 'perform [its] own failure and collapse of voice' in the face of these events with British Muslims at their centre.[26]

* * *

Yasmin Hai's *The Making of Mr Hai's Daughter*, is, like *Greetings*, a coming-of-age memoir structured around a process of self-formation and, to an extent, class mobility. Whereas Hai is from a more privileged background than Manzoor, she too 'progresses', from the lower-middle-class milieu of her north London suburb through Camden School for Girls and Manchester University to the left-liberal high-flying and predominantly secularist world of television journalism. She too tussles with her conscience as she leaves behind mother and *mahalla*. For Hai, however, the trajectory of 'progression' is complex and contradictory: her movement away from *mahalla* to 'mainstream' Britain is one that is facilitated rather than impeded by her father, as is suggested by the memoir's title, which describes her self-formation *as* her father's daughter; and yet it takes her beyond her father's broadly assimilationist attitude to Britishness towards a more nuanced and critical engagement with her culture and religion of heritage. The photograph on the front cover of the paperback edition of a very young Hai clutching a Union Jack with her brother and sister, all three clad in quintessentially English clothes, coupled with the Paisley pattern (which on the hardback cover is 'coloured in' with a Union Jack) and the subtitle 'Becoming British', is clearly suggestive of assimilation. Yet the comic undertones (the exaggerated Englishness of the children's clothes, an arrow pointing from the 'Daughter' of the title to the picture of Hai) implies the gentle ironization and disturbance of this narrative that follows. If Manzoor's *Greetings* is characterized by narrative occlusions and evasions, Hai's self-consciously addresses the contradictions between her father's quest for 'Britishness', the collectivism and communitarianism of the *mahalla*, and the individual freedoms offered by liberal secular middle-class Britain. Indeed, in conjunction with its autobiographical focus on private lives, it engages explicitly with being Muslim in Britain, a focus triggered in part by Hai's experience as a journalist of Muslim heritage in the context of 9/11, 7/7 and their aftermaths.

In Hai's narrative, in contrast to Manzoor's, the hijab, and its fuller, more pious (or, more militant) versions, provide an explicit focal point for exploring the tensions between secularism and faith, individual and community. After describing the bafflement of her colleagues on the BBC programme *Newsnight* at Muslim women's turn to religion, Hai ventures her own opinion on the subject:

> And I must admit that I found it baffling, too. Who were these women who considered themselves secondary to men, shrouded themselves in black cloth to hide their female shame, allowed their husbands to have other wives, walked several steps behind them and happily gave up their careers to be the primary carer at home? Truly baffling—until I remembered that my colleagues were talking about the kind of women I had grown up with. And I didn't know one who usefully fitted their description. (244)

Hai's repetition of the word 'baffling' is redolent of Manzoor's response to Muslim extremism. Yet here bafflement yields to a qualification and illuminating contradiction. In a characteristic narrative move, Hai builds a stereotype, vocalizing—almost ventriloquizing—normative readings of veiled Muslim women, only to dislodge the stereotype, swiftly moving from a

homogenizing position to a deconstructive one. She draws on her own experience—her 'insider' position as a member of a British Muslim community,
albeit one who occupies a peripheral relationship to it—to individualize the
community as well as to distinguish herself from it. A similar move can be
seen in her negotiation of the two social spheres of her teenage years, the
'Bhajis' (her Pakistani British friends from suburban Wembley) and the white,
middle-class Camden girls. When her stories of the liberal and privileged
lifestyle of her Camden friends are not met with admiration and envy by the
'Bhajis', Hai remarks: 'The Bhajis equated these Camden freedoms with burdens. I tried to tell them that this wasn't the case, but they never seemed con-
vinced—though frankly, neither was I' (166). Again, she positions herself in a
borderline position; not only does she straddle cultural boundaries but she is
apparently able to bridge the dividing line between a secular individualism
and a religious communalism, between 'reason' and 'belief', recognizing that
the concept of 'freedom' does not have universal application. Similarly, when
Hai makes a research trip to the north of England in an attempt to learn
more about the so-called segregated Muslim communities of that region she
both echoes and disturbs dominant discourses about Muslim (self-)segrega-
tion when she describes the 'rows and rows of streets teeming with drab, old-
fashioned back-to-backs' as uniquely *white* (303). While this area is mirrored
by a uniquely 'Muslim' one, by making 'whiteness' visible she hints at the root
of segregation in factors such as racism, 'white flight' and economic deprivation, complicating a problematically culturalist understanding of this issue.[27]

While Hai, like Manzoor, is clearly troubled by the entry of religion into
the public or political sphere—something that her secular immigrant father,
whose mission was to make his wife and three children as 'English' as possible, was deeply and passionately opposed to—her rejection of this combination includes an apparently paradoxical tentative admission of its importance:

> Of course, I agree with my father. Religion doesn't have a role to play in
> politics or in our public lives. And yet . . . my father's disapproval of re-
> ligion extended to a disapproval of our old culture and ethnic loyalties.
> He couldn't accept such ideas having any bearing on our modern British
> selves. And yet, that was what provided me with an invaluable sense of
> who I was in later life. (332)

Just as she experiences the importance of an Islamic cultural identity to her
sense of self in the wake of her father's death, so too Hai acknowledges here
the role of religious culture in shaping her identity in more general terms.
In both of these examples, religion can, arguably, remain in the private
domain; her grief for her father, certainly, is private and enacted in the home
or within the *mahalla*. Nevertheless, the potential for an overlapping between
religion-as-private and religion-as-political emerges here in this characteristic
self-contradictory moment in the text, marked by the repeated 'And yet . . . '.

Indeed Hai is explicit in her aim to debunk Muslim stereotypes, describing, for example, her anger at 'hearing another politician bang on about Muslim segregation and Islamic head-dress' in the wake of 9/11 (317). But this anger, and her subtle disturbance of normative discourses surrounding Muslims, is at odds with her own discomfort and anger at her childhood friends' increasing leanings towards religiosity, particularly the decision some of them, including her closest friend Afshan, take to wear the hijab. Despite her apparent understanding of this gesture as individual choice, for Hai her *mahalla* friends have nevertheless 'compromised their individuality'; they 'are ready to go along with every diktat or folly of tribal politics in their desperate need to belong' (333). Echoing her father's burning of her mother's headscarves on her arrival in England from Pakistan decades earlier (25), Hai, by her use of the word 'tribal', implicitly aligns the hijab with the pre-modern, evoking Orientalist conceptions of Islam as incompatible with modernity;[28] and indeed elsewhere, she articulates her difficulty in accepting Afshan's reinterpretation of Islam as feminist, egalitarian and just, as a means of combining faith and belonging with modernity (230–239). For her, Afshan's self-identification as a 'proper Muslim' smacks of the moral absolutism that is *opposed to* modernity (236). Further, the 'belonging' that the *mahalla* girls seek, while explicitly rooted in their 'outsider' status, is aligned with the certainties of assimilation that Hai's father sought and ultimately contrasted with her own ability 'to resist the easy answers', to doubt, to question and to criticize (333). But just as Hai's 'associational' identity as Muslim,[29] her borderline position, entails instability and doubt, so too the choice to embrace and combine the ostensibly conflicting ideologies of religious faith and an individuated post-Enlightenment sense of self arguably carries with it contradiction and conflict that precisely 'resist the easy answers', as well as a considerable degree of agency necessary for the visible adoption of faith in a predominantly secular public sphere. Despite Hai's clear affection for her childhood friends and their importance in her life story, a sense of complexity is lacking in her sketches of Afshan and the other 'Bhajis' who remain little more than stock characters, their individuality subsumed within a quest for 'belonging'. While rooted in the social and material, the choice to assume an overtly Islamic identity is framed in Hai's narrative primarily in terms of conformity, immersion and even submission rather than as an assertion of difference, a form of resistance and a potential means to self-empowerment. The headscarved woman is visibilized or made flesh—in contrast to in *Greetings*—but her voice remains peripheral, leaving the reader wondering: 'How would the Bhajis tell their story?'[30]

The moments of self-contradiction in Hai's narrative can be traced in part to the structural limitations of the individuating, humanistic autobiographical form for accommodating a communitarian Muslim cultural identity. And yet these narrative ruptures also suggest the contradictory nature of the 'ethnic autobiography', including the 'Muslim autobiography' in which a personal engagement with Islam inevitably involves a linking of the private and political, the individual and the collective. If autobiography lends itself to a liberal assertion of individual subjectivity it is also, then, in its 'ethnic' form, potentially subversive of the premise of traditional conceptions of western autobiography. And unlike in Manzoor's memoir, in Hai's the narrator's trajectory towards the formation of an individual subjectivity is complicated by a partial, attenuated gesture towards a Muslim collectivity towards the end of the memoir. Indeed, whereas Manzoor asserts a patriotic Britishness at the end of his memoir, one that silences or occludes the religious culture of his heritage, Hai positions herself as a *British Muslim* in the final sentences of her narrative, asking finally: 'if I don't write and others don't either, how will we Asian Muslims ever contribute to the debate—mostly being conducted by others—about our Britishness? After all, this is our country too' (334).[31]

While Hai's final self-identification as Muslim is on one level an important gesture of claiming a voice for British Muslims, which expresses solidarity and opens out the category of 'Muslim' beyond stereotype, it could also feed into the 'good Muslim'/'bad Muslim' dichotomy that structures liberal understanding of this minority British group. Interestingly, it is a review quote by Muslim journalist Yasmin Alibhai-Brown from the *Mail on Sunday*, reproduced on the paperback edition of the book, that exposes how Hai's memoir could be read along these lines: 'At long last we have a young British Muslim woman writing about her life . . . This book is a gem, from a Briton who needs no lessons on Britishness'. The description is revealingly paradoxical: it implausibly endows Hai with a representative status that she clearly does not have (and, judging from her memoir, would not claim to have); and, with its allusion to 'lessons on Britishness' evoking discourses that have positioned assertive Muslims outside this spurious identity category,[32] it simultaneously suggests another, less savoury 'type' of Muslim that contrasts with the autobiographical subject. In similar vein, a quote from a reviewer for the British Asian magazine *Eastern Eye*, also on the back cover of the paperback edition, states that Hai's portrait 'convinces me that it is entirely possible to be Muslim and British'.[33] However, the compatibility of the autobiographical subject's mode of being Muslim with 'Britishness' conceals the many other British Muslim subjectivities that are sketched in her memoir and are not so consistent with a normative conception of a 'British' identity. Whitlock asks: 'which bodies are breathed into life . . . by autobiography?' and 'What does this product do to the community of origin?'[34] These questions highlight the ways in which these two memoirs that importantly give voice to 'British Muslim' subjects could nevertheless be co-opted into an exclusionary narrative that peripheralizes or even stigmatizes alternative modes of being Muslim. Articulated from the powerful position of 'insider' or 'native informant', Manzoor's denunciation of the 7/7 bombers' anger and hatred as simply unintelligible, and Hai's bafflement at her friends' decision to don the hijab, are all the more compelling, combining with the universalist and emotive address of their autobiographies to potent effect.

The tensions that characterize these memoirs can be traced to the contradictions of a liberal approach to multiculturalism that professes an equality of citizenship but cannot accommodate assertive communitarian Muslim identities in the public sphere. So, the frequent displacement onto a previous generation and an earlier timeframe in Manzoor's text can be seen to operate as a strategy for managing these contradictions, both within his own individual life story and within twenty-first-century Britain. Thus, while Manzoor's narrative frequently fragments and falls silent in the face of these contradictions, by doing so it sheds light on its social conditions and context. In Hai's memoir, these contradictions emerge on the surface of the text. If Manzoor's *Greetings* seems uneasy with the representative status which it will, inevitably, be granted, *The Making of Mr Hai's Daughter* manifests a more confident self-awareness of this status and—through its simultaneous articulation and disarticulation of normative viewpoints—of the preconceptions that may be brought to bear on its subject by a mainstream readership. Although its perspective is circumscribed by her own distance from the *mahalla* and despite its susceptibility to co-option into normative discourses surrounding Muslims, Hai's memoir suggests a will to translate across cultures, and to negotiate between and complicate individualism and communitarianism, 'reason' and 'belief'.

Notes

1. Bart Moore-Gilbert, *Postcolonial Life-Writing: Culture, Politics and Self-Representation* (London and New York: Routledge, 2009), 112.

2. Kobena Mercer, 'Black Art and the Burden of Representation', *Third Text* 10 (Spring 1994): 61–78 (62). Elizabeth Poole and John E. Richardson demonstrate the dominance of negative stories of Muslims in the British media and describe the climate in the last few years as one of 'threat, fear and misunderstanding'. Poole and Richardson, eds, *Muslims and the News Media* (London: I. B. Tauris, 2010), 1.

3. Sarfraz Manzoor, *Greetings from Bury Park: Race, Religion, Rock 'n' Roll* (London: Bloomsbury, 2007); Yasmin Hai, *The Making of Mr Hai's Daughter: Becoming British. A Memoir* (London: Virago, 2008). All references to these texts will be given in parentheses.

4. Gillian Whitlock, *Soft Weapons: Autobiography in Transit* (Chicago: Chicago University Press, 2007), 12.

5. Ibid., 3.

6. Ibid., 17–18, ch. 2.

7. For stereotypes of British Muslims circulating in the media even before 9/11, see Elizabeth Poole, *Reporting Islam: Media Representations of British Muslims* (London: I. B. Tauris, 2002). For a detailed engagement with the potential exclusions of an individualist liberal approach to multiculturalism, see in particular Tariq Modood, *Multicultural Politics: Racism, Ethnicity and Muslims in Britain*

(Edinburgh: Edinburgh University Press, 2005), chs 7–9. I take 'liberal multiculturalism' to mean the reduction of cultural difference to skin colour and/ or individual lifestyle choice, and an ensuing insensitivity to the importance of culture, community and tradition as well as the structural social and economic position of minority groups. In this construction, cultural difference is either co-opted into the normative culture or pushed beyond the boundaries of the 'legitimate' and denounced as irrational, retrogressive and oppressive.

8.   These comments appear on the book covers, with the exception of 'richly humane': Danny Kelly, 'There's Just One Boss in this Family', *Observer*, 27 May 2007, http://www.guardian.co.uk/books/2007/may/27/biography.features (accessed 2 July 2011).

9.   I recognize that this 'type' of reader is a construct and that readers do not form a singular homogeneous group. Readers, however, operate within certain 'regimes of value' formed by specific social relations. See Graham Huggan's discussion, via John Frow, of the readers of postcolonial writing, in Huggan, *The Postcolonial Exotic: Marketing the Margins* (London and New York: Routledge, 2001), 30–31.

10. Mary Louise Pratt, *Imperial Eyes: Travel Writing and Transculturation* (London and New York: Routledge, 1996), 7.

11. Whitlock, *Soft Weapons*, 132.

12. Ibid.

13. Huggan, *Postcolonial Exotic*, 16–17, 158.

14. For a critique of the secularist bid to confine Islam to the private sphere and to separate religion and politics, see S. Sayyid, 'Contemporary Politics of Secularism', in Geoffrey Brahm Levey and Tariq Modood, eds, *Secularism, Religion and Multicultural Citizenship* (Cambridge: Cambridge University Press, 2009), 186–199.

15. Huggan, *Postcolonial Exotic*, 155–176 (163). Huggan's focus here is on Aboriginal autobiography.

16. On the postcolonial writer's embrace of autonomy for these two different reasons, see Moore-Gilbert, *Postcolonial Life-Writing*, 33.

17. Huggan, *Postcolonial Exotic*, 161.

18. See also Manzoor's autobiographical piece 'White Girls' in the 'Pakistan' edition of *Granta* 112 (2010): 243–254.

19. Reina Lewis, 'Veils and Sales: Muslims and the Spaces of Post-Colonial Fashion Retail', in Richard Phillips, ed., *Muslim Spaces of Hope: Geographies of Possibility in Britain and the West* (London: Zed Books, 2009), 69–84 (70).

20. On the quest for self-empowerment among British Muslims, see Anshuman A. Mondal, *Young British Muslim Voices* (Oxford: Greenwood World Publishing, 2008), 20–28.

21. Ibid., 25–26.

22. Robert Eaglestone, '"The Age of Reason is Over . . . an Age of Fury was Dawning": Contemporary Anglo-American Fiction and Terror', *Wasafiri* 22.2 (July 2001): 19–22.

23. To make this point is not to excuse the acts of violence, but to underline the importance of contextualizing them and engaging with them, in order to begin to seek ways of preventing them. See, for example, Tahir Abbas, 'After 7/7: Challenging the Dominant Hegemony', in Phillips, *Muslim Spaces of Hope*, 252–262 (259).

24. The binary also appears in Manzoor's BBC2 film *Luton, Actually*: 'political Islam' is equated with 'a ranting and raving Omar Bakhri' and kept distinct from religion as a 'personal, private faith' (screened 5 March 2005). For the importance of group identity to Muslims, see Tariq Modood, *Multiculturalism: A Civic Idea* (Cambridge: Polity Press, 2007), 106, 39–40, 61.

25. For the importance of distinguishing between the mobilization of Muslims *as Muslim* and 'religious fundamentalism', see ibid., 135.

26. Eaglestone, 'Fiction and Terror', 20.

27. For a deconstruction of the dichotomy of integration versus (self-)segregation, see Ziauddin Sardar, 'Spaces of Hope: Interventions', in Phillips, ed., *Muslim Spaces of Hope*, 13–26 (19–20).

28. See Sayyid, 'Secularism'.

29. Modood, *Multiculturalism*, 106.

30. In Janmahomed's *Love in a Headscarf* the headscarved woman moves to centre stage—the very title of this memoir signalling its deconstruction of the dichotomy of individual choice ('love') and religious communitarian oppression (the 'headscarf', along with the chosen arranged marriage).

31. This implicit difference in the final self-identifications of Manzoor and Hai could be traced in part to gender: Manzoor might feel a particular urgency to distance himself from the hyper-masculinized subjectivities that are so frequently attributed to male Muslim youth, aligning them with criminality and terror. See, for example, Rehana Ahmed, 'British Muslim Masculinities and Cultural Resistance: Kenny Glenaan and Simon Beaufoy's *Yasmin*', *Journal of Postcolonial Writing* 45.3 (September 2009): 285–296.

32. Sardar, 'Spaces of Hope', 20–23; Hai herself criticizes 'phoney definitions' of Britishness (329).

33. While these quotations are of course taken from longer reviews, which may qualify their implications, it is their selection for reproduction on the book itself, and the effect of this, that is of primary interest here.

34. Whitlock, *Soft Weapons*, 9, 15.

4 Voyages Out and In
Two (British) Arab Muslim Women's Bildungsromane

Lindsey Moore

This chapter examines two novels concerned with the experience of Arab Muslim women in national contexts of origin and in migrant situations in Britain, exploring ways in which female protagonists define themselves in relation to national and supra-national communities. The two texts are Ahdaf Soueif's *In the Eye of the Sun* (1992) and Leila Aboulela's *Minaret* (2005). Although both female authors and their main characters identify as Arab and Muslim, the analysis will show that the relative emphasis on these categories varies significantly. Indeed, in bringing together two 'pathfinder' Bildungsromane whose publication dates span thirteen years, I signal a wider turn from Arab to Muslim affiliation. The chapter also assesses, with attention to informing contexts and formal textual qualities, to what extent these novels reflect feminist perspectives.[1]

I have found it instructive, in addressing these core issues, to return to (and complicate) an influential 'second wave' feminist analysis of the Bildungsroman. Rita Felski proposes two meta-structures to the feminist 'self-discovery' narrative, both of which privilege a 'counter-public sphere'.[2] The first comprises a 'voyage out' into society as precondition for an oppositional engagement with gender norms and horizons of expectation. Whereas the Bildungsroman traditionally narrates temporary rebellion but eventual social reconciliation, feminist texts, whilst similarly predicated on separation from an originary context, progress towards the establishment of alternative space in the public domain, sometimes in relation to an elective female (counter-) community. This kind of narrative makes visible the political underpinnings of private experience: in leaving home, protagonists expose and may refuse heteronormative relations.[3] Movement from repetitive domestic time into historical time enables 'a steady accumulation of insights into the structures of power governing relations between men and women'.[4] The plot usually concludes at a point of enhanced self-knowledge that 'functions as a [new] beginning . . . a basis for future negotiation between the subject and society'.[5]

Felski's second model consists of a 'voyage inward', in which female identity is rediscovered by withdrawing from dominant social norms and modes of perception.[6] Here the emphasis is on awakening in a retroactive sense, on recovery or 'a coming to consciousness of a latent female self'.[7] Such narratives feature an underlying circular structure rather than teleological progression. They, like 'voyage out' narratives, are symptomatic of women's alienation from dominant narratives of femininity but, Felski argues, they offer problematic solutions: an essential female identity and/or the privileging of private space already coded as feminine. However, as more recent feminist work emphasizes, staying at or returning home does not necessarily signify a regressive (lack of) movement.[8] One version of the 'voyage in'—the spiritual retreat—has particularly complex resonances, as I will discuss in relation to *Minaret*.

Although Felski privileges the 'voyage out', her focus is not on narratives of transnational migration.[9] As a salient contrast, Mark Stein stresses the politics of arrival for migrant subjects and the transformation, by these subjects and/or their offspring, of postcolonial Britain. For Stein, Bildungsromane represent a first phase of the 'Black British novel of transformation' in which there is a double coming of age: of the protagonist and of the British cultural landscape that s/he transforms. As he summarizes, echoing Felski's 'voyage out' argument about women's texts, 'the black British novel of transformation does not predominantly feature the privatist formation of an *individual*—instead, the text constitutes a symbolic act of carving out of space, of creating a *public sphere*'.[10] However, Stein elaborates on a relatively well-known story of Black and Asian immigration and impact on the British cultural landscape. By contrast, a first generation of British Arab writers has only recently emerged and histories of Arab immigration are less acknowledged in the public domain: witness the inclusion for the first time, in the 2011 Census, of an Arab ethnicity category.[11]

In other ways, of course, Arabs, and especially Arab Muslims, have become hyper-visible in British public space since 9/11. When Amin Malak suggests Islam has cultural as well as spiritual purchase on contemporary identities, he highlights a long *durée* of negative representation that increasingly makes identification as Muslim a *political* choice. Malak's focus on 'identitarian Islam' encompasses believers, those who claim Islam as an important cultural or political identity marker, and others with a looser civilizational affiliation.[12] In what follows, I similarly highlight variety in women's literary engagements with Islam, which functions variously as belief system and set of ritual practices; domain of subtending cultural codes; conduit for political dissent; affirmative identity marker; and/or place of 'arrival' and self-discovery. This latter raises questions about Stein's privileging of the public domain and suggests the possibility of more temporary and/or partial affiliations to British national identity. My analysis, which moves from one context of publication (the early 1990s) to a later one (the mid-2000s), and also from one setting (the 1960s and 1970s) to a more recent one (the late 1980s to the early twenty-first century), traces a shift in modes of identification from Arab to Muslim and assesses its impact on feminist interpretative paradigms.

Ahdaf Soueif, *In the Eye of the Sun* (1992)

Soueif, an Egyptian-born, London-based author, sets her first novel, the Bil-dungsroman of semi-autobiographical Asya, against a background of social, economic and political change in Egypt and the wider Arab world. The novel charts the apotheosis and decline of Nasserite pan-Arabism, described as a 'turning-point' in postcolonial Egyptian history.[13] It maps the character-istics of Felski's 'voyage out' on to a migrant story but with some significant differences, notably in its inclusion of a return 'home'. This, as I will explain, highlights the complexity of the protagonist's cultural definition of self, par-ticularly when it comes to a confrontation between her own and other Egyp-tian women's performances of gender.

The frame narrative opens in 1979 in London. Asya, whilst hosting her uncle while he undergoes cancer treatment, is composing text on birth control:

> Her task right now is . . . to formulate a 'message', and to fashion out of the notes two sets of text . . . : one set detailed and technical for the ex-tension personnel; the health workers, teachers, outreach workers, and village leaders all over the Third World . . . and the other text, simple and punchy for those same health workers, teachers, outreach workers and village leaders to deliver to their target audience: the men, women and children of the villages of the Third World—starting with the Arab Middle East—starting with Egypt. (22)

Important linked concerns are set up in this seemingly innocuous passage: a motif of health/disease; relations between the West and the Arab world; related anxieties about the medium and register of transmitting knowledge from the position of 'native informant'; Asya's ability to 'zoom in' on Egypt from abroad; and sex, particularly as it affects women's lives. As the quota-tion suggests, Asya's perspective is both enabled and circumscribed by her English-educated, urban, privileged and now migrant background, but her consistent impulse is to bridge and translate. Aptly, as we learn in Soueif's *Sandpiper* (1996) collection (in which Asya also features), her name integrates references to Pharaonic Egypt, Islam and Judaism; it also means 'Asia' in Ara-bic, signalling an identity that transcends national/regional definition and—I think ironically—self-Orientalizes.[14] Self-translation is not portrayed as easy: when asked to 'perform' the pronunciation of her name to a linguistics class in the UK, Asya falls temporarily aphasic (354).[15] Then and elsewhere, her perspective on Egypt is mediated by temporal and spatial distance. When a letter arrives in London, detailing her dissident brother-in-law's arrest by President Sadat's Central Security forces, she 'stands up and walks to the window. In the street people come and go. A delivery van is parked on the yellow line and the driver is arguing with the traffic warden. The sun shines' (32). This snapshot of dislocation simultaneously functions as a portal: as the letter jolts Asya's memory, we turn, in an extended flashback, to her young adulthood in Egypt, from 1967 to her departure in 1973.

Asya's personal story is interwoven with diary-like entries relaying historical events and implicitly reflecting upon their mode of transmission. The use of cinematic scenes generates an impression of all the world a-stage around the protagonist's 'less-than-microscopic patch of history' (76); it also exposes processes of historical (mis)construction. A notable example, given the historical shift that Soueif begins to register, is the Egyptian media's false representations of the June 1967 war that President Nasser (Gamal 'Abd al-Nasir) unsuccessfully waged against Israel:

> 8.45 a.m
> Sinai
> Israeli planes finish attacking and destroying most of the Egyptian airforce as it sits on 'secret' military runways. The runways too are rendered useless.
> . . .
>
> 9 a.m
> Cairo, Zamalek
> Soraya Mursi phones her sister Lateefa [Asya's mother] to say that they can hear what sounds like bombs from the direction of Abbassiya.
>   Asya al-Ulama stretches, listens to the phone ring in the living-room, and decides to stay in bed for ten more minutes.
>
> 9 a.m
> Cairo
> The radio and television services begin to broadcast one announcement after another counting the number of enemy planes shot down from the Egyptian skies. (50)

Hilary Mantel suggests that 'high politics and domestic minutiae are juxtaposed' in this novel,[16] but the structure is more accurately one of concentric circles representing the private, the national, the regional and the global. One of the challenges for Asya is to reconcile her inner life with 'the world and action and history taking shape' (61).

Asya's coming-of-age story broadly mirrors Egypt's postcolonial trajectory: each moves from youthful aspiration to a qualified 'independence'. As such, attempts by Egyptian and other Arab leaders to secure self-determining identities in relation to the West (including Israel) are paralleled by Asya's struggle for recognition, particularly in her relationships with men: first Saïf, then (and for a while simultaneously) Gerald, a 'wispy' or neo-Orientalist (473). While (British) Gerald functions as a rather reductive type, unable to see past his exotic construction of Asya, (Egyptian) Saïf is a complex character given first-person interludes, but these—replete with scenes focused on looking at Asya—underline his shared inability to understand her.

Saïf's name, meaning 'piercing sword', is an ironic reference to his inability to 'consummate' his relationship with Asya, and a (seemingly unfounded) suspicion arises that he has lung cancer. Wider allusions to diseased or debilitated male bodies suggest allegorical significance. Notably, the 1967 war is juxtaposed with an injury to Asya's uncle, when an army truck mounts and crushes his car: Malak reads the incident as a metaphor for the self-destructive tendencies of the postcolonial Egyptian state.[17] The central point, for me, is Asya's struggle to define herself independently against the men in her life and, allegorically, the backdrop of a growing crisis of confidence in Egyptian and wider Arab leadership. The protagonist's motives for leaving Egypt, shortly after the 1967 war, are ostensibly educational. However, and significantly, she departs just as Egypt enters a period of increased social mobility, consumerism and collaboration with the West that spur popular backlash. Asya leaves, in short, on a historical cusp: 1967 represents 'a closing chapter' (222) both of her life story and of a dominant (pan)-Arabist construction of Egypt.

After an extended interlude in the UK, Asya attempts to return to a context that, in her absence, has irrevocably changed. In the Epilogue, set in 1980, Egypt is entangled in neo-imperialist politics and new Islamic movements are resurgent. Whereas early Cairo scenes demonstrate the knowledge of a 'local'—for example, a panoramic depiction telescopes to Asya's grandfather in his shop near the Central Market (65)—there can be no Arcadian return to an eponymous 'youth in the eye of the sun' because 'her' Cairo has been overlaid with new historical significance:

> Even on the drive home from the airport . . . she had realised that she would not have found her way home alone: new roads, new buildings, new roundabouts, the great statue of Rameses II, once an imposing landmark outside Cairo Central Station, now slips by insignificantly below them as they speed along '6th October Bridge'!—it used to be that if you didn't want to call a street 26th July Street you could carry right on calling it Fuad Street—and everybody did—but this bridge has no other name: it was *built* as 6th October Bridge. (749)

Asya notes here the redundancy of an imperial and colonial history (King Fuad II's brief reign before Egypt became a Republic in 1952), but the new nomenclature is unwittingly ironic. 6 October was the date of the outbreak of the 1973 attack on Israel, the early phases of which saw Egyptian gains, including the return of Sinai. By the time Asya returns in 1980, though, the Sadat regime has lost credibility, partly due to its unsuccessful manipulation of Islamist groups.[18]

Soueif has emphasized that the novel portrays religion as 'a benign, cohesive factor . . . part of what makes Asya come home'.[19] But when a compatriot visits Asya in Lancaster and asks the direction of the Qibla in order to perform the 'Asr prayers, our protagonist is embarrassingly ignorant: 'Oh God! . . . I should know the answer to this like I know my own name' (547). She perceives Islam as an anchoring aspect of the environment, rather than as a dynamic cultural force: she is therefore baffled by a student who 'is young and has a beard and does his prayers at the right times but he also seems a bit to the left so I can't make him out' (352). When, on her return to Egypt, she encounters a new and pervasive religiosity, Asya objects that 'religion for me . . . and everyone was Ramadan and our grandparents praying and things like that'. She must be told that the old Nasserite slogans of her generation— 'Non-Alignment', 'Socialism', 'Arab Unity' (17)—are no longer the ones that command widespread loyalty.

Whilst teaching at Cairo University, Asya has a tense encounter with a female student wearing a niqab, who writes that she wants to learn English as 'the language of my enemy' but rebuffs invitations to engage in dialogue. Another student has to explain that her classmate 'cannot speak . . . because the voice of a woman is *'awra* [taboo]' (754). Asya initially tries to comprehend this within the static frame of tradition: '[t]he women in the villages Asya has been to visit cover themselves up too. But there they do it naturally, without fuss. They do it because that's what their mothers and grandmothers have always done' (755). On reflection, she grasps what is, in fact, a manifestation of Islamic revivalism, reflecting that the student provides 'some kind of answer to what's happening all around us—all the manifestations of the West', that 'is genuine . . . not imported or borrowed from anywhere' (755).[20] In the immediate aftermath of the scene, however, Asya slips into solipsistic reverie:

> as far as this girl—and the others who thought like her—were concerned she was doing a sort of porno-spread up here on the podium for the world to see . . . What if they knew—what if they had looked through the window of the cottage and seen a blond, blue-eyed man kneeling, his head between her thighs–. (754)

Geoffrey Nash, whilst critical of Soueif's failure to scrutinize the class privilege that constrains Asya's perspective, notes that her female characters tend to 'move in isolation, between boundaries of inimical discourses, implicitly questioning traditional stereotyping of women's role[s] at the same time as negotiating their own way around contemporary Western norms'.[21] This provides a way of (re)viewing Asya contemplating the image of her own (multiply) exposed body. This Bildungsroman continuously negotiates *plural* cultural constructions of the female body. As a young woman, Asya encounters repressive attitudes towards desire when her friends' families attempt to police the boundaries of their daughters' behaviour, particularly when it comes to association with 'outsiders' (notably Palestinians), and Asya's own behaviour is always under (somewhat ineffectual) surveillance and moderated by narrow definitions of normative sexual behaviour.[22] Ironically, the 'voyage out' enmeshes her more thoroughly in heteronormative patterns: Gerard's attitudes are those of a 'sexual imperialist' (723), while Saïf hits and rapes her in a fit of sexual jealousy and then surrounds himself with a 'modern harem' of British and American women (725). Asya's migrant experience underscores the tenaciousness and universality of normative gender scripts even though the *content* of the script differs from one context to another. In the seeming contrast between Asya's ostensibly liberated self and her veiled student, Asya remains caught in the same gaze that the student refutes—but, arguably, negatively reinforces—by veiling her body and voice. As Meyda Yeğenoğlu argues:

> If veiling is a specific practice of situating the body within the prevailing exigencies of power, so is unveiling . . . the unveiled body is no less marked or inscribed; rather a whole battery of disciplinary techniques and practices have [also] produced Western women's bodies and therefore not-to-veil is no less inscriptive than being veiled.[23]

Asya eventually leaves both Saïf and Gerard: reflecting Felski's argument about an exposure of the politics of private relations, this constitutes a crucial aspect of her *Bildung* and enables her to return to Cairo. However, the long preceding period of irresolution is marked by a repeatedly evoked tension between 'art and life' that leads to neurotic symptoms.[24] Her immersion in *English literature* has particularly ambivalent effects. Whereas Asya's academic mother specializes in 'Oriental' influences on the English Romantics and evinces little anxiety about the (post)colonial contexts of her work, the effects of Orientalism, Romantic individualism and colonialism on the daughter remain charged. Asya's identification with a mummified Egyptian woman in the British Museum—'My ancestor, my sister' (429)—is due partly to the state of her own marriage (she calls the woman 'the Princess', Saïf's name for her), but Asya's own cultural and geographical dislocation suggests itself as analogy.

To return to Nash's critique above, Asya's upbringing in a 'determinedly untraditional' family (78) structurally limits her perspective on other Egyptian women. However, formative relationships with women from other social strata enable the author to suggest that gendered politics connect women within Egypt and between 'East' and 'West'. Asya's sexual knowledge is gleaned through conversations with her nanny, 'Dada' Zeina, and her grandmother, whose rural origins connect her with the women for whom Asya will later produce pamphlets on contraception; the link accrues pathos as

Asya's sex life is revealed as unsatisfying and rather damaging. Nevertheless, the scene with the veiled student marks a limit in Asya's—and perhaps
the author's—ability to empathize with particular assertions of cultural identity. Asya's 'voyage out' leads to a heightened feminist awareness, but one
delimited by 'second wave' definitions of spatial and sexual emancipation.
She returns, too, as a relatively unreconstructed, albeit disillusioned, Nasserite, confronting a changing demographic and 'sociocultural vernacular'
informed by mass migration to the urban centres; the rise of an educated
generation with conservative roots; Sadat's Infitah (open-door) policy; and
the growing influence of Wahhabism from the Gulf.[25] Islamism emerges
as a mode of dissent from repressive state politics and western hegemony,
but Asya only partly understands its appeal. Having said this, her tentative
response is not incommensurate with Leila Ahmed's analysis, which sounds
a note of caution about the 'vague' Islamic knowledge of many young adherents and the possibility of their co-optation by conservative groups inimical
to women's rights.[26] In this context, both the elected silence of Asya's veiled
interlocutor and her own confessional narrative gesture towards the ongoing
challenges of defining feminism in the historically, politically and culturally
complex field that is contemporary Egypt.

Leila Aboulela, *Minaret* (2005)

As miriam cooke argues, the rise since the late 1970s of movements that
refute the Arab (pan-)nationalist narrative and instead claim ideological
affiliation to Islam, exacerbated by the post-9/11 'return of the civilizational
binary that structures the logic of empire', means that

> Arab women activists who have long been dealing with the class-patriar-
> chy conundrum within the global system are [now also] deconstructing
> . . . religious texts to find spaces of empowerment for women. Some are
> joining Islamist groups and are working within their logic; others are
> resolutely rejecting implication within such movements. All, however,
> are learning how to situate themselves at the nexus of religion, place,
> and feminist practice.[27]

The strategic connection of religion and location within feminist discourse
is not a new feature of Arab women's writing.[28] It is, though, newly visible in
fiction produced in English and particularly in Arab diaspora fiction.[29]
Leila Aboulela, to date the most high-profile advocate of the Islamic
revival in English-language literature, has connections to Sudan (where she
grew up), Egypt (where she was born), Britain and Qatar (where she currently lives). She has described her work as 'Muslim immigrant fiction',[30]
indicating that geographical specificity is less central to her vision than faith-
based identification. Aboulela explains that her characters are 'ordinary

Muslims trying to practice their faith in difficult circumstances and in a society . . . unsympathetic to religion'.[31] This suggests a retrenchment of the self by (implicitly) migrant subjects who are marginalized in (ostensibly) secular public space. The author also explains that she aims to 'move away from myself, to touch something common, universal . . . lifted up from the ordinary'.[32] Relevant here is her belief that 'for a Muslim, Shari'ah is something personal, something that does not need anyone else to implement it'.[33]

Aboulela's characters can be interpreted in terms of 'neo-Islamic' identity, which emphasizes an individual religiosity that displaces ethnicity and culture. For Olivier Roy, this is a consequence of deterritorialization: Muslim identity 'has to express itself explicitly in a non-Muslim or Western context. The construction of a "deculturalised" Islam . . . can . . . fit with every culture, or, more precisely, could be defined beyond the very notion of culture'.[34] In terms of the horizon of expectation, Talal Asad explains that the *ummatu-l-muslimîn* (*ummah*) 'is neither limited nor sovereign, for unlike Arab nationalism's notion of *al-umma al-'arabiyya*, it can and eventually should embrace all of humanity'.[35] Whilst Aboulela's protagonists also claim a (non-exclusive) British identity, they privilege a *supra*-national space of belonging and thereby challenge the frame, rather than merely the content (as Stein suggests), of the nation.

Minaret, Aboulela's second novel, uses romantic plotting devices—the opening pages stage an encounter between Najwa (the female protagonist) and a young male stranger (to which I will return)—but love is eventually subordinated to personal transformation: reflecting Felski's description of the 'voyage in', the novel is a spiritual Bildungsroman. Its pedagogical aspect manifests in the disjunction between the two versions of Najwa that we encounter in the early stages of the novel and the process of reconciliation that is then narrated.[36] The novel opens in 2003 and returns to 1984–1985, 1989–1990 and 1991, as well as continuing into 2004. It works through the remembered past towards the narrative present: the focus is on what Najwa has become. However, the process of emergence involves the retrieval of something psychologically interior and temporally anterior to the narrated journey. This (migrant, linear) 'voyage out' is really a (spiritual, circular) 'voyage in'. Even as a teenager in Khartoum, Najwa is aware of an inner 'hollow place. A darkness that would suck me in and finish me'.[37] The call to prayer will come to represent an alternative future to the one most readily available to members of her generation and class: 'dreams shaped by pop songs and American films' (35). Interiority, here, is the horizon of expectation and transformation, not, as the above quotation at first suggests, a locus of death.

The catalyst for change is Najwa's exile to London following the execution of her father, due to shifting allegiances amongst Sudan's political elite. Najwa is forced, following her mother's death and her twin brother's imprisonment, to support herself. At the commencement of the frame narrative, she starts work as nanny/housekeeper to a wealthy part-Sudanese family. Outside their apartment, she has a brief initial encounter with Tamer, the younger brother of the woman whose young child Najwa is to care for; he is a devout Muslim. The two become increasingly close until their relationship is discovered; then, paid off by the matriarch, Doctora Zeinab, Najwa resigns herself to a future without family, but with enough money to plan a *Hajj*. While romance is foreclosed, the spiritual journey is further enabled.

At the heart of the text is Najwa's reversion to Islam in 1991.[38] She departs from the secular consumerist values that defined her upper-class life in Khartoum and are further exposed in London, where Najwa gains weight in a grotesque parody of materialism: bending down to pick up coins when buying *Slimming* magazine, 'My stomach was too full. I burped garlic' (129). As Felski argues, the 'voyage in' often involves 'moral and aesthetic revulsion against the very nature of contemporary social reality, which is perceived as alienating and debased'.[39] Najwa's self-loathing is exacerbated when she succumbs to the sexual pressure of Anwar, a secular nationalist forced into exile once the forces that destroyed Najwa's father fall, in turn, to an Islamist coup. Looking in the mirror after sleeping with him, Najwa recalls also being distracted by her own image while her father was being arrested: as these narcissistic moments in the past and the present conflate, she vomits (173). This marks a nadir, concluding a metaphorics of 'falling' (56) and 'sliding' (179). At exactly this point, Najwa 'discovers' an alternative community.[40] The contrast is replicated structurally: the narrative shifts forward to a 2003–2004 scene describing the 'silky, tousled, non-linear' atmosphere—and, to recall Felski again, the counter-public domain—of a women's Eid party (183).

Not long after she starts to attend a women's group at the mosque, Najwa starts to wear hijab. This encourages her to reconceptualize the relationship between self and world. Once again in front of the mirror, she reflects that

> I was another version of myself, regal like my mother, almost mysterious. Perhaps this was attractive in itself, the skill of concealing rather than emphasizing, to restrain rather than to offer . . . Around me was a new gentleness. The builders who had leered down at me from scaffoldings couldn't see me any more. I was invisible and they were quiet. All the frissons, all the sparks died away. Everything went soft. (246, 247)

Najwa's relationship to her veiled body is depicted in ambiguous terms. Saba Mahmood's argument, that veiling is part of the self-*production* of pious identity, does not quite fit Najwa's insistence on an authentic 'concealed' self.[41] The passage also suggests an element of self-exoticization, although our protagonist asserts elsewhere that 'the hijab is a uniform, the official, outdoor version of us'. Without it, her 'nature is exposed' (186); however, wearing it makes her *more* vulnerable, as we see when a stranger assaults her as 'Muslim scum' (80–81). Yeğenoğlu advises that we think of 'the veil' as 'a second skin' but, as Sara Ahmed and Jackie Stacey point out, the skin itself is a 'fleshy interface between bodies and worlds'. Any such interface 'becomes, rather than simply is, meaningful' and 'is always open to being read (and being read differently)'.[42] As is the case for Asya in Soueif's novel, Najwa's gender performance registers conflicting cultural norms; while Asya is exposed as a 'Westernized' woman in Egypt, Najwa's modesty is a provocation in Britain.

As Waïl S. Hassan points out, whereas Soueif's work stages linguistic and cultural interfaces, Aboulela's chooses an alternative to leftist (and Arabist) nationalism and liberal feminism. In the latter's work, 'divine translation negates human agency, interrupts history, and supersedes all worldly affiliations . . . The convert begins life anew, with a clean slate, all previous sins wiped out, and acquires a new identity'.[43] Najwa's 'falling' trajectory leads to a 'settling at the bottom . . . And there, buried below, was the truth' (240). Whereas, I have argued, the confessional detail of Soueif's novel has allegorical import, Aboulela's protagonists withdraw from history and evince 'supra-political' attitudes.[44] Tamer voices frustration with a perceived need, amongst British Muslim youth, to be politicized in order to be a good Muslim. And when Najwa asks him if he sees himself as Sudanese, he replies: 'My mother is Egyptian. I've lived everywhere except Sudan: in Oman, Cairo, here. My education is Western and that makes me feel that I am Western. My English is stronger than my Arabic. So I guess, no, . . . I guess being a Muslim is my identity'. This identification is at odds with his family's self-definition as Arab, but is one which Najwa shares: 'I feel that I am Sudanese but things changed for me when I left Khartoum. Then even while living here in London, I've changed. And now, like you, I just think of myself as Muslim' (110). Najwa further deprivileges (Arab) ethnicity when she suggests that she and her British Asian friend Shahinaz share a crucial elective affinity: they 'both want to become better Muslims' (105).[45]

Although *Minaret* is a migration novel, there is a sense in which geographical movement is instrumentally conceived. As I have suggested, the London environment consolidates a sense of lack already present in Khartoum and the moral compass of Najwa's journey—as the novel's title suggests—is a transnational symbol. Spiritual space is portrayed as an *alternative* to public space and its disciplinary mechanisms. Some of these are historically specific: in 2003, Najwa 'sense[s] the slight unease [Tamer] inspires . . . Tall, young, Arab-looking, dark eyes and the beard, just like a terrorist' (100). The signification of difference also operates in more deeply rooted ways. Complicating her struggle with the appearance of her *female* body are the internalized effects of 'my shitty-coloured skin next to [English] placid paleness' (174) and differentiating markers within a single ethnic group: although they are all from privileged Arab backgrounds, Najwa's supposedly darker complexion, in conjunction with her hijab and occupation, mark her as socially inferior in the eyes of Tamer's family (116).

Najwa's retreat into interior spaces—physical, sartorial and psychologi-cal—strategically forecloses upon this troubling public world, allowing her to 'step away from life and stand in the shade, watch it roll on without me, changeable and aggressive' (255). However, her worldview continues to be informed by a rather unreflective notion of gendered difference, suggesting a championing of *feminine* rather than *feminist* values. When observing fellow students in Khartoum, she differentiates between '[g]irls like me who didn't wear tobes or hijab' and 'boys [who] were members of the [secular National] Front' (43). And when Anwar condemns the Islamist coup in Sudan, Najwa thinks: 'I did not want to look at these big things because they overwhelmed me. I wanted me, my feelings and dreams . . . I did not have the words, the education or the courage . . . I yearned to go back to being safe with God' (241–242). Even within the religious paradigm, whereas Tamer fantasizes about being in the Mahdi's army, Najwa 'would like to pray with them, but I wouldn't like the war' (108). Nowhere in *Minaret* do we find a *structural* critique of gender norms, for example in the conception of public space as normatively masculine that hijab partly reflects.

There are suggestions, however, that Najwa is a *fausse naïve* and not alto-gether reliable narrator. The novel opens: 'I've come down in the world. I've slid to a place where the ceiling is low and there isn't much room to move. *Most of the time* I'm used to it. *Most of the time* I'm good' (1, emphasis added). Immediately before Najwa first encounters Tamer, we have the first of several mirror scenes. This one 'shows a woman in a white headscarf and beige, shapeless coat. Eyes too bright and lashes too long, but still *I look* homely and reliable' (3, emphasis added), suggesting that the self is strategically veiled and not quite out of sight. The opening of the novel also ambiguously juxtaposes the eponymous minaret with a metaphor of unruly womanliness:

> London is at its most beautiful in autumn. In summer it is seedy and swollen . . . and in spring, the season of birth, there is always disappoint-ment. Now it is at its best, now it is poised like a mature woman whose beauty is no longer fresh but still surprisingly potent. (1)

By the end of the novel, maturity has been reconceived as the sublimation of secular desire. However, the final lines describe a dream of a ruined room in which 'Things that must not be seen, shameful things, are exposed. The ceiling has caved in, the floor is gutted and the crumbling walls are smeared with guilt' (276). This recalls the family history that brings Najwa to Lon-don and the reason she is 'afraid of politics' (117). It also exemplifies a point made by Felski, that dreams and hallucinations in women's 'voyages in' often signify repudiation of the past and ritual self-purification.[46] The ruined room of Najwa's nightmare, in recalling her father's corruption and the bad faith of his Sudanese class, functions as 'synecdoche for a westernised Middle-Eastern materialism that is only fit for the fire and which through her faith

Najwa has transcended'.[47] But if an unassimilable history is the root cause of Najwa's investment in the belief that 'Allah . . . will replace the past with something grander, more potent and enhanced' (189), this surely has an ambiguous resonance. Trauma constitutes an *ongoing* threat to identity here; it always potentially 'undoes the self by breaking the ongoing narrative, severing the connections among remembered past, lived present, and anticipated future'.[48] I thus share Hassan's view that faith 'glues the splinters [of Najwa's traumatized self] together and encloses their sharp edges within a protective frame. Yet their danger remains very real and threatening'.[49] For me, Najwa's 'reversion' or 'voyage in' is not altogether credible, although its overdetermined qualities present the possibility of a degree of irony and my reading position, as a non-Muslim, may influence my response.

Both Asya's and Najwa's migrant 'voyages out' are, in important but different ways, also 'voyages in'. Asya's journey, which involves a geographical return, posits imperfect reconciliation with (a changed) 'home' and limited identification with her female compatriots, suggesting that multiple dimensions of self must continually be negotiated. Najwa's journey, which retrieves an anterior self posited as more authentic, does not require a geographical return: the *ummah* transcends national contexts of origin and provides an alternative all-female community. While both texts undoubtedly present a female search for identity, they both also challenge reader perceptions of feminist discourse and practice. Here we should remember not only the problematic engendering of postcolonial nation-states—which Soueif's novel strategically reverses, positing national history as analogue to a central narrative of female self-development—but also problematic *transnational* reiterations of women as bearers and boundary markers of culture.[50]

In the two Bildungsromane I have discussed, we see the difficult process of (trans)cultural insertion of the female self reflected in particular forms of subjectivity: the texts feature multiple or fractured perspectives, refracted through a discontinuous temporal structure. The protagonists must negotiate borders and interfaces between private and public and national and transnational contexts that gender them in particular (classed, ethnic, religious/ non-religious) ways. This is perhaps as it should be, given that the notion of a 'whole self' is an ideological fiction.[51] If replicated uncritically, genre can have a conservative function, and we should not forget the problematic lure of 'insider' perspectives—in English, moreover—on women in Islam.[52] Feroza Jussawalla suggests that in the case of postcolonial Bildungsromane, 'the problem of the *bildung*, of personal growth, is enacted in the narrator's discursive self-understanding rather than in the events which the hero experiences'.[53] Stein, too, emphasizes the centrality of *voicing* identity in migrant/ minority fiction.[54] This highlights processes of articulation, in both senses of the word. I have stressed ways in which movement between different historical and geographical frames underlines the complexity of postcolonial women's self-fashioning and the continuous negotiation that self-identification as Arab and Muslim and (partly) British requires.

The textual comparison I have provided suggests a particular tension or transition. Whereas Soueif's protagonists are in some ways constrained by their privileged social backgrounds but define themselves as (elite) Egyptian Arabs, Aboulela's work illustrates that 'Islam . . . transcends signifiers of race, gender, class and nationalism'.[55] My choice of texts is symptomatic: new modes of affiliation to Islam and hence of recentring the self are emerging in the place of erstwhile nationalist and pan-Arabist loyalties, partly impelled by the need to reject secular space in—not exclusively—migrant settings. *In the Eye of the Sun* ends with Asya identifying with another Pharaonic princess, this time one unearthed 'at home' in Egypt: 'The composure, the serenity, of her smile tells of someone who had always known who she was . . . here she is, delivered back into the sunlight still in complete possession of herself' (785). The 'objective correlative' that regrounds Asya here is pre-colonial and, in contrast with her affinities in the majority of the text, pre-Arab, but definitively Egyptian. By contrast, *Minaret*'s Najwa bypasses national (counter-) identification, affiliating herself instead to the *ummah*. It is too early to comment on the potential for a secular (re)turn in the context of the so-called—but perhaps significantly named—'Arab Spring'. What is clear, though, is that Arab Muslim women's creative work continues to negotiate multiple paradigms that exert pressure upon, even as they may partly enable, women's articulations of individual and collective identity.

Notes

1. This investigation is partly impelled by calls for greater attention to the formal qualities of postcolonial writing: see Elleke Boehmer, 'A Postcolonial Aesthetic: Repeating Upon the Present', in Janet Wilson, Cristina Şandru and Sarah Lawson Welsh, eds, *Rerouting the Postcolonial: New Directions for the New Millenium* (Abingdon: Routledge, 2010). I am reminded of the need to differentiate between women's and feminist writing by Rita Felski, *Beyond Feminist Aesthetics: Feminist Literature and Social Change* (Cambridge, MA: Harvard University Press, 1989).
2. Felski, *Beyond*, 9–12, 126–127.
3. Ibid., 133–141.
4. Ibid., 131.
5. Ibid., 133. Arab women's writing continues to feature struggles to emerge from constraining socio-cultural environments: in, for example, Fadia Faqir's third novel *My Name is Salma* (London: Doubleday, 2007).
6. Felski, *Beyond*, 141–150.
7. Ibid., 143.
8. Sara Ahmed *et al.*, 'Introduction: Uprootings/Regroundings: Questions of Home and Migration', in Sara Ahmed, Claudia Castañeda, Anne-Marie Fortier

and Mimi Sheller, eds, *Uprootings/ Regroundings: Questions of Home and Migration* (Oxford: Berg, 2003), 1–19 (1, 3). For examples pertaining to Arab women writers and filmmakers, see Lindsey Moore, *Arab, Muslim, Woman: Voice and Vision in Postcolonial Literature and Film* (London: Routledge, 1998), ch. 4.

9.   Felski, *Beyond*, 169. Felski focuses upon North American and Western European women's autobiographical realist writing between the 1960s and 1980s.

10. Mark Stein, *Black British Literature: Novels of Transformation* (Columbus, OH: Ohio State University Press, 2004), 30 (emphasis added).

11. See Yousef Awad, 'Cartographies of Identities: Resistance, Diaspora, and Trans-Cultural Dialogue in the Works of Arab British and Arab American Women Writers' (PhD thesis, University of Manchester, 2011).

12. Amin Malak, *Muslim Narratives and the Discourse of English* (Albany, NY: State University of New York Press, 2005), 3–5.

13. Ahdaf Soueif, *In the Eye of the Sun*, 2nd edn. (London: Bloomsbury, 1999), 93. Subsequent references will be included parenthetically in the main text.

14. Malak, *Muslim*, 130; Soueif, 'Mandy', *Sandpiper* (London: Bloomsbury, 1996), 87–104 (93).

15. Interestingly, the other word she fails to pronounce is Quran (354).

16. Hilary Mantel, 'Double Identity: *In the Eye of the Sun*', *New York Review of Books* 60.15 (23 September 1993): 28 (28).

17. Malak, *Muslim*, 133, 131.

18. See Leila Ahmed, *Women & Gender in Islam: Historical Roots of a Modern Debate* (New Haven: Yale University Press, 1992), 217. Sadat supported Islamist groups in order to suppress the left, but was assassinated by officers affiliated to radical offshoots of the Muslim Brotherhood in 1981.

19. Saïdeh Pakravan, 'An Interview with Ahdaf Soueif', *Edebiyat: The Journal of Middle Eastern Literature* 6.2 (1995): 275–286 (281).

20. On new forms of Islamic dress that have arisen in Egypt and beyond since the 1970s, see Ahmed, *Women*, 217–234.

21. Geoffrey Nash, *The Anglo-Arab Encounter: Fiction and Autobiography by Arab Writers in English* (Bern: Peter Lang, 2007), 75.

22. For example, after watching Fellini's sexually explicit film *Satyricon*, Asya's uncle explains away female desire as an 'ill[ness]' (6).

23. Meyda Yeğenoğlu, *Colonial Fantasies: Towards a Feminist Reading of Orientalism* (Cambridge: Cambridge University Press, 1998), 115.

24. Asya's sexual inhibitions are related to restraints placed upon her relationship before marriage. Her excessive beauty regime might also be read as the effect of two sets of cultural pressures on the female body.

25. Ahmed, *Women*, 225, 217–223.

26. Ibid., 230–234.

27. miriam cooke, 'Islamic Feminism Before and After September 11th', *Duke Journal of Gender Law and Policy* 9 (2002): 227–235 (234). cooke does not define Islamist, but uses it to describe political ideologies grounded in Islamic doctrine (for example 232).

28. Examples include Leila Abouzeid's *Year of the Elephant: A Moroccan Woman's Journey toward Independence*, trans. Barbara Parmenter (Austin: University of Texas Press, 1989 ['*Ām al Fīl*, 1983]) and Farida Ben Lyazid's film *A Door to the Sky* (*Bab al-Sama' Maftouh*, 1989).

29. Other examples are Mohja Kahf's *The Girl in the Tangerine Scarf* (New York: Carroll & Graf, 2006) and Shelina Zahra Janmohamed's *Love in a Headscarf* (London: Aurum, 2009).
30. Waïl S. Hassan, 'Leila Aboulela and the Ideology of Muslim Immigrant Fiction', *Novel* 41.2–3 (2008): 298–318 (299).
31. Ibid., 310.
32. Ibid., 307.
33. Claire Chambers, 'An Interview with Leila Aboulela', *Contemporary Women's Writing* 3.1 (2009): 86–102 (97).
34. Olivier Roy, *Globalized Islam: The Search for a New Ummah* (London: Hurst, 2004), 23–24.
35. Talal Asad, *Formations of the Secular: Christianity, Islam, Modernity* (Stanford: Stanford University Press, 2003), 197–198.
36. Nash, *Anglo-Arab*, 136, 145.
37. Leila Aboulela, *Minaret* (London: Bloomsbury, 2005), 31. Subsequent references will be included parenthetically in the main text.
38. Her newfound religiosity is a reversion or recognition. In the mosque, 'The words were clear, as if I had known all this before and somehow, along the way, forgotten it' (240).
39. Felski, *Beyond*, 142.
40. Wafaa only apparently calls 'out of the blue'; the catalyst is Najwa's new receptivity.
41. Saba Mahmood, *Politics of Piety: The Islamic Revival and the Feminist Subject* (Princeton: Princeton University Press, 2005), 51.
42. Sara Ahmed and Jackie Stacey, 'Introduction: Dermographies', in Sara Ahmed and Jackie Stacey, eds, *Thinking Through the Skin* (London: Routledge, 2001), 1.
43. Hassan, 'Leila Aboulela', 307–308, contrasts two structures of 'translation' in Soueif's and Aboulela's work, with particular reference to the latter's *The Translator* (Edinburgh: Polygon, 1999).
44. Nash, *Anglo-Arab*, 30. See Felski, *Beyond*, 144, for a similar evocation of progress towards the self as *tabula rasa*.
45. This privileging of religion over ethnicity is reflected in the novels referenced in note 29 above.
46. Felski, *Beyond*, 144.
47. Nash, *Anglo-Arab*, 149.
48. Susan J. Brison, 'Trauma Narratives and the Remaking of the Self', in Mieke Bal, Jonathan Crewe and Leo Spitzer, eds, *Acts of Memory: Cultural Recall in the Present* (Hanover: University Press of New England, 1999), 41, cited in Ulrike Tancke, '"Original Traumas": Narrating Migrant Identity in British Muslim Women's Writing', *Postcolonial Text* 6.2 (2011): np.
49. Hassan, 'Leila Aboulela', 311.
50. See Elleke Boehmer, *Stories of Women: Gender and Narrative in the Postcolonial Nation* (Manchester: Manchester University Press, 2005), 3–6.
51. Bart Moore-Gilbert, *Postcolonial Life-Writing: Culture, Politics and Self-Representation* (Abingdon: Routledge, 2009), 72.
52. Nash, *Anglo-Arab*, 15, 16; Amal Amireh and Lisa Suhair Majaj, 'Introduction', in Amal Amireh and Lisa Suhair Majaj, eds, *Going Global: The Transnational Reception of Third World Women Writers* (New York: Garland, 2000), 1–25.

53. Feroza Jussawalla, 'Kim, Huck and Naipaul: Using the Postcolonial Bildungsroman to (Re)define Postcoloniality', *Links & Letters* 4 (1997): 25–38 (28).
54. Stein, *Black*, 30.
55. Malak, *Muslim*, 3.

Part II
Migrant Islam

5 Infinite Hijra
Migrant Islam, Muslim American Literature and the Anti-Mimesis of *The Taqwacores*

Salah D. Hassan

Introduction

There is no end to the migrations of Islam, and therefore Islam has no limit as a source for the many cultural formations that sit at the horizon of the present. The limitlessness of the many Islams is identical with Islam's universality. Not only can anyone and everyone be a Muslim, but anyone and everyone has been touched by the forms and histories of Islam. The idea of an uncontained migrant Islam, spreading across the globe and multiplying Muslims, is frightening to Islamophobes who fear its potentialities. To Islamists, who seek to capture migrant Islams and imprison them in a non-existent past, these potentialities constitute a threat to orthodoxy and advance the spectre of innovation (*bid'ah*). Islamophobes and Islamists have equally reduced Islam to a monolith of dogma and practice that is mobilized to instill hatred of Muslims and to inspire Muslims to hate. Despite the reckless bombast of Islamophobes and Islamists, the many Islams continue their migrations, moving into the future, giving rise to newness as they combine with other forms of culture, whose identities have yet to be determined. This movement and hybridization of a polymorphous monotheistic tradition is not historically unique to Islam, but in the present context, there is a uniqueness to the many forms of Muslim cultural expression, notably in those North American places of twentieth-century migration, where Muslim minorities are enabled by the ideal of religious freedom and at the same time are subject to the violence of religious intolerance. It is in the simultaneous embrace and rejection of the non-Islamic that Muslims generate often out of necessity and without calculation the most fantastic forms of migrant Islam.

Migrant Islam is not intended to refer necessarily to Muslims who immigrate and carry their religion with them from Africa, Asia or the Middle East to those inhospitable geographies of Europe and North America; rather migrant Islam signifies the movement of ideas, values, words and styles of thought that are productively at home with new technologies and emerging social environments that give rise to new forms of Muslimness beyond the abode of Islam

(*Dar al-Islam*). These new forms of Muslimness co-exist with, but are often in tension with, conventional immigrant Muslim communities that have long dominated mosques and regulated the social and cultural world of Muslims in North America. In this regard, migrant Islam in the North American context—but elsewhere as well—has given rise to subjecthood that embodies and gives expression to a Muslim Americanness that is neither conventionally Muslim nor conventionally American. Furthermore, migrant Islam refers to a kind of cultural reach that has an impact also on non-Muslims, a 'hemispheric Islam' that Wai Chee Dimock describes in the following terms:

> And indeed, Islam is 'hemispheric' in every conceivable sense. It is spread, that is, across the northern hemisphere as well as the southern hemisphere, defining the term latitudinally as well as longitudinally, and bringing the pressures of the East–West axis to bear on the North–South. Robert Irwin speaks of the emergence of an 'Islamic world system' between the years 1000 and 1500. . . . This hemispheric spread meant that it was multilingual from the first, becoming a 'civilization' (and not just a religion) through the mixing of these languages and through the mixing of its core faith with a wealth of secular forms, from poetry and philosophy to law, architecture, the visual arts, medicine, mathematics, and the natural sciences.[1]

Dimock subsequently turns to Ralph Waldo Emerson, the nineteenth-century US poet and essayist, and Washington Irving, the nineteenth-century US essayist and historian, to show the importance of Islam in conditioning early nineteenth-century American literary sensibility. These new world manifestations of Islam at the core of the canon of US letters are not isolated, but can be linked backward in time to Jefferson's interest in Islam, as Denis Spellman has shown,[2] and forward in time to the inclusion of Muhammad among the lawgivers in the frieze of the US Supreme Court marble room. Islam's migrations to the US have taken other forms as well, notably and perhaps most significantly with the founding of the Nation of Islam in the 1930s and its continuing legacy, as is partially reflected by the lasting impact of Malcolm X and Muhammad Ali, undoubtedly two of the most recognizable Muslim American names.

The name of another American Black man is a further sign of Islam's varied migrations to the US: Barack Hussein Obama. Obama's name is a form of Muslimness that disrupts and cannot easily be reconciled with the dominant notion of Americanness, defined in terms of a largely Anglo Judeo-Christian cultural configuration. And even though Obama disavows any affiliation with Islam, his name is a public assertion of Muslimness and almost any form of Muslimness in the contemporary US unsettles. American paranoia about the Islamization of the US, as is evident by recent controversies about the construction of a mosque in Manhattan, the opposition to the use of Sharia in US legal matters, and Congressional Hearings on the radicalization of Muslim Americans, extends to the suspicion that Obama is a crypto-Muslim. Indeed, one of the incomprehensible events in recent US history is that a Black man with a Muslim name is elected President in the very era when Muslims are especially under suspicion and entire mosque communities are under surveillance. So while Muslimness disrupts US national identity, Americanness also has the potential of unsettling Islam. 'Muslim American' has the potential to be mobilized as a critical concept that performs a double critique, one that is directed against an Islamophobic US public discourse and another that targets the social traditionalism of immigrant Muslim communities.

In what follows, I begin by examining the distinct ways that writing categorized under the heading Muslim American needs to be understood not simply as a product of recent immigrations by Muslims to the United States, but as part of the long history of Islam's migrations. In other words, even though much of the literature that is defined as Muslim American might also be understood as immigrant literature, such as Mohsin Hamid's *The Reluctant Fundamentalist* (2007), it also can be viewed as a quasi-indigenous US ethnic literature, as is the case with *The Autobiography of Malcolm X* (1965).[3] Both *The Reluctant Fundamentalist* and *The Autobiography of Malcolm X* expose the violence of US international and domestic policies and contest reductive notions of Islam; but at the same time these two narratives retain a certain kind of conventionality in representing Muslims as exceptionally religious, leaving little space for imagining Muslim alternatives to traditionalism in the US context.

Subsequently, I focus on the specific example of Michael Muhammad Knight's *The Taqwacores*, a novel published by Autonomedia in 2004, whose impact is partly registered by the production of documentary and feature films inspired by the original text. Knight has since the appearance of *The Taqwacores* produced a substantial body of writing that is located at the margins of US letters and institutional Islam, and at the same time occupies a central place in the corpus of contemporary Muslim American literature, even as it resists incorporation into the mainstream.[4] For many readers, Muslim and non-Muslim, *The Taqwacores* (and its sequel *Osama Van Halen* (2009)) is likely to be an especially unsettling novel; it is perhaps the only contemporary work of fiction that brings together Americanness and Muslimness not in some happy hybridity, but rather in a destabilizing marriage of American punk culture and Islamic heterodoxy, aggressively pushing against polite Muslim Americans and their progressive non-Muslim allies, who seek a cosy accommodation of Islam within the middle-class norms of US culture and politics.

Migrant Islam and Muslim American Literature

Islam defines itself historically, not with the birth of the prophet, nor at the moment of revelation, but rather with the event of migration. The revelation of the Quran to Muhammad, at least in the Meccan period, can be under-stood as a profoundly personal experience, whereas *Hijra*, the migration of Muhammad and his followers from Mecca to Medina in 622 of the Common Era, is that collective event that sets in motion the endless movements of Islam across the globe. It is from the year of the *Hijra* that Muslims mark the beginning of the Islamic calendar, giving value to migration as a temporal experience in contrast with the transcendental quality of revelation, a phe-nomenon outside of time and place.

Perhaps more importantly, that foundational migration of the first Mus-lims is politically significant and complicates some of the more current atti-tudes about Muslims and among some Muslims. The condition of Muslim migrancy challenges the very idea of an exclusivist Islam, or a narrowly defined notion of *Dar al-Islam*, a state in which Muslims are the politically dominant majority. The emergence of a hegemonic orthodox Islam in the later seventh century foreclosed the era of Muslims as a migrant minority in seventh-century Arabia, but across the centuries and into the present, there have been countless migrations of Muslims of a different sort beyond the realms of *Dar al-Islam*, where they have negotiated and renegotiated their relation to Islam and to the dominant cultures.

Nowhere have the effects of these migrations been more complex and contradictory than in the United States, where many migrant Islams and Islam-inspired religious formations have put to the test the ambivalent plural-ism of US political culture. Despite the relatively small number of Muslims in the US, estimated at around 2,500,000 in 2009 by the PEW Research Center, Muslims have occupied a significant place in US public discourse and policy, especially since 9/11.[5] That is to say, the volume of statements on Muslims in the US is disproportionate to their demographic importance. In effect, images of Muslims are one of the mainstays of US news reporting, popular news magazine articles, television shows, Hollywood movies and blogs. The mediated image of Muslims characterized in large part by misinformation has produced a culture of suspicion and a generalized fear of Islam that is portrayed as essentially violent and repressive. Even in works by well-known US authors, such as John Updike, whose novel *Terrorist* (2006) makes an effort to understand something about Islam, Muslim and terrorist often go hand in hand.[6]

For writers, such as Mohja Kahf or Mohsin Hamid, whose works have contributed to the elaboration of a specifically Muslim American literary culture, the challenge is to generate a counter-narrative to the negative figu-ration of Islam without falling into the traps of apologetics.[7] Over the last ten years, perhaps partially as a response to the increased attention on Mus-lims as a menacing presence in the US, a body of writing has formed under the rubric Muslim American literature and includes everything from insider accounts such as *The Muslim Next Door: The Qur'an, the Media, and that Veil Thing* (2009) by Sumbul Ali-Karamali to the youth novel *Muslim Teens In*

Pitfalls and Pranks (2008) by Maryam Mahmoodian to the celebrated post-modern poetry of Khaled Mattawa.[8]

There are two dominant trends in thinking about Muslim American literature, one that tends to emphasize the properly Islamic quality of the writing, its ability to inspire good living and to provide ethical models for Muslims who find themselves in the minority and must work to maintain their faith and resist social assimilation. The readership for these books is almost exclusively Muslim, many of the authors are affiliated with the Islamic Writers Alliance, and the books are listed on the website of Islamic Fiction Books.[9] The proliferation of Muslim children's literature and teen literature may be linked in part to the curricular needs of Muslim American schools, often associated with Islamic Centers.

The other trend locates Muslim American within the broader field of ethnic and minority literatures, suggesting that to be Muslim in the US is to belong to an ethnicized or racialized group, not unlike African Americans, Latino Americans, Asian Americans or Native Americans. A *New York Times* article cites Mohja Kahf, who has actively promoted the idea of Muslim American literature as a subgenre within US letters:

> 'Islam makes you this other race,' Ms. Kahf told a literature class at Stanford University, noting that the genre should appeal to both American Muslims and outsiders seeking a better understanding of the minority. 'I can't not write ethnically, because my characters don't eat pork and they do use incense.'[10]

Increasingly, Muslim American is used more as an inclusive category in contrast with ethnic rubrics, such as Arab American, Iranian American and Pakistani American, even though these categories, which emphasize national origin over religious affiliation, often remain operative for many authors. So for instance, the Poetry Foundation has posted a podcast titled 'Five Muslim American Poets' on its website that records a 2009 discussion at Northwestern University moderated by the poet Paul Breslin with Raza Ali Hasan, Ibtisam Barakat, Fady Joudah, Kazim Ali and Khaled Mattawa.[11] Barakat, Joudah and Mattawa are established Arab American writers, whose works are heavily influenced by Arab world affairs and Arab literary traditions, but only incidentally refer to Islam or Muslims. To think of them as Muslim American writers makes possible the inclusion of Raza Ali Hasan and Kazim Ali in the discussion, but constitutes a significant recategorization of their work. This relabelling of Barakat, Joudah and Mattawa positions them awkwardly in relation to the secular Arab nationalist cultural formations that take some distance from Islam and allow for pan-Arab American cultural alignments.

This redefining of some Arab American writers into the category of Muslim American is not produced merely by necessity; it can be traced as part of a much more important tendency to assert Muslim Americanness. Prior to 2001, research on Muslim Americans could be usefully contrasted with research on Arab Americans, in large part because the majority of Arab Americans are not Muslim. Indeed, one of the often repeated points within the dominant discourse in Arab American studies is that Arabs are not to be confused with Muslims. Similarly, scholars of Islam and many non-Arab Muslims in the US regularly note that most Muslims in the US and in the world are not Arabs. Since 9/11, these tendencies continue, especially in the face of ignorance about Muslims and Arabs in US popular discourse. However, among those who have studied Arab Americans, there is an increasing trend to align Muslims and Arabs in the US. Some of the most interesting research in the field of Arab American studies links Arab and Muslim, which testifies to an increasing identification among Arab American activists, community organizers, advocacy groups and experts with what is happening more generally to Muslims in the US. This is evident in social science publications of note such as Elaine Hagopian's 2004 volume *Civil Rights In Peril: The Targeting of Arabs and Muslims*, Yvonne Yazbeck Haddad's *Not Quite American?: The Shaping of Arab and Muslim Identity in the United States*, also published in 2004, and Louise Cainkar's recent book *Homeland Insecurity: The Arab American and Muslim American Experience after 9/11* (2011).[12]

These trends in post-9/11 social science research on Muslims in the US are finding expression also in the field of literary studies. The establishment of the *Journal of Muslim-American Literature* (JML), whose first issue is scheduled for publication in Fall 2011, is part of an official policy aimed at incorporating Muslim cultural production into US academic study. The journal's first call for papers announces its state sponsorship and its critical mission: 'The *Journal of Muslim-American Literature* (JML) is a pilot project made possible by a United States Department of State grant. Its main purpose is to help establish the critical terms and parameters of Muslim-American literature/cultural production, clearly distinguishing it from any ethnic, racial or cultural identifier'.[13] The Department of State's involvement in this scholarly endeavour is noteworthy for several reasons: 1) it suggests the linkages between US foreign and domestic policies that relate to Muslims; 2) it reveals the effort to obtain more intelligence about Muslim Americans; and 3) it demonstrates that the humanities are a site of significant policy action. To be sure, the Department of State's interest in advancing scholarship on Muslim Americans can be also understood as a cynical effort to domesticate recalcitrant cultural expression, to make American that which on the surface appears to be foreign.

By peeling away the ethnic, racial and cultural markers associated with immigrant Muslims, the *Journal of Muslim-American Literature* defines the field of literary production in terms of those American writers who no longer see themselves according to immigrant origins or racial formations, such as Black or Latino, but instead primarily as Muslim. This development can be read as the social formation of a Muslim American religious-ethnic category, similar

to Jewish American or even Catholic American, which simultaneously domes-
ticates and deracializes Muslimness, but also marks Muslim as other. This
trend links with older, more politicized efforts to deracialize Muslimness in
the US context. For example, in his analysis of Islam among Black Americans,
Moustafa Bayoumi notes through a reference to *The Autobiography of Malcolm X*
that Malcolm opposed racial distinctions among Muslims in the US:

> In 1960, after the scholar C. Eric Lincoln coined the term 'Black Muslims'
> for Nation followers, Malcolm objected vehemently. 'I tried for at least
> two years to kill off that "*Black* Muslims,"' he said. 'Every newspaper and
> magazine writer and microphone I got close to [I would say] "*No!* We are
> black *people* here in America. Our *religion* is Islam. We are properly called
> 'Muslims'!" But that "Black Muslims" name never got dislodged.'[14]

Malcolm X understood Islam among Blacks as part of a worldwide phenomenon, through which the effects of North American racialization—enslavement, Jim Crow, segregation, and criminalization—might be overcome.
Accordingly, Islam for Blacks offered the possibility of understanding oneself
beyond the categories of race that had long served to separate.

Mohja Kahf has argued more recently for a very broad notion of Muslim
American writing that acknowledges the overlap with 'ethnic, racial and
cultural identifiers', but at the same time wants to advance the idea of literary
Muslimness: 'It is a cultural, not religious, notion of Muslim that is relevant.
A "lapsed Muslim" author, as one poet on my roster called himself, is still a
Muslim author for my purposes. I am not interested in levels of commitment
or practice, but in literary Muslimness'.[15] Kahf's conceptualization of literary
Muslimness creates a space for a creative secular Muslim identity that operates fully outside of the conventions of Islamic religious practice, yet does
not disavow Islam.

Anti-Mimesis, Knight's *Taqwacores* and the Imagining of Muslim Cool

Inflected as much by US history and cultural icons as by the interpretative
possibilities of Islamic textual traditions, *The Taqwacores* imagines a 'community' of young Muslim Americans whose consciousness of God (*taqwa*) finds
expression in the counter-cultural aesthetics of 'punk rawk'. Freed from the
constraints of Islamic dogma, the authority of imams and familial expectations, the mostly male characters, who live together in a house in Buffalo,
New York, hold *jum'ah* prayer on Friday afternoon and taqwacore parties on
Friday night:

> that night all of Jehangir's kufr cronies filed in and trashed the place as
> he stood in a corner watching it all go down with a sly satisfaction that

only hours ago our house had been a masjid and now it was a riot, as though real salvation hinged on having a little taste of everything. Then Jehangir reached the point of drunkenness at which he could talk about nothing but Allah, his tragic fallings as a mumin and the promise that within the next twenty American years or so Islam would blossom into something that you could not witness anywhere else in the world.[16]

The novel imagines taqwacore as a US cultural formation constituted out of the counter-intuitive union of a deritualized Islam and an anarchic hedonism that exists only to disrupt and disturb the comfortable and established communities of respectable Muslim Americans.

At a certain level, *The Taqwacores* can be read as a coming-of-age narrative of Yusef Ali, a Pakistani college student who takes up residence in a Muslim co-op house on Elmwood Ave, the main street in what has become a trendy youth culture district of Buffalo, New York. The house is rented to a community of Muslim American youth, who have created a *mihrab* (niche in a mosque that marks the direction of prayer) by smashing a hole in a plaster wall of the living room. The living room functions as the *jum'ah* prayer room on Friday afternoons and the punk party room on Friday evenings. At the centre of the community is Jehangir Tabari, whose drunken philosophizing, sexual promiscuity and punk rock vision represent the main force behind the heterodoxy of taqwacore culture. But other aspects of taqwacore are figured through the more religiously observant Umar, the burqa-wearing Rebeya and the pot-smoking Fasiq, who have made the house their communal home, rejecting the conventions of the *masjid* and generating an alternative *jum'ah* that is defined more by competing musical tastes, refashioning Muslim religious practices, and disrupting US middle-class social norms. The narrative develops through Yusef Ali's naïve dialogues with these other characters, which become the occasion for him to reconsider what it means to be a young Muslim American in the twenty-first century. Yusef Ali is mostly a passive spectator throughout the novel, whose spiritual crisis is paralleled by a sexual awakening that takes the form of masturbation. Self-pleasuring and self-inflicted pain are two of the central themes of the novel, which builds toward Jehangir's main event, the massive taqwacore concert that is the rapturous and tragic climax of the narrative.

The Taqwacores can easily be dismissed as the fantasy of a white Muslim American convert whose wet dream is an emancipated American Islam, liberated not only from Muslim normativity, but also from American political correctness. I will return in the conclusion to the relationship between literary and sexual fantasy in the novel, but for the moment, I want to address the ways that Knight's vision of a punk Islam is in part realized in its cultural effects. To be sure, *The Taqwacores* is a product of Knight's imagination; that said, the elaboration of the taqwacore concept and its figuration in the life and death of Jehangir Tabari, who organizes the great taqwacore concert that is the climax of the novel, has moved from literature into the world. Since the publication of the novel, taqwacore bands, such as The Kominas, The Secret Trial Five and Al-Thawra, have emerged, identifying Michael Muhammed Knight's novel as an influential inspiration. This development is documented in Omar Majeed's 2009 film titled *Taqwacores*, a feature-length documentary that records the performances of several punk Muslim bands on tour with Knight who provides commentary.[17]

Viewed from this perspective, *The Taqwacores* exemplifies the anti-mimetic notion that life imitates art, in keeping with Oscar Wilde's assertion of the primacy of representation over reality. Anti-mimesis understands art as principally transformative, changing the very nature of things by unleashing the imagination and allowing those ideas, forms, and figures to condition our experience of the real. As Vivian explains to Cyril in Oscar Wilde's *The Decay of Lying*, 'Paradox though it may seem—and paradoxes are always dangerous things—it is none the less true that Life imitates art far more than Art imitates life'.[18] For Wilde, great art rejects mimesis and seeks to create a new awareness through the work of the imagination, which in no way is dependent on nature and life, but rather brings them into existence. Accordingly, for Vivian (and Wilde) only through art can newness enter the world. To privilege anti-mimesis over mimesis in art and literature is to value change over status quo, future over the present, new over old, innovation over tradition. Anti-mimesis is the promotion of small revolutions through images or words that have the potential of unsettling received ideas, custom and convention. Understanding *The Taqwacores* in terms of anti-mimesis credits the fiction with the production of a social reality that was awaiting articulation. It is as if Knight imagined the underground self of American Islam, the resistant and consequently repressed double whose offences and offensiveness could only first take shape in the novel, but now can no longer be contained or denied. Like it or not, taqwacore will forever be part of the lexicon of Muslim American culture.

If Jehangir Tabari is the taqwacore visionary in the novel, then Yusef Ali bears witness to the realization of Jehangir's vision. The relationship between Jehangir and Yusef is not quite analogous to that of prophet and disciple; Jehangir is the living embodiment of taqwacore, while Yusef admits that he 'stands for almost everything that taqwacore is not' (212). When Yusef Ali first moves into the house, he takes the room of Mustafa, a previous housemate, who 'lived firmly by Islamic principles' (16). Mustafa's legacy remains in the room in the form of a collection of Islamic religious texts—'nine volumes of Sahih Bukhari bound in green leather, a copy of *The Spectacle of Death* and a cardboard box filled with gorgeously ornamented Qurans' (17). Yusef Ali does not strive to follow Mustafa's example and has little interest in the books he left behind, but he does observe a certain Islamic orthodoxy, an orthodoxy that is more mainstream than the angry repressiveness of the heavily tattooed Umar or the feminist revisionism of Rabeya behind her burqa.

While the punk Muslim characters with crazy names, like Amazing Ayyub and Rude Dawud, and the very notion of taqwacore spring from the wild imaginings of Michael Muhammad Knight, Yusef Ali represents, at least in his exteriority, a recognizable and pseudo-realist figuration of the good Muslim American boy. Yusef Ali's character is pseudo-realist because he functions primarily as a narrative device through which the outrageous actions of the other characters are mediated. His conventional middle-class immigrant relationship to Islam stands always against the coolness of the other Muslim American characters, who are far more educated in both the orthodoxies and heterodoxies of their *deen* (religion). Yusef Ali explains to Lynn, the cute convert to Islam:

> You weren't raised in a Muslim family so you can just take things on your own terms. For me it's hard because I got all of this stuff in one big lump package. Some of it's worthwhile guidance that I would like to hold on to for the rest of my life, some is just culture that's a part of who I am and then there's a lot of traditional things that I can't understand. (86–87)

As Yusef and Lynn discuss religious belonging, she cites a line from Attar's *Conference of the Birds*—'forget what is and is not Islam'. The irony of this scene is that Yusef has never heard of Attar or his famous twelfth-century Sufi poem and has to be educated in the lyricism of heterodox Islam by a lapsed American convert.

Even as Yusef Ali envies the individualized Islam of converts, who choose to become Muslims, and values a punk Islam that vomits and urinates on family, culture and tradition, his Islam is normative, dispassionate and distinctly uncool. The dilemma for Yusef Ali is not framed in terms of the opposition between Islam and American culture, but instead in terms of the opposition between mainstream Islam and taqwacore. Yusef is the perfect foil to Jehangir, because his mainstream identification, innocence and nerdiness validate Jehangir's taqwacore lifestyle. Yusef Ali, the straightedge middle-class South Asian engineering student from Syracuse, narrates *The Taqwacores* from within the household, but from outside of taqwacore culture. His narrative is marked by a sympathetic neutrality that positions him as an ally even though he remains firmly located within the conventionalities of American Islam. Because Yusef Ali is a sober, respectful *mumin* (believer) who accepts his drunken, stoned and fornicating Muslim housemates as brothers, the behaviour of Jehangir and the others is elevated to acceptability. Only toward the end of the novel does Yusef Ali begin to understand the cultural and political ideals that underwrite taqwacore:

> Punk Rock means deliberately bad music, deliberately bad clothing, deliberately bad language and deliberately bad behavior. Means shooting yourself in the foot when it comes to every expectation society will

ever have for you but still standing tall about it, loving who you are and somehow forging a shared community with all the other fuck-ups.

Taqwacore is the application of this virtue to Islam. I was surrounded by deliberately bad Muslims but they loved Allah with a gonzo kind of passion that escaped sleepy brainless ritualism and the dumb fantasy-camp Islams claiming that our deen had some inherent moral superiority making the world rightfully ours.

I think it's a good thing. (212)

Here Knight uses Yusef Ali to elaborate explicitly the meaning of taqwacore and its import as a critical social movement aimed primarily at exposing the hypocrisy of the mainstream forms of Islam. This passage, which appears in one of the last chapters of the novel, just before the punk Muslim concert, is an unnecessary and overly contrived attempt to fill the concept of taqwacore with a significant discourse. But throughout the book, Jehangir and others in the house have given expression to these very ideas through their statements and actions, which are often criticized by the more upright Umar. Yusef Ali's assessment of the worth of taqwacore indicates that he has intellectually embraced its virtues, even if he is unable fully to inhabit the social identity of a Muslim punk. The authoritative narrative mode, which implies his proprietary relationship to taqwacore, can usefully be contrasted with a slightly earlier moment in the same chapter when he affirms his outsiderness: 'I walked through my house feeling more like an anthropologist than actual member of this strange society' (211). At this point in the novel, Yusef has spent many months in the house, often in the company of Jehangir whom he idolizes, but still remains an observer of the alien taqwacore world that surrounds him.

To return to the passage above, for Yusef Ali, the bad behaviour of the taqwacores is ennobled because they 'loved Allah with a gonzo kind of passion'. This passion is a form of fanaticism, characterized by an extremist pursuit of existential authenticity that is itself an affirmation of *taqwa*. The novel presents taqwacore as an absolutely unmediated form of Islam characterized by a direct relationship between the *mumin* and Allah. While the fanaticism of the taqwacores contrasts with that of Islamist political movements, Jehangir links them by comparison with the Taliban: 'Who's to say that we won't fuck things up, in our own way, as much as the Taliban' (224). And earlier in the novel, Yusef describes Jehangir's appearance as 'a post-apocalytic mujahideen like the Taliban met Mad Max' (197). Taqwacore is the alternative Islamic fanaticism, one that does not reject Americanness, but rather sees in it the possibilities of subverting all other forms of Islam and also their antithesis:

Fuck the local imam, fuck PhDs at al-Madina al-Munawwara, fuck Siraj Wahhaj, fuck Cat Stevens. Fuck the traditionalists and fuck the apostates too—fuck Ibn Warraq, fuck Anwar Sheikh, fuck Ali Sina, fuck them all, let me puke out every book I've consumed, give me the Islam of a starry-night cornfield with wind rustling through my shirt. (252)

The fanaticism of taqwacore is directed against traditionalist Islam, represented by religious authority (imams), Saudi Arabia (al-Madina al-Munawwara), the Taqwa Mosque in Brooklyn (founded by Siraj Wahhaj) and the piety of the white convert (Cat Stevens); but at the same time, the rejection of these forms of Islam does not entail a denial of faith in Allah as is the case with the apostates (Ibn Warraq, Anwar Sheikh and Ali Sina) who can be seen as examples of anti-Islamic fanaticism.[19]

Taqwacore fanaticism finds expression also in the *fantasticism* of the novel that is built around unreal figurations of an American Islam, such as the Sufi trucker poet Buzz Sawyer and the science fiction writer Abu Afaq. By incorporating these fantastic figures and their writings into the narrative, Knight seeks to evoke an obscure American Islam that can serve as a source text for taqwacore culture. Jehangir introduces Yusef Ali to the poetry of Buzz Sawyer, claiming that he was 'a Sufi of the Uwayysi Mashrab' (187). By including one of his poems in the novel and attributing to Buzz Sawyer the literary influence of Rumi and spiritual affiliation with an actual Sufi order, Knight gives the impression that such a poet actually exists, when in fact Buzz Sawyer was the ring name of Bruce Woyan, a professional wrestler, who died in 1992. The reference to Abu Afaq is similar, but more significant and more complex. Jehangir gives Yusef Ali a copy of Abu Afaq's *Twenty-Four Septendecillion*, which he calls the 'great Islamic pulp novel' and explains that 'It's from the 1940s—the heyday of *Amazing Stories* and all that shit, the shit that guys like Ray Bradbury grew up on. Abu Afaq, he was like a fuckin' philosopher disguising his ideas in cornball outer-space stories. He was like Islam's Robert Heinlein' (195). Abu Afaq is the name of an elderly Jewish man in Medina at the time of Muhammad, who was assassinated because he insulted the prophet of Allah.[20] As with Buzz Sawyer, the fantastic is concealed behind the veil of literary history, a series of references (Ray Bradbury and Robert Heinlein) and quotations from the novels that suggest the factual existence of Abu Afaq, the great Muslim American science fiction writer. Like the taqwacore bands, Buzz Sawyer's Sufi poetry and Abu Afaq's science fiction are Michael Muhammad Knight's fantasies of a Muslim American iconoclasm: 'Muhammad was a punk rocker / He tore everything down / Muhammad was a punk rocker / and he rocked that town' (3).

Despite the success of *The Taqwacores* as a manifesto for Muslim American punk culture, the novel needs also to be read critically as yet another example of a white US author's cultural simulation of otherness. Knight does this especially with Yusef Ali, who serves as a foil through which the author conveys his authorial presumption about mainstream Muslim America. It is not at all that Knight projects himself onto Yusef—there is no collapsing of author and narrator. Rather Knight uses Yusef as a way to make the novel accessible to second-generation immigrant Muslim male youths, even as he parodies their sexually repressed condition. But in doing so, Knight also produces a self-parody, as one cannot fail to see how Yusef's growing obsession with masturbation operates as a clichéd metaphor for Knight's writing of the novel. In other words, there is an inescapable parallel between Michael Knight's cultural self-pleasuring as he imagines a non-existent taqwacore community and the sexual pleasure that Yusef Ali gives himself while fantasizing about Victoria Secret models. That said, even at its representational limit, *The Taqwacores* and Knight's other writings address the self-fashioning of Muslim American cultural formations and contribute to the future migrations of Islam.

Notes

1. Wai Chee Dimock, 'Hemispheric Islam: Continents and Centuries for American Literature', *American Literary History* 21.1 (Spring 2009): 28–52 (32–33).
2. D. A. Spellman, 'Could a Muslim Be President? An Eighteenth-Century Constitutional Debate', *Eighteenth-Century Studies* 39.4 (Summer 2006): 485–506.
3. Alex Haley, *The Autobiography of Malcolm X* (New York: Ballatine, 1965); Mohsin Hamid, *The Reluctant Fundamentalist* (New York: Harcourt Books, 2007).
4. Michael Muhammad Knight, *The Taqwacores* (Brooklyn: Autonomedia, 2004); Michael Muhammad Knight, *Blue-Eyed Devil: A Road Odyssey Through Islamic America* (Brooklyn: Autonomedia, 2006); Michael Muhammad Knight, *Osama Van Halen* (Brooklyn: Soft Skull Press, 2009).
5. According to the 2009 PEW Foundation report, *Mapping the Global Muslim Population*, 20 per cent of all Muslims live as minorities, www.pewforum.org/newassets/images/reports/Muslimpopulation/Muslimpopulation.pdf (accessed 28 May 2011).
6. John Updike, *Terrorist* (New York: Knopf, 2006).
7. See for example, Neil MacFarquhar, 'She Carries a Weapon, They Are Called Words', *New York Times*, 12 May 2007, http://www.nytimes.com/2007/05/12/books/12veil.html (accessed 28 May 2011).
8. Sumbul Ali-Karamali, *The Muslim Next Door: The Qur'an, the Media, and that Veil Thing* (Ashland, Oregon: White Cloud Press, 2009); Maryam Mahmoodian, *Muslim Teens In Pitfalls and Pranks* (Muslim Writers, 2008).
9. See the list of books at www.islamicfictionbooks.com/, a website that includes a link to the Islamic Writers Alliance (http://www.islamicwritersalliance.net/home.html) (accessed 30 May 2011).
10. MacFarquhar, 'She Carries a Weapon'.
11. 'Five Muslim American Poets: Literary discussion featuring readings by poets Raza Ali Hasan, Ibtisam Barakat, Fady Joudah, Kazim Ali, and Khaled Mattawa', The Poetry Foundation, 27 October 2009, http://www.poetryfoundation.org/features/audioitem/2040 (accessed 28 May 2011).
12. Louise Cainkar, *Homeland Insecurity: The Arab American and Muslim American Experience after 9/11* (New York: Russell Sage Foundation Publications, 2011);

Elaine Hagopian, *Civil Rights in Peril: The Targeting of Arabs and Muslims* (London: Pluto Press, 2004); Yvonne Yazbeck Haddad, *Not Quite American?: The Shaping of Arab and Muslim Identity in the United States* (Waco, TX: Baylor University Press, 2004).

13. . Call for Papers, *The Journal of Muslim-American Literature*, 27 April 2011, http://call-for-papers.sas.upenn.edu/node/41247 (accessed 28 May 2011).

14. Moustafa Bayoumi, 'East of the Sun (West of the Moon): Islam, the Ahmadis, and African America', *Journal of Asian American Studies* 4.3 (October 2001): 251–263 (258).

15. Mohja Kahf, 'Teaching Diaspora Literature: Muslim American Literature as an Emerging Field', *The Journal of Pan African Studies* 4.2 (December 2010): 162–167 (167).

16. Michael Muhammad Knight, *The Taqwacores*, 90. Citations will hereafter be inserted in the text.

17. Omar Majeed, dir., *Taqwacore* (EyeSteelFilm, 2009). Information about the film and the bands is available at the film website: http://www.taqwacore.com/ (accessed 28 June 2011).

18. Oscar Wilde. 'The Decay of Lying', in *Intentions* (Volume 7 of *The Complete Writings of Oscar Wilde*) (New York: The Nottingham Society, 1909), 3–57. Online version: http://www.victorianweb.org/authors/wilde/decay.html (accessed 28 June 2011).

19. Ibn Warraq is the pen name of the author of *Why I Am Not A Muslim* (1995) and several other books. He is admired by many critics of Islam in the US, such as Daniel Pipes, who has praised his work. Anwar Sheikh (1928–2006) was a Pakistani who resided in the United Kingdom and wrote critically about Islam. He authored several books attacking Islam, most notably associating it with Arab nationalism and Arab imperialism in the subcontinent. Ali Sina is the pseudonym for a Canadian Iranian whose blog alisina.org is dedicated to attacking Islam.

20. There is little serious scholarship on Abu Afaq. Much of the writing that is readily available online about the killing of Abu Afaq tends to be anti-Islamic propaganda or Muslim apologia. For anti-Islamic writings, see for example the posting by Silas on the answering-Islam website (http://www.answering-islam.org/Silas/abu-afak.htm.org). For Muslim apologetics, see for example, Hesham Azmy's rebuttal of Silas on the answering-Christianity website (http://www.answering-christianity.com/abu-afak_rebuttal.htm). The Wikipedia entry on Abu Afaq includes the following note: 'As an elderly man, Abu 'Afak Arwan wrote a politically charged poem against Muhammad and his followers that is preserved in the Sira. The affair was recorded by Ibn Ishaq in "*Sirat Rasul Allah*" (The Life of the Prophet of God), the oldest biography of Muhammad'. As Ibn Ishaq recounts the story, Muhammad then ordered the assassination of Abu Afaq (http://en.wikipedia.org/wiki/Abu_%27Afak). Michael Beard refers to the Abu Afaq story in his essay 'Distance and Reception: Islamic Literary History and the Western Reader' (*Alif: Journal of Comparative Poetics* 6 (Spring 1986): 45–56). Beard notes in passing: 'There are numerous reasons which have nothing to do with esthetics which suggest why the poets as a class might be subject to attack in the Islamic community. Among the most troublesome of opponents of the new religion were the poetess Asma' bint Marwan and the poet Abu 'Afak' (50).

6 Muslims as Multicultural Misfits in Nadeem Aslam's *Maps for Lost Lovers*

Amina Yaqin

'Pakistan is not just a wife-beating country, it's a wife-murdering one', or so says a character in Nadeem Aslam's 2004 novel *Maps for Lost Lovers.*[1] As a British Pakistani author, Aslam carries the burden of representing both the diasporic community and his country of origin in narrating the often contentious issue of 'honour crimes' in this novel. The stark brutality of this statement indicates a willingness on the part of the writer to explore the uncomfortable byways of a claustrophobic provincial minority community. In Britain today broader debate on this issue seems caught in an impasse, endlessly repeating the stereotypes of a traditional pre-modern Islamic society and a secular liberalism entrenched in European tradition. Aslam's novel makes an important literary contribution to this 'clash of cultures' debate in a post-9/11 world. Yet a number of readers have commented on the slightly disorientating experience of reading a novel that seems in many ways to reiterate populist clichés in its story of a pair of ill-fated lovers whose transgression is punished with death, and a closed community who shield and support the murderers. They have expressed uncertainty about whether, in the end, Aslam is challenging or confirming popular images of backward and atavistic Pakistani immigrant behaviour. My contention here is that *Maps for Lost Lovers* offers an uneven and contradictory engagement with honour crime. On the one hand it is concerned to provide a forensic, pseudo-documentary analysis of a sociological phenomenon—albeit one already overdetermined by Orientalist moral projections. On the other, the story of two lovers killed for their transgression is complicated by the additional factors of ghettoization and lack of material resources and cultural capital. However, in the end, the novel foregoes these tensions in favour of a family saga of incestuous relations and doomed love.

In order to explore this trajectory and understand the implications of the novel's key theme it is important to establish a broader political sense of how honour killings and honour crimes are recognized and discussed in Britain. Primarily associated with the immigrant Muslim population, the phenomenon of honour crime in modern Britain is immediately taken to affirm the perceived polarization between a secular West and its ethnic and religious minorities. Of course, case studies in Britain have shown that honour crimes are not just a Muslim issue but they are almost always portrayed as such in the press and popular media. They cut across South Asian ethnicities, cultures and classes but are often presented in a one-dimensional sensational style with an emphasis on gory descriptions of violence. They are fodder for a media keen to point the finger at the troubled hotspots of multiculturalism in Britain. Such a highly charged topic might be expected to be of interest to a novelist of Aslam's calibre. However, when does excoriating and honest community criticism by an 'insider' tip over into mere reiteration of majority prejudice?

In the year 2000, discussions took place in the UN General Assembly on the subject of honour crimes. A fraught debate was marked by many disagreements on the acceptable definition of 'crimes of honour', with certain Muslim majority states expressing an objection to what they felt was an implicated association with Islam. Eventually Resolution 55/66 was adopted by the General Assembly to 'address the elimination of crimes against women committed in the name of honour'.[2] In both human rights and national discourses on honour crimes, Muslim societies were identified as key locations for the continuation of what was seen as a barbaric pre-modern practice. In the same year, a newspaper article in the *Sunday Observer,* entitled 'Love, Honour and Obey—or Die', looked at honour killings in Britain in relation to the high occurrence of domestic violence for Asian women. Yet the correspondent, Jason Burke, chose to begin his article with an evocative description of the rugged and dry northern hills of Pakistan, from where, supposedly, the insidious foreign disease of honour crime had been imported into England, along with Islam and its attendant cultural practices. In Bradford, Derby or Huddersfield, he reports, 'Old men, their beards dyed orange with henna, rest in the evening sunlight on their way to the mosque. Boys, in white round prayer caps and the traditional baggy trousers worn in Karachi or Peshawar, play cricket with a makeshift bat. Women pull their headscarves tight up to their eyes when a stranger walks past'.[3] This sense of an exotic but essentially alien presence within Britain—bringing with it values that are at odds with those of the civilized West—has become widespread, especially in the post-9/11 context. It feeds a news agenda in which journalists—particularly in the early years after the terrorist attacks—have been ravenous for instances of aberrant behaviour to underline supposed civilizational differences between the West and its Other.

In particular, honour crimes have become fodder for the tabloid press, with their penchant for moral absolutes and defence of the 'British way of life'. Popular reportage on honour crime shares the overall tendency to equate it with Islam and Muslim practices, often with an added dose of sensationalism. Sometimes a connection is made with contemporary concerns in order to refute liberal notions that Muslims are being unfairly targeted over other groups. This is nowhere more evident than in tabloid reporting of honour crimes. For example, on the third anniversary of the 7/7 attacks in

London, Trevor Kavanagh in an article in *The Sun*, entitled 'Islamophobia
. . . or cold hard truth', is keen to assert that he is not an Islamophobe while
nevertheless insisting that amongst Muslims, 'Forced marriages are common. Honour killings and beatings are far from rare. Women are refused
education or a chance to learn English'. He too is keen to communicate to
his readers that the 'barbaric treatment of women has been imported and
thrives here'.[4] There is certainly nothing to be gained by whitewashing or
ignoring the appalling practices in which women especially are victimized,
brutalized and murdered. However, the high moral tone of much reporting,
and the implication that reporters such as Burke or Kavanagh—in their different ways—are contributing to an enlightened project of saving Asian women
from patriarchal oppression, is as dubious as it is self-aggrandizing.[5]

Aslam's novelistic representation is by no means as crude as those tabloid
caricatures. However, it does have a didactic element and Aslam himself
is sometimes seen as one of those Pakistani representative spokespersons—
along with Kamila Shamsie and Mohsin Hamid—to whom the press turn for
an authoritative 'inside' perspective. Born in Gujranwala, Pakistan, Aslam
moved with his father, a communist, poet and film producer, to Huddersfield
when he was fourteen years old. His father left Pakistan for political reasons
and thereafter gained employment as a factory worker and a bin man so, as
Aslam was growing up, there was very little money but there was an emphasis on the freedom of thought. He describes himself as a non-believer and is
generally recognized as a cultural Muslim rather than a practising adherent
of the faith.[6]

Such representative positionality is, of course, highly problematic and
there is a danger that an ethnographic dimension, in which Aslam and company feature as native informants, is at work in the media's repeated recourse
to such 'expert' voices.[7] Beyond this, there is the matter of the diversity of
Muslim diaspora experience, of which Pakistani migrants are only a small
part. Add to this the regional and doctrinal variations evident among Muslim
immigrant groups and the idea that one voice can adequately represent them
all—and in the notoriously creative and slippery form of the novel too—begins
to look strained. From the perspective of political anthropology, Haideh
Moghissi, Saeed Rahnema and Mark Goodman suggest that what helps forge
a group identity amongst migrant Muslim populations from majority Muslim societies is a 'commonality in the sense of being deported to the culture of not belonging, of becoming a permanent target for stereotyping and
bigotry'.[8] Moreover, 'the shift to a heightened "Muslim" identity' does not
represent an increasing faith-based spirituality but instead utilizes Islam as a
powerful ideological tool of resistance in a climate of continuing colonial and
neo-colonial policies against Muslim societies, accompanied by an intolerant
atmosphere in the new country of residence. In this sense, diasporic Muslim
identity becomes transnational, deeply riven by the experiences of race, class
and ethnicity. In Britain the old South Asian diaspora with its ethnic variants

of Pakistani, Indian and Bangladeshi has regrouped and partly reinvented itself as a 'new' Muslim diaspora with activist agendas in a post-9/11 climate. Nadeem Aslam is aware of this and his novel speaks of a pre-9/11 'culture of not belonging' amongst a provincial immigrant Muslim populace in Britain who have always been at the margins of integration policies. Underwritten by the specificity of the Pakistani context it explores the stories behind the stereotype of Muslim women as victims of honour crimes and presents us with transnational identifications amongst his characters borne out of the complex relationships to gender, race, class and ethnicity.

Lila Abu-Lughod has argued that in scholarship and campaigns which claim to understand honour crimes as a 'distinctive and specific cultural complex', western society and integrated immigrants are upheld as the models of liberal and human values 'embodied in a free sexuality and personal autonomy'.[9] Abu-Lughod's sharp analysis alerts us to the difficulties of adequately representing honour killings. Human rights activism, the judicial and legal system, media representation, fiction and fantasy and anthropological study all conspire to fix and 'solidify honour crimes as timeless cultural practices' affiliated to a particular kind of community at odds with western society. Thus the public imagination is caught both by the scientific mode of factual reporting in human rights data collection and by imaginative storytelling. What also gets fixed is the female body as a receptacle of honour-based violence and it becomes the carrier of an entire discourse by no means exclusive to women.

Honour is, therefore, one of those key issues which underline the contemporary tension between Islam and secular democracy in the United Kingdom. The debate has mutated into one about the value or otherwise of Britain's multiculturalism. Honour crimes, forced marriages and other 'Muslim issues' have found their way into a more general critique of the supposed lack of integration amongst Muslim immigrants in Britain. For instance, Prime Minister David Cameron's February 2011 criticism of 'state multiculturalism' as a failure because of radicalization and terrorism is a prime example of a dialogue which targets Muslim immigrants as the failed ingredient in a multicultural experiment looked on critically by the state at a moment of national crisis. Cameron's controversial speech brought the usual mixture of plaudits and rebuttals. What went unremarked at the time was the way in which it offered an implicit critique of a previous Prime Minister, Tony Blair's statement about multiculturalism, given on 8 December 2006 in the aftermath of the 7/7 attacks, espousing a particular model of integration.[10] For David Cameron, state multiculturalism has failed young Muslims in particular because they feel 'rootless'. Significantly, Cameron also says it has encouraged some to ignore 'the horrors of forced marriage'.[11] In a rather ungenerous response to his predecessor's tribute to British values characterized by a 'common culture of tolerance', Cameron responds with a vision where Muslims will be scrutinized more closely, especially with regards to public funding and should expect 'a lot less of the passive tolerance of recent years and much more active, muscular liberalism'. Does this 'muscular liberalism' amount to a rollback of state multiculturalism and a reinvigoration of the 'little England' Toryism of the Thatcher years? This seems unlikely, given the Cameron government's general espousal of a social liberalism to go along with a relentlessly pursued free market economic liberalism. (It also seems unlikely, given that, at the time of writing, the Conservative Party chair is a Muslim woman, Baroness Sayeeda Warsi, whose altogether more sympathetic intervention on the evils of 'respectable' Islamophobia was rather eclipsed by Cameron's speech.) Whatever is meant by the phrase 'muscular liberalism', the danger must be that its animus is assimilationist rather than integrationist and that it could allow the state to further criminalize British Asian Muslim youth as part of its continuing campaign against terror.

Whatever the overall impulse, Cameron's speech articulated the need to police variants of British identity, indicating which are permissible and which are not. This quest is tied to the desire to inspect Muslim organizations to ensure they meet certain standards. This is in contrast to Blair's vision for a modern Britain that includes an accommodation of religious groups in the strategy for community cohesion and integration to present a country 'at ease with different races, religions, and cultures'.[12] Cameron reiterates the principles of liberalism which must be upheld and promoted as part of the British value-system, 'Freedom of speech. Freedom of worship. Democracy. The rule of law. Equal rights, regardless of race, sex or sexuality'.[13] Yet, for all the seemingly uncontroversial attractiveness of these attributes, it seems that the model of liberalism being espoused by Cameron is one that does not include a diversity of cultures but is the 'political expression' of one type of culture demanding precedence over a host of others.[14]

Alongside these heated public political manifestos are the lived realities of multicultural experience and those subjects who must perforce bring their cultural traditions into line with a new demanded conformity. What do they make of their so-called 'lack of integration'? Can a governmental dream of what ought to constitute 'modern Britain' be brought into line with everyday realities? Is ghettoization, as a mental as well as physical state, avoidable? Can national belonging supersede ethnic and religious difference? All these questions matter to the characters of *Maps for Lost Lovers*, who are continually searching for their identities in a strange land, away from their home, their customs and traditions. In the end their only constant companion is loneliness and the pain of separation from their loved ones. Underwriting this lyrical theme of loss is the very 'real' code of honour which defines their everyday lives in a tightknit community.

Yet it should be remembered that ideas of honour are not only characteristic of eastern cultural traditions. In the West, the notion of defending one's honour nowadays often appears quaint—a throwback to the days of duelling aristocrats, courtly love and closeted and chaste females. In fact, of course, codes of honour are alive and well and found in numerous locations, from criminal and gangster fraternities to team sports. Martin Hollis discusses the relevance of honour to cultural codes of practice. He states that honour makes categorical demands, circumventing spontaneous reasoning behaviour by providing particular interpretations and sanctioning certain types of action in particular circumstances. Most importantly, such honour codes are socially specific; they do not hold sway over others beyond a particular in-group. Hollis underlines the point that 'the demands of codes defining proper conduct for particular groups of people are not universal or uniform and are likely to conflict with Enlightenment ideas of morality'.[15] One of the examples he refers to is that of the paradigmatic British officer in India during the Raj who, while obsessed with defending the honour of his white womenfolk, was free to treat 'native' women in any way he wished.[16]

The double standard of honour in unequal situations is, of course, a scenario beloved of British novelists on India, from E. M. Forster's *A Passage to India* (1924) to Paul Scott's *Raj Quartet* (1966–75). Earlier in the history of Indian English fiction, the question of an 'exotic' Indian honour code was something that intrigued the Anglo Indian writer Rudyard Kipling who wrote about it in his short story, 'Beyond the Pale',[17] where a British officer's clandestine affair with an Indian Sikh widow, Bisesa, is an outrageous transgression of racial boundaries and a contravention of honourable behaviour. The officer, Trejago, nightly romances Bisesa, who remains concealed in purdah behind a small iron-grilled window. Yet at the same time as he is falling deeper in love with his hidden paramour, Trejago continues to court an Englishwoman by day. The tale's bloody denouement when the cross-cultural affair is discovered—Bisesa is mutilated by her outraged father and Trejago wounded in the groin—illustrates the price to be paid for the wilful flaunting of established social conventions in two closed and antipathetic communities. The narrative reiterates the 'unknowability' of women's lives in oriental courtyards that are not open to the otherwise panoptic gaze of the colonizer. Bisesa and Trejago's butchered bodies signify the horrible consequences of venturing into the honour-coded gender domain in which men assert their control over women through violence. Dignity is restored at the end through the reimposition of a strict societal moral code that does not allow for transgressive sexual behaviour.

This fascination with honour codes and female sexual behaviour has continued in the world of postcolonial fiction and has been a subject of representation for migrant writers who translate their cultures for what is often presumed to be a western reading public. Honour's twin emotion, shame, has been notably satirized by Salman Rushdie in his 1983 novel of the same name. Shame is the symbolic characteristic governing 'Peccavistan', Rushdie's phantasmagorical rendering of the real Pakistan. Shame, or the lack of an appropriate amount of it, conditions the behaviour of most of the characters in the novel.[18] At one point in his metafictional work, Rushdie's narrator pulls up his magical realist narrative to inform us that its inspiration was, in part, the true story of a Pakistani immigrant in the East End of London who murdered his only child because 'by making love to a white boy' she had committed an act of such dishonour that it could only be expunged through her death.[19] We are told that her father's violent act was supported by the Asian community who refused to condemn him publicly on radio and television despite being aware of the fact that she had not even 'gone all the way' with her white boyfriend. Characteristically, Rushdie projects the culture of honour and shame as an East/West divide, having to do with a warped morality pitting godliness against godlessness. He says, 'We who have grown up on a diet of honour and shame can still grasp what must seem unthinkable to peoples living in the aftermath of the death of God and of tragedy: that men will sacrifice their dearest love on the implacable altars of their pride'.[20]

In a sense, Nadeem Aslam's novel, *Maps for Lost Lovers*, takes its cue from this anecdotal intervention in *Shame* since it focuses on an Asian, specifically Pakistani community—this time in a northern town in England—confronted by the disappearance of two lovers, Jugnu and Chanda, who have been openly living in sin. The novel was published to largely favourable reviews in the British and American press. Reviewers have compared Aslam either to Rushdie because his novel valorized Muslims 'who flout the conventions of their religion' or to Monica Ali for its exposure of the immense 'cultural gulf' between Britain and its immigrant community.[21]

Ron Charles in *The Washington Post* states that Aslam is 'either very brave or very naïve' to write what he calls a 'devastating anti-Islamic novel'. He goes on to say that *Maps for Lost Lovers* is 'every faith-culture's worst nightmare' because 'the frontal attack by a prejudiced outsider is relatively easy to repel . . . But Aslam, a Pakistani-born writer who lives in England, speaks in the quiet, sympathetic voice of an insider as he portrays the physical and psychological violence committed in the name of God'.[22] Interestingly, similar sentiments were expressed to the present writer by students at the Punjab University in Lahore in 2011 who felt that Aslam had betrayed Pakistan with his stereotypes of forced marriages, honour crimes and illiterate followers of Islam.[23] Interviewing Aslam for *Newsline* magazine in Pakistan, Kamila Shamsie tentatively broaches this question of the reception of his book in Pakistan, but she ends by asking him to explain why the West needs a book which is 'unflinching in its portrayal of some of the worst aspects of life in Pakistani communities—honour killings, religious obscurantism, gender inequities' and so on. Aslam's response focuses on the hard-hitting portrayals that characterize his book. He describes himself as someone who lives in the West and is therefore aware of 'its injustices and subtle repressions, but I also know this other world, and I have to bring news of it too'.[24] During the interview he tells Shamsie the story of a paedophile Maulvi from Tipton who was allowed to get away with his actions because of the community's sense of shame in reporting it to the police once he had been found out by a child's parents. Similar concerns come across in the novel. Paedophiles and sexual repression feature in the chapter entitled 'Leopold Bloom and the Koh-i-Noor', which begins with the statement 'Semen was found on the mosque floor late last evening' (234). Subsequently, Shamas walks in on a junior cleric, 'a bachelor in his fifties, with his erect penis in a child's mouth'. Further details emerge as the novel progresses regarding the cleric's prison record for sexual assaults on children in a mosque in Brick Lane in London and his identification on the sex-offender's register. The novel depicts the trauma faced by parents and families of those affected, especially where it involves young girls as their marriage prospects are seen to be hindered by such revelations being made public.

Aslam it seems feels a social responsibility toward those Muslim communities in Britain whose lives mimic the desolation of his fictionalized cold and hostile neighbourhood of Dasht-e Tanhaii, variously translated as 'The Wilderness of Solitude' and 'The Desert of Loneliness'. We learn that:

> The whites were already moving out of here by the end of the 1970s, and within the decade the Hindus became the first immigrant group to move out to the rich suburbs . . . leaving behind the Pakistanis, the Bangladeshis, and a few Indians, all of whom work in restaurants, drive taxis or are unemployed. (46)

As one of the residents puts it:

> *Nobody* deserves this rundown neighbourhood of one suicide attempt a year, 29 people registered insane, and so many break-ins a month . . . more and more of the burglaries are being done by the sons of the immigrants themselves, almost all of whom are unemployed. (46)

It is this wasteland that serves as the backdrop for the crime that lies at the heart of the story.

The narrator is always concerned with the fate of girls and young women who are shown to be at the forefront of their community's absolutist approach to personal morality. We are told that,

> A Pakistani man mounted the footpath and ran over his sister-in-law—repeatedly, in broad daylight—because he suspected she was cheating on his brother. . . . This was here in England and, according to the statistics, in one Pakistani province alone, a woman is murdered every thirty-eight hours solely because her virtue is in doubt. (136)

Aslam sees such atrocities, which often go almost unnoticed by the surrounding white majority society, as every bit as worthy of note as those more eye-catching spectacular acts of violence, such as that seen on September 11, 2001. For instance, in an interview with the *Independent* newspaper, he nails his colours firmly to the mast when asked how he might have framed the novel if he had set it in 2001 instead of 1997. He states, 'In a way, the book is about September 11'. He recounts how, when visiting Ground Zero in New York, he felt 'disappointed and angry' with himself as a writer for not having been 'rigorous enough to condemn the small scale September 11s that go on every day'. For him, 'Jugnu and Chanda are the September 11 of this book'. For Aslam as a novelist, there is an awareness of living in a post-9/11 world, 'Most ordinary Muslims say, "We just want to get on with our lives. Don't identify us with fundamentalists." But it's a luxury. We moderate Muslims have to stand up'.[25]

Maps for Lost Lovers is ostensibly a novel about the deep emotions of love and faith amongst ordinary British Muslims. It deals with a family conflicted by the pressures of community, religion, nationality and culture. The story of Chanda and Jugnu's murder is told through the voice of Jugnu's brother, Shamas, who is sixty-four years old, a poet, a socialist and the Director of the Community Relations Council, and his devout wife Kaukab. The narrator tells us at the start, 'Perspective tricks the eyes', and as readers we are introduced to the differing viewpoints of the community and the police investigation. Shamas, cast as the progressive father and husband, is a curiously passive character who in his personal life seems to be activated only once by his sexual desire, which overpowers him and leads to an affair with the beautiful Suraya, another victim of a drunk and violent Pakistani husband. In his public role he lives to serve the needs of his community over and above those of his family. People of the community regard Shamas as a good brother because despite having the financial means to move away he has stayed on, much to the dissatisfaction of his wife Kaukab.

A cleric's daughter, Kaukab embodies conservatism and a blind adherence to faith. Her character's rigidity is emphasized by the narrator's ironic refrain, 'Allah's law was Allah's law and nothing could be done' (159). She is ignorant and devout: a deadly combination which has led her to unknowingly poison her own younger son and alienate her eldest boy. Her younger son Ujala was a rebellious teenager and Kaukab unable to cope with his highly strung temperament sought the help of a cleric who gave her a powder to help calm the boy. Kaukab, unaware that the powder had bromide in it, fed it to Ujala who subsequently made the discovery and left home. Charag, the older boy in whom Kaukab invested all her dreams of betterment and success is, to her disappointment, an artist, a profession which she thinks is a waste of time, and is also married to a white woman. Her daughter, Mah-Jabin, is close to her but feels unable to communicate openly about the failure of her arranged marriage to a cousin in Pakistan—a failure for which Kaukab holds her responsible because of her western ways. Kaukab idealizes Pakistan as a place of purity and wants only to hear good things about it. However she cannot envisage going back there to live: 'There is nothing on this planet that I loathe more than this country, but I won't go to live in Pakistan as long as my children are here' (146).

Toward the end of the novel when she discovers that the real reason for her daughter's marriage break-up in Pakistan was her violent husband, she is beside herself, having until then believed in the fabrication of a happy union between Mah-Jabin and her husband's nephew. She lashes out at Shamas,

> I want you to know that Mah-Jabin's chances in life were ruined by you, her father. You didn't want to move to a better neighbourhood, and no decent family was ever going to ask for the hand of a girl living in this third-class neighbourhood of people who are mill labourers or work at The Jewel in the Crown and The Star of Punjab. (328)

In her rage she accuses him of putting his principles before the needs of his family: declining an OBE; not leaving this town of white flight for a better environment so that Charag could pursue a career in medicine; allowing Ujala to leave school at fifteen as was the norm in the neighbourhood; and generally being more interested in the welfare of the community than his own family. Her children are strangers to her because they do not hold the same values as her. When her eldest son Charag has a vasectomy Kaukab is horrified. She thinks that, 'The vasectomy was a Christian conspiracy to stop the number of Muslims from increasing' (59). She repeatedly tells her children, 'My religion is not the British legal system, it's Islam' (115). She disapproves of Jugnu and Chanda's relationship outside the sanctity of marriage. When the two lovers go undercover as friends to Pakistan to visit Jugnu's parental home, she makes a call to let the people of the house know that they had 'two sinners under their roof' (59). Thus Kaukab is inwardly torn by her family's actions. Her neighbours never miss an opportunity to taunt her about her family's failures in upholding respectability and religious tradition. In one sense, Kaukab's is the real tragedy of this novel: she is a woman who courts her own fate with her blind faith and enslavement to convention.

The Pakistan known to the people of Dasht-e Tanhaii is a dark place and, according to the narrator, 'life is a trial if not a punishment for most of the people born there' (9). So when Shamas says to his lover Suraya, 'Pakistan is not just a wife-beating country, it's a wife-murdering one' he is warning her of the wrath she faces from her husband who is also a drunk (226). As we become embroiled in the lives of the different characters the honour killing seems to recede into the background and the narrative is taken over by stories of repressed sexualities, a lack of tolerance amongst the immigrant community toward strangers, and an unwillingness to cross moral borders when they are faced with the age-old quest for love. The balancing act for the people who inhabit Dasht-e Tanhaii is between religion, community and duty. Those who remain within the boundaries of the community carry their moral borders with them despite having made the journey from Pakistan to Britain. We hear about unruly girls beaten to death in an effort to exorcise them, young boys raped by clerics, helpless wives divorced on a whim by drunk husbands.

The novel's central plot of the investigation into the murder of Jugnu and Chanda is self-consciously framed as one of an honour killing, albeit committed in a moment of rage by Chanda's two brothers. At the very beginning, the question is asked, 'had Chanda brought shame on her family by living with Jugnu?' (16) We are told that when she left the family home above their grocery shop and moved in with Jugnu next door, her brothers had 'threatened revenge to preserve their honour. *We'll make you lick our injuries.* They had broken in and put out a cigarette in their bed' (20).

Jugnu is a highly educated well-travelled cosmopolitan lepidopterist who has journeyed from Pakistan, via Moscow, to England, the US and finally back to England. Initially he lives with his brother and sister-in-law, Shamas and Kaukab, before moving into his own house next door to them. In contrast to the orthodox values which rule Shamas and Kaukab's household, Jugnu is a rationalist: he has chosen a career in science, has broadened his horizons through travel, and even owns a speedboat he has named 'Darwin'. Other than family affiliation it is difficult to understand why this cosmopolitan figure chooses to live in the claustrophobic town of Dasht-e Tanhaii, a place riddled by high unemployment and crime. Initially he is welcomed into the community and the neighbours encourage their children to seek his company as 'he was educated and they wanted some of his intelligence to rub off on them' (46). But this worldliness soon leads to his fall from grace. First he is seen mixing with white women and then 'living openly in sin' with the shopkeeper's twice-divorced daughter Chanda. In due course he comes to be viewed as an outsider who cannot be trusted.

Chanda is the victim of a badly arranged marriage between first cousins at the age of sixteen. Divorced at seventeen, married again by another Pakistani cousin and divorced a few months later, she returns to England to live with her family and help out at the grocery shop. The family marries her off to an illegal immigrant who disappears as soon as he has got his legal status, leaving Chanda trapped in a marriage without a husband. She meets Jugnu while delivering butterfly food to his house and the two fall in love. The furore in the neighbourhood over this coupling is caused by the illegitimacy of the relationship. It cannot be sanctioned as an official Islamic marriage until the missing husband divorces her. It seems that there is no escape for Chanda from the prison of failed marriages arranged by her parents. Indeed, to some extent her experiences call into question the neat distinction between arranged and forced marriages that official policy seeks to draw.[26] In the novel, this ambivalence of interpretation hangs over the story. For instance, Mah-Jabin sees the female conversations in which marriages are plotted as a kind of 'organized crime' against the neighbourhood girls (106).

To Chanda the love relationship with Jugnu offers her a first opportunity to exercise her free will in choosing a partner. To her he becomes a saviour who will rescue her from the intimidation of her parents and brothers, but instead he unknowingly carries her death warrant.[27]

It is the local matchmaker whose conversation with Kaukab sums up the perilous position the community finds itself in:

> 'Sister-ji, the white police are interested in us Pakistanis only when there is a chance to prove that we are savages who slaughter our sons and daughters, brothers and sisters.' . . . 'I know Chanda's brothers are innocent because those who commit crimes of honour give themselves up proudly, their duty done. They never deny or sulk.' . . . The matchmaker nods vehemently. 'And as for Chanda: What a shameless girl she was, sister-ji, so brazen. She not only had poor Jugnu killed by moving in with him, she also ruined the lives of her own poor brothers who had to kill them—if that was what happened, of course. . . . But what I fail to understand is how Shamas-brother-ji could have allowed the two of them to live together in sin? And how did you, Kaukab, manage to tolerate it, you who are a cleric's daughter—born and brought up in a mosque all your life?' (41–42)

There is a willed blindness in the immigrant community toward the law of the land and a pride in retaining a cultural authenticity which values honour above all else. The matchmaker's speech emphasizes a binary opposition between individual desire and collective morality that is played out in the fate of the characters. Their society does not allow for sexual transgressions and those who violate this rule must be punished, especially women when they are seen to be willing participants.

Yet, in the end it is not God's law that makes the brothers commit the crime, it is an act driven by anger and rage. Both brothers are known to have dabbled in the drug trade but have been restrained under the watchful eye of their father and their employment in the family business. Ironically, Chotta is having a clandestine affair with a local Sikh woman. The night before he murders his sister he discovers his lover, Kiran, in bed with another man. Rage over his lover's betrayal inspires him to seek out Jugnu and punish him for having an affair with his sister. Barra is recovering from the shock that the doctors had made a mistake in identifying his wife's sixth foetus as female, an error only discovered after the termination had taken place at the abortion clinic. After five daughters this would have been his saving grace as a man and instead he has been emasculated. He is a partner to his brother's crime and attacks his sister, unintentionally breaking her neck while trying to silence her screams. Yet when confessing to the murder during a visit to Pakistan they insist, 'It was a matter of honour' (347). Even so, their act seems to owe less to religious motivation than to personal grievances.

However, this is not how their crimes are understood in the British judicial system, where they are placed according to the agendas outlined earlier:

> [Shamas] heard the judge say that the killers had found a cure to their problem through an immoral, indefensible act; a cure, a remedy—and their religion and background took care of the bitter aftertaste. Their religion and background assured them that, yes, they were murderers but that they had murdered only *sinners.* (278)

After the trial the narrative splits and we are given the perspectives of several different parties with an interest in creating a definitive narrative around the event. The local newspaper *The Afternoon* describes the brothers as,

> *the kind of people who don't realize that not everything in life is to do with them* . . . A distinguished Pakistani commentator on the Asian radio too would be forthright: 'Some immigrants think that just because they belong to a minority they are nice people, that they should be forgiven everything just because they are oppressed'. (348)

On hearing the verdict the murderers cry 'racism' and 'prejudice', concluding England to be a 'country of prostitutes and homosexuals'. This cacophony of voices is not truly dialogic as nobody is prepared to listen to one another. It simply reiterates the conflicting readings that reflect the agendas of different parties. The book shows us that 'state multiculturalism' is a meaningless notion for an immigrant working class and a rootless underclass who cling to an unforgiving mode of belonging in an alien environment. The behaviour and actions of the community as a whole cast it outside normative British values and it only becomes prominent when its outrageous practices create ripples across the smooth surface of civil society. The characters in the novel challenge us to think through the construction of identities as they occur within the territorial boundaries of the nation and what happens to those identities when they come into conflict with the values upheld by the metropolitan centre. Certain characters are able to step outside the narrow boundaries of the Dasht-e Tanhaii enclave, experience the world beyond and gain a broader view, while others are trapped in a self-perpetuating inward-looking moral universe.

The different receptions accorded to *Maps for Lost Lovers*—either as an eye-opening account of alien practices among Muslim migrants, or as a muck-raking reiteration of negative stereotypes—indicate its inherent ambivalence, despite the presence of a didactic omniscient narrator. Pakistanis are represented as settlers and illegal immigrants in Britain, both working class and an unemployed underclass, some of whom are progressive, others pre-modern, but amongst whom the practices of arranged marriages, honour crimes and female infanticide are common. Such practices cannot be reconciled with the normative values of liberal society. Aslam's narrative unsettles because it seems to be indulging an anthropological—and possibly prurient—interest in such closed societies among its non-Muslim readers, while, at the same time, acknowledging the impoverished, disenfranchised and ignored position of Muslim communities beyond the glare of metropolitan attention. The novel is, in a sense, about internal borders, those barriers of belief and practice that prevent communication and condemn those living behind them to a life fighting the shadows of perceived slights and dishonour. It is not so much a novel about Islamism or honour crimes as a matter of human rights, more a story about working-class diasporic Pakistanis in Britain who are unwilling or unable to change. In contrast to other famous South Asian authors who celebrate cosmopolitan migrancy and hybridity, Aslam has carved a niche for himself as a British Pakistani writer of repute with an eye for addressing social causes such as honour crimes or arranged marriages in painstaking prose which disturbs and unsettles with its depictions of class, gender, ethnicity and religion. However his prose style is embedded with a liberalism characteristic of the British left in that it deliberately critiques a conservative Islamic consciousness to underline progressive secular principles and in doing so flattens the complexities of faith based identities.

Notes

1. Nadeem Aslam, *Maps for Lost Lovers* (London: Faber and Faber, 2004). All subsequent references to the novel will be given in the text.
2. Jane Connors, 'United Nations Approaches to "Crimes of Honour"', in Lynn Welchman and Sara Hossain, eds, *'Honour': Crimes, Paradigms, and Violence Against Women* (London: Zed Books, 2005), 22–41.
3. Jason Burke, 'Love, Honour and Obey—or Die', *The Observer*, 8 October 2000.
4. Trevor Kavanagh, 'Islamophobia . . . or Cold, Hard Truth', *The Sun*, 13 July 2008, http://www.thesun.co.uk/sol/homepage/news/columnists/kavanagh/article1417495.ece (accessed 29 June 2011).
5. For a detailed analysis of media representations and the specific theme of honour killings as a Muslim issue, see my co-authored book with Peter Morey, *Framing Muslims: Stereotyping and Representation after 9/11* (Cambridge, MA: Harvard University Press, 2011), 71–77.
6. Marianne Brace, 'Nadeem Aslam: A Question of Honour', *The Independent*, 11 June 2004, http://www.independent.co.uk/arts-entertainment/books/features/nadeem-aslam-a-question-of-honour-731732.html (accessed 7 March 2006).
7. For a detailed discussion of the Muslim native informant in contemporary culture see my essay, 'Inside the Harem, Outside the Nation: Framing Muslims in Radio Journalism', *Interventions* 12.2 (2010): 226–238.
8. Haideh Moghissi, Saeed Rahnema and Mark J. Goodman, *Diaspora by Design: Muslim Immigrants in Canada and Beyond* (Toronto: University of Toronto Press, 2009), 13.
9. Lila Abu-Lughod, 'Seductions of the "Honor Crime"', *differences* 22.1 (2011), 17–63 (32).

10. The full text of Tony Blair's 8 December 2006 speech on multiculturalism is available on http://forum.stirpes.net/ethnopolitics/9647-tony-blair-speech-multi-culturalism.html (accessed 7 July 2011).

11. 'State Multiculturalism has Failed, Says David Cameron', 5 February 2011, BBC News, http://www.bbc.co.uk/news/uk-politics-12371994 (accessed 28 April 2011).

12. See note 10.

13. See note 11.

14. See Charles Taylor, 'The Politics of Recognition', in Amy Gutmann, ed., *Multi-culturalism: Examining the Politics of Recognition* (Princeton: Princeton University Press, 1994), 25–73 (62).

15. Martin Hollis, *Trust Within Reason* (Cambridge: Cambridge University Press, 1998).

16. Ibid., 123.

17. Rudyard Kipling, 'Beyond the Pale', *Plain Tales from the Hills* (London: Penguin, 1987 [1890]), 162–167.

18. Salman Rushdie, *Shame* (London: Jonathan Cape, 1983), 139.

19. I have discussed the complexity of gender in *Shame* in my chapter on 'Family and Gender in Rushdie's Writing', in Abdulrazak Gurnah, ed., *The Cambridge Companion to Salman Rushdie* (Cambridge: Cambridge University Press, 2007), 61–74.

20. Rushdie, *Shame*, 115.

21. Anonymous review, 'A Travesty of Honour', *The Economist*, 1 July 2004, http://www.economist.com/node/2876737 (accessed 4 October 2005); David Robson, 'The Deadly Honour', *The Telegraph*, 13 July 2004, http://www.telegraph.co.uk/culture/books/3620449/The-deadly-honour.html (accessed 5 October 2004).

22. Ron Charles, 'Holy Terrors', *Washington Post*, 18 May 2005.

23. In April 2011, I delivered an introductory lecture on Postcolonialism at the English Department of the Punjab University in Lahore and presented Nadeem Aslam's novel, *Maps for Lost Lovers*, as an example of postcolonial writing which goes beyond the strategy of writing back to the centre. There was a very heated response to the book and many students felt that the novel offered a gross mis-representation of Pakistani society.

24. Kamila Shamsie, 'Writer at Heart', *Newsline*, 1 July 2004, http://www.news-linemagazine.com/2004/07/writer-at-heart/ (accessed 15 June 2011).

25. Brace, 'Nadeem Aslam: A Question of Honour'.

26. In 1999 the Home Office set up a Working Group on Forced Marriage to look into the problem of 'forced marriage' in England and Wales and to advise on policy. The unit was relaunched as the joint Forced Marriage Unit (FMU) in January 2005 by the Foreign and Commonwealth Office in collaboration with the Home Office, in order to broaden the previously exclusive focus on over-seas marriages to those taking place within Britain. This unit, according to the Home Secretary at the time, Charles Clarke, had the intention of being a 'one-stop shop' for offering assistance and information to those affected by the issue. Baroness Symons, the FCO Minister, focused on the important role that the unit would play in 'protecting young people from forced marriage' (http://www.fco.gov.uk/en/newsroom/latest-news/?view=PressR&id=2002651 (accessed 16 March 2009)). In March 2006 the FMU launched a national

publicity campaign on forced marriage (http://www.fco.gov.uk/en/newsroom/latest-news/?view=PressR&id=2000471# (accessed 16 March 2009)).

27. Chanda's entrapment is similar to that of the Great Peacock female moth caged by Jugnu which when hatched attracts the nineteen male Peacock moths with its noisy call but is motionless except for the flapping of its wings expressing a fantastical yearning for the beloved, echoing a well-known metaphorical device in lyric poetry.

7 'Sexy Identity-Assertion'

Choosing Between Sacred and Secular
Identities in Robin Yassin-Kassab's
The Road from Damascus

Claire Chambers

The British Syrian novelist Robin Yassin-Kassab is often marketed as a writer
of 'postcolonial London', and the dustjacket to the hardback edition of his
debut novel, *The Road from Damascus* (2008), features a drawing of Harrow
Road in west London lined with the migrant-run fried chicken restaurants
humorously discussed in the novel.[1] Yet the novel provides more than just
a glimpse into the lives of Arabs in the capital—a topic already explored in
Hanan al-Shaykh's Arabic-language novel, *Only in London* (2002)[2]—addressing broad issues relating to migration, faith, identity, love and politics. Yassin-
Kassab's plot unfolds over a tumultuous period in 2001, during which Sami
is thrown out of London's School of Oriental and African Studies (SOAS)
where he has long been struggling to write a PhD thesis on Arab literature.
He reacts by taking his customary drink and drugs consumption to new
levels, leading to a one-night stand and crisis in his marriage to Muntaha.
The summer culminates, first, in Sami being caught up in a riot during a talk
by the controversial writer Rashid Iqbal (who is clearly based on Salman
Rushdie), and, second, in the attacks on the World Trade Center. Soon after
September 11, Sami is briefly arrested, as he had been earlier that year for
cannabis possession, although in the Islamophobic post-9/11 atmosphere it
is for his newly-grown beard and attendance at a mosque. This tallies with
Peter Hopkins' evidence that young Muslim men came under 'increasing
levels of harassment, violence and scrutiny' after the attacks on the World
Trade Center and Pentagon.[3] The novel ends with the reconciled Sami and
Muntaha holidaying in Scotland where they pray together for the first time,
and Sami realizes that he has 'developed a trembling, contingent faith' (347).

This chapter argues that Sami, the novel's British protagonist of Syrian
Muslim heritage, is confronted with a choice between sacred and secular
identities, which he comes some way towards resolving by the end of the
novel. The French Lebanese author Amin Maalouf suggests that there are
two forms of identity. One is a lived experience of identities as performative, multifarious and improvised,[4] which Yassin-Kassab terms 'the theatre

of everyday living' (122). The other is a seemingly assured identity *politics*, which Maalouf intimates is closely linked with identity *crisis*. Gabriele Marranci posits a similar binarism when he argues that identity is 'a process with two functions. On the one hand, it allows human beings to make sense of their autobiographical self; on the other, it allows them to express the autobiographical self through symbols'.[5] Maalouf laments that this second 'tribal' concept of identity is the one 'most commonly accepted everywhere, not only amongst fanatics', and he focuses closely and critically on this version of identity as a simplifying, often violent, way of asserting difference from the Other. He excoriates identity as 'a matter of symbols', describing Muslim headscarves, for example, as 'reactionary, backward-looking',[6] but I would suggest that he neglects the colonial, neo-colonial, racist and Islamophobic currents that contribute significantly to the current attractiveness of donning hijabs and niqabs.

Inattention to colonialism is not a charge that could be levelled at Nawal El Saadawi who, in her essay 'Why Keep Asking Me About My Identity?' points out that identity politics is a problem assigned solely to those 'who are being postcolonized', and that 'American "identity", American culture' is assumed not to need probing because it is taken to be normative.[7] Anticipating Mahmood Mamdani's identification of a post-Cold War drift towards 'Culture Talk',[8] El Saadawi rejects the recent tendency to discuss identity separately from class, gender, politics and economics.[9] Even apparently unequivocal sacred and secular identities are highly diverse amalgamations, which are constantly shifting and interpenetrating. As Stuart Hall writes, 'Diaspora identities are those which are constantly producing and reproducing themselves anew, through transformation and difference'.[10] Lawrence Grossberg similarly describes identity as 'relational and incomplete',[11] while Robin Cohen describes the recent 'fragmented', context-specific model of identity, noting that any subject can assume 'a number of possible social identities, depending on the situation'.[12]

Recently, there has been a turn away from this postmodern emphasis on identity as being always already under erasure and in flux. For example, Olivier Roy describes a process that he terms 're-Islamisation', in which 'Muslim identity, self-evident so long as it belonged to an inherited cultural legacy, has to express itself explicitly in a non-Muslim or Western context'.[13] Writing from within this context, Tariq Modood, in his recent book, *Multiculturalism* (2007), argues that Wittgenstein's concept of 'family resemblance' allows us to recognize distinct ethnic and religious groups, although these groups alter in different times and space, and are internally heterogeneous.[14] Modood's contention that we can identify Muslims as a group despite all their differences, just as we can detect members of the same family despite great variations in their eye colour, physique, posture, personality, and so on, is helpful when thinking about figures such as Yassin-Kassab as Muslim writers. While contemporary writers of Muslim heritage exhibit very different features, styles, and affiliations, we can usefully speak of them as part of a loosely connected and often discordant family.

I use this idea of 'family resemblance' to argue that certain common attributes are shared by writers from a Muslim cultural background, whether their ancestry is in South Asia, Africa or the Middle East. As I will show, Robin Yassin-Kassab's intertextual evocations of other well-known Muslim writers and texts are imaginative and critical. The novel contains an implied challenge to the overall optimism about 'British values' found in Monica Ali's *Brick Lane*. Yet, Yassin-Kassab occupies territory in-between Nadeem Aslam's pessimism and Leila Aboulela's idealism about Muslim communities in Britain. Most overtly, he satirizes and transvalues the writing and aggressive secularism of Salman Rushdie. As is well-known, in *The Satanic Verses* and many of his other texts, Rushdie repeatedly characterizes secular worldviews as being productively uncertain, compared to the stagnant dogmatism of religious perspectives. In contrast, early in Yassin-Kassab's novel, Sami sees secularism as representing a side (or tribe) that he can belong to, making him pugnaciously assert that 'He couldn't accept a supernatural truth' (56). By the end of the novel, however, he reflectively concludes that (notwithstanding Rushdie's stereotypes) belief in Islam can involve 'a doctrine of radical unknowing and the beginnings of acceptance' (347). The book therefore ironically undermines attempts to brand Muslims as adherents of an intolerant absolutism and to portray secularism as synonymous with humanism, and it is also self-conscious about its place in the dynamic, emergent canon of fiction by writers of Muslim heritage.

My belief in the existence of close interconnections between writers of Muslim heritage does not come out of a naïve belief in a transcendental *ummah* (the idea of a unified global Muslim community) and nor do I mean to ignore the very real tensions between different Muslim groups within an in any case divided Britain. But, as I argue in my book *British Muslim Fictions* (2011), British-resident authors of Muslim heritage share certain preoccupations (relating to gender, class, the war on terror, Muslim Spain, the Rushdie Affair and cosmopolitanism, among other issues), and are producing some of the most interesting fiction in the UK today. Recognition that their work forms a unique generic category is growing, as is testified by Peter Morey and Amina Yaqin in their Framing Muslims research project,[15] and by the new literary prize the Muslim Writers Awards. Although largely being produced by the numerically dominant South Asian community, writers of Arab descent, such as Robin Yassin-Kassab, are increasingly gaining prominence.

The Road from Damascus to some extent focuses upon the *ummah*, as it portrays a cast of mostly Muslim characters from around the world. For example, Sami's identity is pulled between the two contradictory poles of postmodernism and Arabism. As an undergraduate, he sports various t-shirts emblazoned with Palestinian flags or slogans underneath a PVC jacket celebrating the hedonism of the Acid House movement. He often teams this with a checked Arab kuffiyeh, although he recognizes that 'A member of his class in Syria would never wear one' (13). Sami's nationalism and anti-imperialism is displaced and infused with other meanings: in an almost Baudrillardian statement, the narrator claims that 'the significance of signs had swivelled away from their original focus' (13). In his early twenties, Sami constructs his identity out of the building blocks of Black music (including hip hop and jazz) and Arabic poetry, which he passionately declaims to English girls in bars, who admire 'the sexiness of Sami's Arabism' (14). Yet a decade later, he is overcome by ennui as he considers Arab culture and politics to be decaying: 'Poets died and were not replaced. Religion grew in response' (35). He finds renewal in the start of the Second Intifada (April 2000) when, paraphrasing William Wordsworth, he thinks, 'to be young in that morning of the rejuvenated Arabs was very heaven' (38). Yet this feeling is short-lived, and the novel revolves around the identity crisis that ensues when Sami's pick-'n'-mix blend of secular Arabism and western popular culture no longer sustains him.

Apart from Sami, the most important of the novel's international characters are his Iraqi wife, Muntaha; her firebrand younger brother, Ammar; various South Asian, African and white convert associates from the mosque Ammar attends; and Gabor, a British-born Hungarian Russian Jew (whose grandfather had the Tolstoyan name of Vronsky). Gabor shows signs of being in love with Muntaha after her split from Sami when the latter has a debauched 'lost weekend' and misses the *ta'ziya*, or condolence ceremony, to commemorate the death of Muntaha's father. After a summer of getting closer as friends, Gabor plans to seduce Muntaha by impressing her with his paintings which blend Muslim concepts, such as *tawheed* (divine unity), with art. He fantasizes over Muntaha's appearance, which he considers at once 'erotic' and 'terrible':

> The thing about Arabs—they're freakish. More like us than Africans are, or Chinese, so like us sometimes they're almost interchangeble—but the thing an Arab face must have to distinguish it from a European is at least one element of freakishness, of disproportion. . . . And Muntaha—she's rich in freakishness, her nose, mouth, in particular her eyes, big like baby eyes, and bigger top to bottom than side to side. (291)

This chimes with Joseph Massad's argument in *Desiring Arabs* (2007) that 'sex [acts] as one of the main axes by which civilization and barbarism can be classified',[16] and that Arabs tend to be portrayed in western discourses as deviant, desirous and desirable, and as representing a radical alterity. Perhaps there is some truth in Maya Jaggi's assertion that Gabor acts as 'a straw man set up to embody a predatory orientalism'.[17] However, Gabor's efforts prove fruitless, as Muntaha reminds him that although she and Sami are currently separated, she still considers herself married. As he makes his crestfallen way home from Spitalfields, the narrator comments, 'She said no, and so prevented the story from moving into the universal territory we can all relate to' (293), which may be a swipe at that other novel of London's East End, Monica Ali's *Brick Lane* (2004),[18] which was greeted with broad commercial and critical plaudits in part because its protagonist Nazneen chooses not to stay in her 'religio-cultural space' (293) and has an affair with the younger British Muslim Karim.

However, in his representations of Muslims at least, Yassin-Kassab treads a careful middle ground between Nadeem Aslam's lyrical, but condemnatory depictions of a claustrophobic, abuse-ridden Muslim community in *Maps for Lost Lovers* (2004), and celebrations of a supportive, class-free mosque in such novels as Leila Aboulela's *Minaret* (2005).[19] In many ways, *The Road from Damascus* is a novel of ideas and, as such, its Muslim characters enunciate diverse and often clashing views of Islam. For instance, Sami has his secularist assumptions and image challenged by Muntaha's decision to wear the symbolically-charged hijab:

> Sami supposed they must look like a proper Muslim couple, what with the hijab, Muslims out on dark business, their trauma children and a string of austere relatives left behind in an unfurnished overcrowded room. Four or five children already, that's what it probably looked like. These two Muslims at large. (110)

Sami feels antipathy to Muntaha's headscarf because of the stereotyping he thinks it will engender, and because he himself views it as a marker of 'supernaturalism [or] backwardness' (2). *The Road from Damascus* thus tacitly accords with Aboulela's *Minaret* and with Emma Tarlo's research in illustrating that, far from being the symbol of female passivity, invisibility and oppression it is often represented as being, in many situations wearing the hijab is a highly conspicuous demonstration of personal agency, often against the wishes of a woman's (male) relatives.[20]

The Road from Damascus is a novel about contrasting religious and secular worldviews, and Sami has to weigh up the attractiveness of atheism (represented by his father) and religion (represented by his mother, wife, brother-in-law and others). Within this broad bifurcation, there are of course various shades of sacredness and secularity, from Gabor's brand of spiritual agnosticism, to Muntaha's personal devotion, to Ammar's crude slogan 'Don't fuck with [Islam]'. Ultimately, the sentiment expressed in the novel's epigraph from the Sufi mystic and poet Ahmad Yasavi hangs over the text: 'unbelief itself is a religion with its own form of belief' (141). We see this in the actions of Sami's father, who condemns his own brother-in-law to decades of imprisonment and torture all for the sake of doctrinaire ideas about the necessity of secularism in Syria. The Syrian Ba'athist government's massacre in Hama of 20,000–30,000 members of the Muslim Brotherhood and others in 1982,[21] which Sami and his father support because of their opposition to Islamism, is a forerunner of the brutal crackdowns being perpetrated by Bashar al-Asad's regime in 2011 and 2012 against Syria's Arab Spring uprisings. The novel tilts away from all dogma, and yet its ending on a tranquil note of prayer and marital reconciliation suggests the attractions of cultivating a flexible belief system.

Yassin-Kassab also represents sacred and secular alternatives as being anything but neatly separated from each other. For instance, the novel illustrates that the Muslims' holy book, the Quran, shares concerns with its pagan precursor, *The Epic of Gilgamesh*, while much of the supposedly secular hip hop which Sami enthusiastically consumes is influenced by movements such as the Nation of Islam. Such sacred/secular juxtapositions suggest that the novel explores a 'third space' connecting the two, in which the interplay between religion and secularism is apparent.[22]

Gilgamesh is an epic dating back to the third millennium BCE, from what is arguably the first literate civilization, the Sumerians of Mesopotamia. His atheist father presents Sami with the epic as a substitute for religion, teaching him the legend that the constellation Orion was originally known as Gilgamesh. As a child, Sami's religious mother tells him the Quranic stories of Ibrahim and Moses, and about *djinns* and the Rightly Guided Caliphs, while his father teaches him the history of Middle Eastern pre-Islamic societies, before moving on to instill respect in him for contemporary Arab poets, such as the secular Syrian Nizar Qabbani and the Palestinian nationalist poet, Mahmoud Darwish. As Sami himself recognizes, his parents are divided in their approach to his education: 'Qabbani versus Qur'an. [His father]'s bookish noise, and the unspoken but resistant verses of the Book. These were the opposing camps' (56). While Sami feels some temptation to join in the attractive religious 'chorus' (59) sung by his mother, ultimately he sides with his father's view of religion as 'the long childhood of a people' (60).

Although *The Epic of Gilgamesh* has been termed 'as much a secular poem as the *Odyssey*',[23] there is no reason to distinguish religions of the Book from *Gilgamesh* in this way, as they share themes, concerns and ambiance. Like the Bible, the Torah and the Quran, *Gilgamesh* contains a flood myth, one of the earliest extant deluge fables. In the clay tablet known as 'The Story of the Flood', the tale is told of the gods angrily deciding to destroy mankind by means of a terrible tempest. However, a god informs one man, Utnapishtim, of the plan, so he builds a huge boat and collects on board his family and many animals. When the flood subsides, Utnapishtim moors the boat at the side of a mountain, and sends a dove, followed by a swallow and a raven, to seek dry land. After this he arranges a sacrifice to propitiate the gods.

As N. K. Sandars observes, 'There is a remarkable resemblance between the story told in Genesis and the Gilgamesh tablet'.[24] What she does not mention is that the parable also contains parallels with the Quranic story of the Great Flood, which is told twice in the Quran, in Surahs 11 and 71. The Quranic story of Nuh places more emphasis on Nuh's remonstrations with the sinful people to repent and recognize Allah, and is less obviously indebted to *Gilgamesh* than the Biblical Noah—for instance, it contains no reference to releasing birds to look for land—but the Quran nonetheless shares similarities with the ancient Mesopotamian myth. Furthermore, towards the end of *Gilgamesh*, a serpent eats the plant of Youth Regained, which the protagonist has with difficulty procured from the bottom of the sea. Not only does this have congruence with the Genesis story of the snake which persuades Eve to eat from the Tree of Knowledge,[25] thus denying man immortality, but it also reverberates with the story, common to Bible and Quran, in which Moses, or Musa, turns his stick into a serpent.[26] The juxtaposition of pre-Islamic literature and the Quran allows Yassin-Kassab to make an elegantly indirect point about the cross-fertilization of seemingly opposed traditions, and also to refute the apparent conflict between ideas of the secular and the sacred. He may also be anticipating the claims of thinkers such as Talal Asad and Timothy Fitzgerald that this dichotomy is a product of western Enlightenment thought, and that the categories of 'religion' and 'secularism' should not be uncritically accepted, but interrogated for their Eurocentric assumptions.[27]

Finally, Yassin-Kassab brings in ecocritical issues through the characters of GR (Global Resister), her Reclaim the Streets environmental activists, and Tom Field, a counter-cultural academic, all of whom offer Sami an alternative to 'Muslim or Arab controversies' (307). The *Gilgamesh* flood myth, with its story of the obliteration of humanity by a weather catastrophe, thus links in with early twenty-first-century concerns about climate change. The novel suggests that if we are to survive global warming, then the solutions are not just technological but spiritual. Sami becomes increasingly repelled by the zombie consumerism of millennial Britain, and adopts a vegetarian diet, eschews chemicals such as deodorant and embarks on Islamicate fasts and ablutions. Yassin-Kassab is not the only writer to make the link between *The Epic of Gilgamesh* and human hubris leading to climate change. In *Hell and High Water*, Alastair McIntosh also makes the connection,[28] arguing further that the Enlightenment arose concurrently with full-scale imperialism and unbridled capitalism. However, like Yassin-Kassab he suggests that this created a spiritual gap, because it deadens the spirit to view the world and its peoples through the lens of logical positivism as objects to be used. In addition to the main choice that Sami has to make between sacred and secular texts and modes of living, he must negotiate a whole series of further apparent dichotomies, which include father and mother; storytelling and religion; green politics and alternative millenarianisms; drugs and prayer. The opposition that the fictional writer Rashid Iqbal believes exists between storytelling and religion is suggested by the novel to be ambivalent at best. Even before we are told that one of Iqbal's novels was described as 'a continent finding its voice' (297),[29] parallels between the fictional character and Salman Rushdie are compelling. He is described as being of Indian origin and British nationality, a 'postmodernist, controversialist', and the author of several books which sound suspiciously anti-Islamic (294). However, this satirical portrait of Rushdie as singularly opposed to Islam is not the full picture that we get from *The Satanic Verses*, or others among Rushdie's early texts.[30] Yassin-Kassab also includes an unflattering physical depiction, which refers to the writer's famously 'hooded' eyes (297).

The name is also resonant for those familiar with Rushdie's oeuvre. 'Rashid' is probably an allusion to Rushdie's first post-fatwa text, *Haroun and the Sea of Stories*,[31] in which Haroun's storyteller father is called Rashid Khalifa (the two names together also evoke Harun al-Rashid, the caliph fictionalized in *One Thousand and One Arabian Nights*). By including this reference to Rushdie's text that attempts to recuperate the relationship between Islamic cultures and storytelling, Yassin-Kassab appears to have a greater awareness of other possible interpretations of the controversial writer than might at first be assumed. Also 'Iqbal', while a common name, may contain a reference to the poet Iqbal, and his articulations of desire for a Muslim homeland eventually realized in the creation of Pakistan. When Rashid Iqbal makes a speech in which he begins with the image of a book-burner and a suicide bomber, and goes on to espouse storytelling, literature, songs and films in opposition to religion (300), it clearly parodies Rushdie's own lecture, 'Is Nothing Sacred?', which was first presented *in absentia* by Harold Pinter in 1990, when Rushdie was in hiding after the fatwa.[32] This speech, although more sophisticated than the bombastic version given by Rashid in the novel, nonetheless contains a similar explicit message about the demise of religion, and the idea that the resulting 'god-shaped hole'[33] can be filled with art, narratives and stories.

Anyone with an awareness of Rushdie's increasingly conservative media soundbites, including his declaration that 'veils suck',[34] will find familiar the depiction of Rashid Iqbal as a 'self-satisf[ied]' extoller of 'progress' (298), who calls for a ban on the hijab in British educational institutions. In his lecture, a distinction is made between a chutnified, impure, mongrelized literature and the pure, austere religion of Islam, which Iqbal controversially asserts is 'not a civilization of narratives' (299). We see the Muslim convert academic who has been chosen by the university to respond to Iqbal's speech furiously

> Scribbling about the spicy mix that was Islamic Spain. About the Greco-Judaic-Indo-Persian masala of medieval Baghdad. About Qur'anic allusions to Alexander the Great. About syncretism and Sufi visions and Muslim travelogues. (300)

Contrary to prevalent stereotypes of Islam as a 'registered trademark of illiberalism—the ideational source of countless malignant practices',[35] this quotation opens up an entirely countervailing image of pluralism, tolerance, sophistication and hybridity. It also immediately evokes Rushdie's novel, *The Moor's Last Sigh* (1995), as one of its chapters is actually entitled 'Malabar Masala', and the entire work alludes to Moorish Granada as well as interchange between Hinduism and the three religions of the book in twentieth-century India.[36] Again, Yassin-Kassab intends a distinction to be made between his Iqbal character and the more multifaceted thinker, Salman Rushdie. Ultimately, the novel indicates that the Muslim religion, far from being opposed to narratives as Iqbal claims, is in fact replete with them, whether stories that derive from the Quran, or the Sunna (life of the Prophet), and *hadiths* (narrations about the ways and deeds of Muhammad). As the quotation demonstrates, Rashid Iqbal's suggestion that Islam is a consistent single entity is also erroneous.

Yassin-Kassab explores Islam, indeed religion itself, in all its multiformity. The city, theorized by such scholars as John McLeod as 'postcolonial London', is an arena where such differences are staged and heightened, although as McLeod carefully points out, the term 'does not factually denote a given place or mark a stable location on a map'.[37] Sami recalls his childhood days in London:

> Just on his bus route to school there were as many one-and-only truths jostling for attention as there were fast food outlets. Jehovah's Witnesses and Seventh Day Adventists. The Nation of Islam in natty suits and carved hair. Rastafarians, both black and (absurdly) white. Anglicans, sagely complacent despite the colonization of their churches. Hare Krishnas singing while lapsed Catholics wolfed their free curry. Sikhs with daggers and briefcases. Freemasons with briefcases only. A Hindu incarnated as the bus conductor bowing inwardly to the elephant god. Scientologists offering personality tests. Grinning Discordians. A Sufi roadworker at his drill, pruning the rose garden within. Rebirthers. Crystal healers. Buddhists of the latest version. To name but some. All of whom had found the exclusive answer. (56–57)

Here Yassin-Kassab also evokes the often-forgotten multiplicity of western religions, from mainstream Anglicanism and Catholicism, to the fringe Christianity of Seventh Day Adventists and Jehovah's Witnesses, the new ageism of crystal healing, the downright weirdness of Scientology and Discordianism and the more secular but nonetheless dogmatic practices of Freemasons and capitalists (the latter in the shape of 'fast food outlets').

Among the hybridized religions of the East mentioned in the above quotation, two related to Islam stand out, the first of which is an esoteric tradition of the religion, Sufism. The reference to the 'rose garden within' probably alludes to the mystic poet Rumi (1207–1273), whose poetry contains many images of spring rose gardens, denoting the need to cherish love, the intellect or the soul.[38] As such, the Sufi roadworker appears to be thinking benign thoughts in order to cultivate the 'rose garden' of his inner spirit. Sufis are often seen as tolerant, syncretic and peaceful, and Sufism's practices include music, dance, devotion at saints' shrines and meditation. Yet the term 'Sufi' in all likelihood derives from the coarse garment of wool (*suf*) worn by the early Arab ascetic who sought to develop an alternative philosophy to combat the decadence and worldliness of a Muslim empire gaining in strength.[39] Contrary to stereotypes of bohemian westerners dabbling in Sufi mysticism and dervish-like whirling, the Path promotes pronounced austerity. Sufism encourages direct experiences of God, and its classic texts, such as *A Tale of Four Dervishes*, or *The Life of Rabia of Basra*, are difficult and uncompromising.[40] Rabia of Basra, the great ninth- and tenth-century mystic, is remembered by Muntaha, who thinks of her countrywoman's lines about loving Allah only for himself and not out of fear of hell or desire for heaven (93).

In contrast, the Nation of Islam is the other, violent variant of Islam mentioned in this passage about London's multifarious religions. Elsewhere in the novel Ammar is described as 'reading pamphlets about how the mad scientist Yaqoob invented the white devil race by genetic experiment' (215–216), which is genuine Nation of Islam theology.[41] In his phase as a hip hop aficionado, Ammar dabbles in militant ideas like these, and also those preached by the Nation of Islam's more extremist offshoot, the Five Percenters. In this way, Yassin-Kassab makes clear that there are strong parallels between hip hop and Islamism (rap stars such as Wu-Tang Clan and Brand Nubian, both of whom Ammar admires, propagated Five Percenter ideology in their lyrics). Rather than the contraposition of the sacred and secular which Islamism and hip hop at first appear to be, then, the two are both concerned with what Sami terms 'sexy identity-assertion' (218): the swagger found in identifying with a 'posse' or 'crew'. It is hard to make generalizations about Islamism which, as Philip Lewis points out, is a 'complex' category, encompassing groups as mainstream as the parties who participate in the current Turkish government, and the violent conglomerate al-Qaeda.[42] Nonetheless, the unspecified, yet distinctively British brand of political Islam to which Aamer subscribes is isolationist—he excludes non-Muslims such as Gabor from the conversation—corrosive, and simplistic—he wears a t-shirt that declares, 'Islam: The Only True Religion' (113).

As a teenager, however, Ammar felt strong affinity with hip hop artists like Public Enemy and Schoolly D, and Sami first bonds with his future brother-in-law by pseudo-intellectualizing about Public Enemy, whom he claims 'have taken music to a new level. It isn't even music any more, which I mean as a compliment. It's the news, it's politics, it's preaching. And also the roar of the crowd, and the noise of the metropolis'. Ammar's appreciative, but monosyllabic response: 'Wicked! . . . Yeah man. . . . Word' and Muntaha's wry comment that Sami is writing a doctoral thesis puncture his pretentions so that he feels his identity shrivel to 'a face painted on a balloon' (213). Questions as to whether Arabs can share a Black identity concern Ammar in his hip hop phase, and hang over the novel. In my interview with him, Robin

Yassin-Kassab expressed his love for non-commercial hip hop, both African American and Arabic. He described in his youth buying a hip hop album, which had 'All praise is due to Allah' written on the cover: 'people like me would latch on to this, thinking "It's us!", because it was a creative, powerful, urban image'.[43] In the chapter entitled 'It Soon Come', Yassin-Kassab layers images of Ammar's new 'pared-down protestant' mosque with flashbacks to Sami's and Ammar's attendance at a Public Enemy gig almost a decade earlier. In the style of the hip hop sample described at the beginning of his chapter, Yassin-Kassab intercuts his prose with cacophonic lines from Linton Kwesi Johnson's 'Time Come', quoting the iterative menace in 'Look out! look out! look out!' (211).[44]

Elsewhere in the text, Yassin-Kassab makes passing reference to the 'hijab posse' (152), largely second- and third-generation Bengalis who have become far more orthodox Sunnis than their parents. He also depicts the jumbled-up mimicry of Ammar's mosque: 'The white convert in Pakistani gear. The two subcontinentals dressed like Arabs, in white gellabiyas. The Arabs and the Somali . . . in tracksuits, like Ammar' (222). Finally, he evokes the evolving religiosity of men like Marwan, Muntaha's father, who, like many Arabs of his generation, was an urbane, anti-religious intellectual, but who discovers a nascent faith during his weekly torture sessions in an Iraqi jail. As a refugee in Britain, he finds comfort in the Regent's Park mosque, and his faith develops into a conservative nostalgia. In his newfound orthodoxy, Marwan views Sami as 'this failed Syrian, this fake Englishman, neither fish nor fowl, his head full of froth' (115). As well as evoking what Homi Bhabha describes as the productive and enabling in-between space of migrants, Yassin-Kassab suggests that second-generation hybridity is also grounded in traumatic experiences and identity confusion.

Another popular art form which Sami enjoys is film, the iconography and music of which gives him an almost spiritual release from the loss of meaning and destabilization of his identity he has felt since his father's untimely death. However, Sami also watches movies for the 'apocalyptic buzz of victimized self-righteousness' he derives from their anti-Arab representations (151). Jack Shaheen rightly identifies Arabs in Hollywood films as symbolizing 'Public Enemy #1—brutal, heartless, uncivilized religious fanatics and money-mad cultural "others" bent on terrorizing civilized Westerners, especially Christians and Jews'.[45] Sami's personal favourites are *Raiders of the Lost Ark* (1981), with Indiana Jones nonchalantly shooting a sabre-wielding Arab after allowing him to show off his swordsmanship; *True Lies* (1994), James Cameron's risible depiction of the Palestinian struggle and the 'Crimson Jihad' gang; and *The Siege* (1998), which Sami critiques for its metonymic juxtapositions of men at prayer with explosions. Although the films' overt racism is clearly lampooned here, Sami's indignation is undercut by the fact that he watches these films stoned while Muntaha is at work and seemingly enjoys his martyrdom: 'Humiliation hits Sami in the gut. Wonderful' (152).

Even between members of particular Muslim groups, the novel depicts a healthy debate taking place, which finds precedent in Islam's endorsement of *ijtihad*, or independent reasoning. When there is no clear guidance from the Quran or *hadiths*, Muslims take part in *ijtihad* to formulate their own protocols. In relation to this process, Tariq Ramadan asserts: 'There is absolutely no contradiction . . . between the realm of faith and the realm of reason. On the contrary, the spark of faith, born in the original testimony, needs intellect to confirm that testimony'.[46] We see such reasoning at work when Muntaha and her extremist brother Ammar quarrel about the meaning of the word jihad (318–319), which is conventionally defined as 'holy war', but is more usefully translated as 'struggle in the way of Allah'[47] or an 'ethic of striving'.[48] As Noorani observes, the Prophet Muhammad declared that 'The highest form of jihad is to speak the truth in the face of an unjust ruler'.[49] It is often argued that jihad should not be interpreted as a sixth pillar of Islam, but that the other pillars all come out of it, as the profession of faith, praying, giving alms to the poor, fasting and performing *Hajj* all require spiritual effort. Neither Ammar nor Muntaha questions the concept itself, central as it is to Islamic thought, but rather each disagrees over expositions of its meaning. Muntaha rejects Ammar's simplistic and dangerous interpretation that jihad means killing the *kuffar*, maintaining instead that it means the intellectual, moral and spiritual struggle within, to assert one's belief, pray and maintain a happy marriage, and that different temporal and spatial factors determine its significance (319–320).

Yassin-Kassab thus educates non-Muslim readers as to diverse Islamic interpretations of those ubiquitous topics—rendered in one-dimensional ways by most western media outlets—such as jihad, Sharia law and issues surrounding women's bodies, including veiling, 'forced marriage' and polygamy. During the course of *The Road from Damascus*, we watch the ebullience of postmodern secularism give way to a quieter, more serious Islamic faith, which nonetheless makes room for doubt and uncertainty (Muntaha declares, 'Hoping so, believing so, that's all Islam is' (147)). Identity, 'This short lifelong struggle to balance an oily bubble of selfhood atop this body' (116), is given greater meaning via a conditional, inclusive spirituality.

Ultimately, many of the text's Muslim characters come to view religion in Amin Malak's phrase as 'a key component of their identity that could rival, if not supersede, their class, race, gender, or ethnic affiliation'.[50] Although everyday lived identity is malleable and performed, this chapter has demonstrated that the decades either side of 9/11 have witnessed an upsurge in rigid identity politics and attention to symbols. Mainstream British society puts increasing pressure on young cultural and/or religious Muslims to choose between the sacred and secular components of their identity. Yet in *The Road from Damascus*, Robin Yassin-Kassab indicates that these apparently separate mechanisms of faith and secularism are in fact meshed together in all of us, creating friction, but also intertwining in creative ways. Through his energetic and original use of intertextuality, including references to the Quran and recent cinema stereotyping of Muslims, Yassin-Kassab explores overlaps and interplay between what otherwise seem antithetical positions.

Notes

1. Robin Yassin-Kassab, *The Road from Damascus* (London: Hamish Hamilton, 2008). All page references are to this edition.
2. Hanan al-Shaykh, *Only in London*, trans. Catherine Cobham (London: Bloomsbury, 2002 [2001]).
3. Peter Hopkins, 'Young Muslim Men's Experiences of Local Landscapes After 11 September 2011', in Cara Aitchison, Peter Hopkins and Mei-Po Kwan, eds, *Geographies of Muslim Identities: Diaspora, Gender and Belonging* (Aldershot: Ashgate, 2007), 189–200 (191).
4. Amin Maalouf, *In the Name of Identity: Violence and the Need to Belong*, trans. Barbara Bray (New York: Penguin, 2003 [1996]), 38–39.
5. Gabriele Marranci, *Understanding Muslim Identity: Rethinking Fundamentalism* (Basingstoke: Palgrave, 2009), 20.
6. Maalouf, *Name*, 34, 120, 43.
7. Nawal El Saadawi, 'Why Keep Asking Me About My Identity?', *The Nawal El Saadawi Reader* (London: Zed, 1997), 117–33 (117).
8. Mahmood Mamdani, *Good Muslim, Bad Muslim: America, the Cold War and the Roots of Terror* (New York: Three Leaves, 2004), 18–20.
9. El Saadawi, 'Identity?', 129.
10. Stuart Hall, 'Cultural Identity and Diaspora', in Patrick Williams and Laura Chrisman, eds, *Colonial Discourse and Post-colonial Theory: A Reader* (New York: Columbia University Press, 1994), 392–403 (402).
11. Lawrence Grossberg, 'Identity and Cultural Studies: Is that All There is?', in Stuart Hall and Paul du Gay, eds, *Questions of Cultural Identity* (London: Sage, 1996 [1997]), 87–107 (89).
12. Robin Cohen, *Frontiers of Identity: The British and the Others* (Essex: Longman, 1994), 204–205.
13. Olivier Roy, *Globalised Islam: The Search for a New Ummah* (London: Hurst, 2004), 23.
14. Tariq Modood, *Multiculturalism: A Civic Idea* (London: Polity, 2007), 87–119.
15. See www.framingmuslims.org (accessed 15 May 2011), and Peter Morey and Amina Yaqin, *Framing Muslims: Stereotyping and Representations After 9/11* (Cambridge, MA: Harvard University Press, 2011).
16. Joseph Massad, *Desiring Arabs* (Chicago: University of Chicago Press, 2007), 6.
17. Maya Jaggi, 'Beyond Belief: Review of *The Road From Damascus* by Robin Yassin-Kassab', *Guardian Review*, 14 June 2008, 11.
18. Monica Ali, *Brick Lane* (London: Black Swan, 2004 [2003]).
19. Nadeem Aslam, *Maps for Lost Lovers* (London: Faber, 2004); and Leila Aboulela, *Minaret* (London: Bloomsbury, 2005).
20. Tarlo argues that 'many women consciously adopt forms of dress that are more conspicuously Islamic than their parents or husbands desire or expect'. Emma Tarlo, 'Hijab in London: Metamorphosis, Resonance and Effects', *Journal of*

Material Culture 12.2 (2007): 131–156 (139). For an autobiographical account of Yassin-Kassab's own objections when his wife first started wearing *hijab*, see Robin Yassin-Kassab, 'My Wife Wears the Hijab. I Wish She Didn't', *Observer*, 2 November 2008, 38.

21. See Kathrin Nina Wiedl, *The Hama Massacre: Reasons, Supporters of the Rebellion, Consequences* (Munich: Grin Verlag, 2006).

22. Homi K. Bhabha, *The Location of Culture* (London: Routledge, 1994), 53–56.

23. N. K. Sandars, ed. and trans., *The Epic of Gilgamesh* (Harmondsworth: Penguin, 1987 [1960]), 30.

24. Ibid., 40.

25. Genesis 3:1–6.

26. Surah 26:32.

27. Talal Asad, *Formations of the Secular: Christianity, Islam, Modernity* (Stanford: Stanford University Press, 2003); and Timothy Fitzgerald, *Discourse of Civility and Barbarity: A Critical History of Religion and Related Categories* (Oxford: Oxford University Press, 2009).

28. Alastair McIntosh, *Hell and High Water: Climate Change, Hope and the Human Condition* (Edinburgh: Birlinn, 2008), 15, 139, 144, 158–159.

29. Early editions of Salman Rushdie's *Midnight's Children* were famously emblazoned with a quotation from Clark Blaise's review in *The New York Times*, proclaiming, 'It sounds like a continent finding its voice'. See Salman Rushdie, *Midnight's Children* (London: Picador, 1982 [1981]), front cover.

30. Rushdie is undoubtedly worried about the ways in which Islam is put to ideological use or joined to nation-state ideology, but in terms of his influence by Islamic culture, art, and so on (particularly forms arising from Sufism), he cannot entirely be described as anti-Islamic.

31. Salman Rushdie, *Haroun and the Sea of Stories* (London: Granta, 1991 [1990]).

32. Salman Rushdie, 'Is Nothing Sacred?', *Imaginary Homelands* (London: Granta, 1991), 415–429.

33. See Salman Rushdie, *Midnight's Children* (London: Picador, 1982 [1981]), 10–12.

34. See Riazat Butt, 'Rushdie backs Straw in Row over Muslim Veils', *Guardian*, 11 October 2006, 12.

35. Peter G. Mandaville, *Traditional Muslim Politics: Reimagining the Umma* (London: Routledge, 2001), xi.

36. Salman Rushdie, *The Moor's Last Sigh* (London: Jonathan Cape, 1995).

37. See John McLeod, *Postcolonial London* (Abingdon: Routledge, 2004), 7.

38. Jalal ad-Din Rumi, *A Rumi Anthology*, trans. Reynold A. Nicholson (Oxford: Oneworld, 2000), 183, and *The Sufi Path of Love: The Spiritual Teachings of Rumi*, trans. William C. Chittick (Albany: State University of New York Press, 1983), 280–285.

39. Philip Lewis, *Islamic Britain: Religion, Politics and Identity Among British Muslims* (London: I. B. Tauris, 1994), 28–29.

40. Mir Amman, *A Tale of Four Dervishes*, trans. Mohammed Zakir (Harmondsworth: Penguin, 2006); and Widad El Sakkakini, *First Among Sufis: The Life and Thought of Rabia al-Adawiyya, the Woman Saint of Basra*, trans. Nabil Safwat, intro. Doris Lessing (London: Octagon Press, 1982).

41. See Elijah Muhammad, *Message to the Blackman in America* (Phoenix, AZ: Secretarius Memps Publications, 1997).

42. Philip Lewis, *Young, British and Muslim* (London: Continuum, 2007), xiv.

43. Claire Chambers, unpublished section from 'Robin Yassin-Kassab', *British Muslim Fictions: Interviews with Contemporary Writers* (Basingstoke: Palgrave, 2011), 189–204.

44. Linton Kwesi Johnson, 'Time Come', *Mi Revalueshanary Fren: Selected Poems* (London: Penguin, 2002), 23–24.

45. Jack G. Shaheen, *Reel Bad Arabs: How Hollywood Vilifies a People* (New York: Olive Branch, 2001), 2.

46. Tariq Ramadan, *Western Muslims and the Future of Islam* (Oxford: Oxford University Press, 2004), 17.

47. David Waines, *An Introduction to Islam* (Cambridge: Cambridge University Press, 2003 [1995]), 162.

48. Francis E. Peters, *The Monotheists: Jews, Christians, and Muslims in Conflict and Competition, Volume I: The Peoples of God* (Princeton: Princeton University Press, 2005), 269.

49. A. G. Noorani, *Islam and Jihad: Prejudice Versus Reality* (London: Zed, 2002), 45.

50. Amin Malak, *Muslim Narratives and the Discourse of English* (Albany: State University of New York Press, 2005), 3.

Part III
(Mis)reading Muslims

8 Writing Islam in Post-9/11 America

John Updike's *Terrorist*

Anna Hartnell

Introduction: Writing 'Islam'

John Updike's penultimate novel, *Terrorist* (2006), signals the attempt on the part of one of America's most well-known and prolific writers to take on Islam in the wake of 9/11. 'Islam' has long been, as Edward Said tells us, 'news'. In *Covering Islam* (1981), Said explains that a monolithic 'Islam' has long served as a watchword for violence and terrorism in the western media.[1] The violent penetration of US space occasioned by the 9/11 attacks served to make hyper-visible a narrative that has for decades demonized Islam as anti-modern and anti-western. Though drawing on very different discursive paradigms, since the latter stages of the Cold War this narrative has to an extent replaced the Communist 'menace' in American national mythology. In this sense 9/11 has renewed and intensified, if not resurrected, tendencies in US culture that have sought to police a religion apparently intent on transgressing its assigned place in the American religious mosaic by asserting itself in the public sphere. By explicitly tackling Islam's perceived relationship with violence, Updike's novel conjures an economy of representation identified by Said in 1978 as the dominant frame in which western understandings of the Muslim 'other' emerge.[2] How far *Terrorist* travels from the familiar terrain of Orientalist discourse will be the focus of this essay.

Said's designation of Orientalism posited a rigid binary relation between East and West, and while his early ground-breaking study has been much criticized for its own maintenance of this Manichean division, his later work pointed to its transcendence through contrapuntal readings carefully attuned to the unravelling of colonial power.[3] Only a very generous reading of Updike could credit *Terrorist* with deconstructing the colonial binary. In spite of his apparently genuine attempt to displace reductive readings of Islamist violence, 'Islam' does ultimately emerge as Other in Updike's novel, its practitioners sometimes drawn in commonplace Orientalist stereotypes. Moreover, the overwhelmingly religious register of *Terrorist* sharply contrasts the values of 'Islam' with those of what is a recognizably 'Judeo-Christian' culture. Yet Updike's 'clash of civilizations' is significant nonetheless for the fact that, almost unwittingly, it insinuates a series of ruptures between religious, ethnic and national poles of identity, in ways that interrupt seamless accounts of 'Americanness' as much as they undermine coherent accounts of 'Islam'.

In this sense *Terrorist* emerges as an intervention into the duplicitous nature of western discourses of secularism which, as Judith Butler observes, may well be 'a fugitive way' for certain kinds of 'religion to survive'.[4] Ronald Grimes's observation that the American-led response to 9/11 was as much a form of religious expression as was the initial attack suggests that September 11 has exposed the subterranean agenda of secularization: 'our wars are no less holy than theirs—just holy in a different way. Holy war: war for which no price is too high. Holy war—the kind that is waged when God is on our side'.[5] Updike approaches this reactive crusade on the part of western countries by sympathetically positioning his own narrative voice *vis-à-vis* an Arab American Muslim convert. This essay opens by exploring the novel's somewhat problematic treatment of the relationship between Islam and violence, and goes on to suggest that this relationship inheres in a certain rendering of Enlightenment discourses of secularism that privilege Christian—and specifically Protestant—forms of faith. And yet I argue that the novel simultaneously articulates a form of self-critique via its interrogation of an often racist post-9/11 US nationalism, which exerts such totalizing claims on Muslim loyalties.

Islam and Spectres of Violence

Nowhere is Updike's attempt to ventriloquize the mind of a would-be Islamist terrorist clearer than in the novel's treatment of the Quran. As John Strawson notes,

> like the Orientalists of the eighteenth and nineteenth centuries, language holds a special place for him—thus [in *Terrorist*] we are faced with a significant amount of transliterated Qur'anic Arabic. This draws on the Orientalist trope that to know the language is to know the mind of the other.[6]

And indeed much of the novel's rationale for Islamist violence seems to come from the Quran—Updike claimed in an interview that 'more than most religions this is a religion of the book'.[7] Updike makes no secret of the fact that when rereading the Quran for the purposes of writing *Terrorist* he was surprised to find Allah so 'angry' and claims that 'a lot of the Koran does not speak very eloquently to a Westerner'.[8] While he stresses that all religious traditions contain the seeds of violence, he was struck by 'how much hostility toward non-believers' the Quran expresses.[9] Thus throughout the novel Ahmad, its central protagonist, repeatedly looks on at his fellow

Americans as 'devils' and 'infidels' made up of 'weak Christians and non-observant Jews' who embrace a society that testifies to a 'God known to have died'.[10] Against this fallen world Ahmad posits a literal reading of the Quran that projects 'Paradise' as 'a real place' (107). This desire to render physical what his mentor—Shaikh Rashid—presents as the Quran's metaphoric suggestiveness is arguably indicative of Ahmad's susceptibility to the idea that the Quran's injunctions about faith demand both internal and external application. *Terrorist* thus somewhat problematically projects a neat identity between Ahmad's faith—gleaned from the holy book—and his later decision to embrace violence.

And yet the instinctive repulsion towards Islam betrayed in *Terrorist* by the character Jack Levy does not seem to be Updike's own. Far from wanting to write a novel that vilifies Islam, he in fact claimed to be engaging the reader's imaginative sympathies for its critique of American culture:

> Writers in so far as they perform a public service try to expand your sympathies and lead the readers' sympathies into places where they wouldn't ordinarily go. I thought a terrorist could be a good place for Americans to try to see from within.[11]

Ahmad perceives a morally exhausted world, intoxicated by sex and consumerism and enslaved to its own images. 'America', reads the novel, 'is paved solid with fat and tar', governed by a 'Jewish-Protestant God' committed to the suppression of the Palestinians in Israel on the international stage, and on the home front characterized by the lazy 'lackluster sameness' encapsulated by Beth and Jack Levy (25–27). Ahmad's contrasting desire to ride 'the Straight Path' stands out in favourable contrast. While his strong sense that America is populated by 'devils' is not unlike the America painted by Sayyid Qutb—whose experiences of the US in the 1940s led to an indictment of a 'decadent' western culture that was to have a significant influence on the development of contemporary Islamist ideology—it is one that Updike partially identifies with as well. In an interview for the *New York Times*, Updike said 'I think I felt I could understand the animosity and hatred which an Islamic believer would have for our system'.[12]

Ahmad's faith marks him out from the brash high school crowd and is in many ways, as his mother Terry remarks, 'beautiful'. This faith is accompanied by a personal gentleness that leads Jack Levy to conclude that Ahmad has the 'dignity' and 'presence' to be a doctor—'I'd trust him with my life' (92). The irony that Ahmad's religion would ultimately set him on the path of mass murder is the central preoccupation of the novel. One of the fascinating aspects of Updike's exploration of Ahmad's turn to violence is that it poses a religious dilemma not dissimilar to that which confronts many of the characters that have populated the pages of Updike's previous works. As Marshall Boswell points out, Updike's own religious vision is deeply shaped by readings of Søren Kierkegaard and Karl Barth. In 1958 Updike suffered an existential crisis revolving around the fear of death, and he claims to have been drawn back from this abyss by reading these two philosophers. The consequence for Updike, as Boswell writes, is a 'dialectical approach to religious issues in which defining oppositions do not resolve into a satisfying synthesis but rather remain in sustained tension and ambiguity'.[13] It is just this kind of tension that in turn makes its way into the 'moral debates' that Updike believes shape the fictional worlds offered up to his readers. The book that Updike claims to have most changed his life is Kierkegaard's *Fear and Trembling* (1843), and I suggest that some of its motivating dilemmas make their way into Ahmad's own crisis of faith in *Terrorist*.

In *Fear and Trembling* Kierkegaard stages a 'clash between ethics and the inner call to faith' by dramatizing the biblical story in which Abraham believes he has been divinely summoned to sacrifice his only son, Isaac.[14] For Kierkegaard the religious situation is precisely the leap of faith that separates the believer from the realm of universal morals militated by the social order— Abraham's willingness to isolate himself from society by slaughtering his son signals for Kierkegaard the abyssal, and ultimately admirable, quality of this leap. *Terrorist* itself includes numerous references to this particular biblical story, and as the novel draws to a close it is clear that a similar dilemma conditions Ahmad's faith—which will also somehow be proven via the sacrifice of innocent Americans in an act which will pit Ahmad's religious leap of faith against the demands of society's moral standards. Ahmad's sense of himself becomes increasingly elevated and distanced from the concerns of the everyday as his supposed martyrdom draws near; as Shaikh Rashid briefs him, we are told 'he yearned to savor his solitary hours in this clean, safe room, alone with God' (270). Just as Abraham brackets off his own intentions from all thought of society's judgements in a pure 'leap of faith', Ahmad too wishes to preserve the purity of his own faith from outside pressures. Yet it is at this point where the two narratives decisively depart.

There is a fundamental difference between the religious dramas portrayed by Kierkegaard in *Fear and Trembling* and Updike in *Terrorist*. Where Abraham's anticipated act of religious violence depends on a suspension of the ethical, Ahmad's religious suspension of the morals of mainstream American society relies on embracing the ethics espoused by another shared culture. Thus where Abraham's leap rests on faith alone, Ahmad's leap of faith is subject to considerable manipulation by those around him. In other words, where Abraham's dilemma hinges on a tension between the internal relationship with God and the external demands of society—and ultimately privileges the voice of God over and above that of society—the tension experienced by Ahmad is between competing US and Islamist ideologies, both of which pollute his desire to be 'alone with his God'. In contrast to Abraham's faith, Ahmad's is subject to the constant interference of Shaikh Rashid insistently asking 'Is your faith still strong?' (269). The sinister character of

Rashid tells Ahmad that a warrior is needed 'whose love of God is unqualified, and who impatiently thirsts for the glory of Paradise' and he asks him 'are you such a one, Ahmad?' (234). Ahmad's desire that his faith be somehow 'protected' from the influence of Rashid at the last hour is consequently both futile and ironic: *Terrorist*'s implication is that Ahmad's faith is from the outset irremediably conditioned by that of his 'teacher'.

At the beginning of the novel Updike's Barthian sense that God is 'wholly other' is consonant with Ahmad's perception that the African American church he witnesses is altogether too 'cosy' with their God. But towards the end of the novel it becomes clear that Updike's critique of Ahmad's faith is that it becomes altogether too 'cosy' with the people around him and less sharpened by his own individual conscience. As the moment of Ahmad's violent act approaches we read that 'a certain simplicity does lay hold of Ahmad in the troughs between surges of terror and then of exaltation'. This 'newly elevated and simplified sense of himself' takes on the absolutist shades of black-and-white that colour Ahmad's daily uniform (250–251). This signifies the very opposite of the dialectical confrontation that shapes the Kierkegaardian clash between the religious and the ethical that Updike so admires. Rather, Ahmad's faith has apparently become fully reconciled to the politicized Islam to which both Charlie and Rashid have exposed him.

Interestingly then, while Updike insisted that he had written a book about religion and not politics, his plot is unable to extricate the latter from the former. For the clash engendered by Ahmad's intended act of violence is not between ethics and religion but rather between two very different social—and thus political—systems. The initially private terrains of Ahmad's faith have been polluted by the politics of others in the community of believers and thrown off course. As Ahmad emerges from the Lincoln Tunnel having failed to detonate his bombs the loss of faith he fears throughout the text seems to have been realized: '*these devils . . . have taken away my God*' (310). So we are left with the potentially problematic situation in which the intervention of Ahmad's individual conscience—his repudiation of violence—has deprived him of Islam. It is hard not to draw the conclusion that what emerges as sinister in Updike's novel are the consequences of a communal faith.

Ahmad's initial attitudes towards Islam are comparable to the workings of a Protestant interiority that Updike can relate to and respect. Thus in contrast to 'the masses of ordinary, hard-pressed men and plain, practical women' who populate the Arab American neighbourhoods, and who are, according to Ahmad, 'enrolled in Islam as a lazy matter of ethnic identity', Ahmad prefers to experience his faith in 'isolation' (177). Yet ultimately the novel cannot sustain Ahmad's desire to rely on 'faith alone'—*Terrorist* moves ineluctably towards the pollution of such interiority by external forces that lead to the assumption of violence. In this particular case there is every reason to critique and condemn the influence of these external forces; the 'social system' influencing Ahmad here is a form of political Islam that equates acts of violence and the murder of innocents with sacred duty. The question to ask though is whether Updike construes violence as an inevitable result of collective religion—if so, we might also want to question the extent to which Updike succeeds in translating the mind of a Muslim. Karen Armstrong writes that 'we have a long history of Islamophobia in Western culture that dates back to the time of the Crusades. In the twelfth century, Christian monks in Europe insisted that Islam was a violent religion of the sword' and this one-dimensional view of Islam has persisted ever since.[15] To the extent that Ahmad's personal jihad inevitably evolves to take the shape of public violence in *Terrorist*, Updike himself participates in this long tradition. The Quranic saying that *'idolatry is worse than carnage'*, one that also found its way into the instructions left by the September 11 hijackers, reverberates throughout the novel and seemingly provides a scriptural basis for the suggestion that Islam is irremediably haunted by violence (201).[16]

Jihad and the Problem of the Secular

Updike's novel is arguably part of what Yvonne Haddad identifies as an 'American hostility to non-privatized Islam'.[17] While large sections of American Christianity have transgressed into so-called 'secular' territory with relatively little censure, Updike appears to take Islam to task for this transgression in *Terrorist*. Contemporary debates about the much contested Arabic term jihad throw light on this move, in large part because understandings of jihad circulated in the West are bound up with notions of the public and private realms: at one end of the spectrum of western commentators, the term is projected as meaning nothing less than a universal call for 'holy war', and at the other there is the impulse to somehow sanitize the term and claim for it the status of a largely personal 'struggle'. The notion that jihad also translates to mean the striving for 'social justice' sits between these two positions—it certainly implies the penetration of the public realm but does not necessarily entail violence—and presents a challenge to both extremes of this spectrum. Yet as *Terrorist* shows, once jihad pervades the social realm its significations become increasingly ominous to western spectators like Updike. This stems in part, I suggest, from the fact that, in Adam Zachary Newton's words, 'at least since Epicurus', discussions of religion in the West have had 'Christianity at least subliminally in mind'.[18]

As Bruce Lincoln notes, most studies of religion undertaken in the West have been up until very recently modelled on Clifford Geertz's definition of religion which turns on symbols, moods, motivations and conceptions:

> A religion is (1) a system of symbols which acts to (2) establish powerful, pervasive, and long-lasting moods and motivations in men by (3) formulating conceptions of a general order of existence and (4) clothing

these conceptions with such an aura of factuality that (5) the moods and motivations seem uniquely realistic.[19]

This definition has, however, fallen out of favour in recent decades largely as the result of Talal Asad's critique. This critique picks up on two points, the first being that Geertz's definition works well for certain styles of religiosity, mainly Protestantism, which becomes the implicit model for religion as such. This then leads to the neglect of embodied practice and community that are vital aspects of many religions, not only Islam but Catholicism and Judaism as well. Asad's second and more radical point concerns the very nature of Geertz's definitional project, and is summarized here by Lincoln:

> Insofar as the task of defining anything presumes a discrete object that can be identified in contradistinction to others, this implies a model of 'religion' that emerged only with the Enlightenment. Prior to that time, even in western Europe religion cannot be analytically (or practically) disarticulated from virtually all other aspects of culture.[20]

As Asad's work has vividly illustrated, the Enlightenment separation of the religious from the secular—which, as Charles Taylor has argued, para-doxically privileges certain kinds of 'religious' affiliation from the outset[21]—became a central imposition of the colonial project.[22] It is therefore hardly surprising that the development of Islamist ideology—which itself evolved from centuries of Muslim anti-colonial struggle against the West—frequently identifies secularism as a key aspect of western decadence. As Lincoln explains, this critique of secularism lies behind much of Sayyid Qutb's diag-nosis of America as in a state of *jahiliyyah*. Lincoln explains that

> traditionally, this term designates the age of spiritual ignorance charac-terizing the pre-Islamic period of barbarism, and he [Qutb] extended its usage to describe the modern world's malaise, where *jahiliyyah* was not just a matter of ignorance, but a more active state of rebellion against God's sovereignty on earth.[23]

As already noted, Ahmad's own perceptions of America are not dissimi-lar to Qutb's, who discerned a disturbing rupture between religious spaces and those designated 'secular'. Qutb's well-known description of the church dance in Greeley, Colorado, at which he witnessed members of the opposite sex engaging in what he believed to be inappropriate behaviour, relays these kinds of concerns; as Lincoln writes:

> Qutb was not disturbed simply by the eroticism he took to be inde-corous and improper. More troubling, but analytically most revealing, was the enabling condition of this offensive spectacle: the disconnection

between the preceding 'religious' church service and the 'social' event that followed.[24]

Ahmad detects something similar when he finds himself in an African American church and is repelled by the association he feels between 'songs of Jesus' and those of 'sexual longing' (8). Thus Ahmad's sense of Islam is an all-encompassing one which claims all spheres of life, yet his faith is nonetheless founded on a certain interiority, as evidenced by his consistent desire for privacy, to 'be alone with his God'. Updike thus projects onto Ahmad's faith an interesting mixture of high Protestantism and a *political* Islam that Updike cannot really relate to *as* religion. This is because for Updike—whose understanding of religion is consistent with Geertz's definition—politics and faith should not intersect. Updike claims that *Terrorist* 'is really not so much a political take . . . this is more a religious novel';[25] it is about the lengths to which the central protagonist will go to defend his faith. Updike's attempt to isolate this 'religious' discussion from the 'political' domain leaves us with a largely creedal clash that projects Islam in monolithic terms. Updike does not so much fail to understand the communal aspects of Islam as condemn them, alongside, it should be added, fundamentalist Christianity, as attacks on western freedoms. Thus what began as an exercise in empathy arguably finds its solution in the repudiation of Islam. And what is outwardly a realist novel possibly interrupts its own 'seamless' claim on reality via the production of familiar Orientalist archetypes.

Updike claimed in an interview that 'in other ways, *apart from Islam*' Ahmad is 'a nice boy, a nice boy who believes, and belief entails certain uneasy-making consequences in the real world'.[26] In another interview, when asked if his portrayal of Ahmad's imam did not seem rather Orientalist, Updike unconvincingly defends himself by saying that 'clichés contain a certain amount of truth or they wouldn't have arisen in the first place' and claims his right as a writer to 'let loose' his feelings.[27] In a world in which people increasingly grant themselves permission to 'let loose' their feelings on Islam, this response is in many ways problematic. Updike's America, then, though under fire in *Terrorist*, is markedly Christian, as are Updike's frames of reference for understanding religion of any kind. For this reason his novel ultimately finds Islam wanting, and participates in the assumption that 'Islamic terrorism is locked in an existentialist battle with the West'.[28] So while Updike's 'Muslim' is very far from the racist visions of Muslims and Arabs that emerge from the pens of many journalists, his is nonetheless a peculiarly 'disembodied Islam'. Its defining referent seems not to be the Islamic East but a Christian West.

As Strawson shows, Ahmad's motivations for being drawn into the conspiracy are shallow at best; he 'seems untouched by the politics of the Islamic world itself'. Parallel to discussions of Qutb in the West that tend to focus solely on his writings on America, the implication is that opposition to the

United States, and not internal power struggles within the Islamic world, is the motivating factor for Islamist terrorism. But, as Strawson writes, 'the West is not the principal concern of Islamist groups', and, as Iraq painfully highlights, neither are western civilians its most numerous victims.[29] Indeed, the division of the world—by some Muslim and particularly Islamist groups—into '*dar al-Islam* (the world of Islam) and *dar al-Harb* (the world of war)' has often entailed particularly virulent attacks on the so-called unbelieving 'hypocrites' within nominal Muslim territories.[30] The failure to acknowledge the internal dynamics within the Islamic world leads to the emergence of a peculiarly decontextualized 'Islam' in *Terrorist*—largely 'religious', not 'political'—and in part affirms Said's observation that the real subject of Orientalist discourse is the West itself.[31]

That *Terrorist* was initially conceived as a novel about Christian fundamentalist violence—Islam was later substituted as somehow more appropriate to today's world—raises questions as to how far Updike has succeeded in creating a realistic psychological portrait of a Muslim character.[32] It also points to the fact that Christianity polices Updike's religious vision, and further highlights his own secularist stance, one that, I have argued, puts an inherently sinister spin on any notion of the *ummah*, the Muslim community. Yet while the path from faith to violence in *Terrorist* seems inevitable, there is an attempt to project an alternative, in some senses 'private' path for the course of jihad. Ahmad counters Charlie's apparent militancy by saying, much to the approval of Charlie's father, that 'Jihad doesn't have to mean war' (149). Both Charlie and Rashid gradually and insidiously draw Ahmad's sense of jihad away from the potentially internal 'struggle to become holy and closer to God' (108)—as Rashid tells Ahmad, Charlie 'informs me that you have expressed a willingness to die for jihad' (233). And yet interestingly, this supposed 'willingness' to become a martyr conflicts with Ahmad's sense throughout the novel that 'infidels do not know how to die' (174). Ahmad's observation seems to highlight a culture unaware of its own limits, its own finitude, and ironically Ahmad's desire to bring home the knowledge of life's destination towards death—via the act of mass murder—is precisely a transgression of his own finite possibility. For his this-worldly claim to otherworldly 'justice' contradicts the notion that the ultimate will of God must remain a mystery. Once again, Updike privileges the religious as 'faith alone' and sanitizes Ahmad's initial critique of US culture and notion of jihad by divorcing it from the 'action' that Charlie, Ahmad's Janus-faced mentor, is so keen on.

Here Updike joins a growing debate in the West as to the 'true' nature of jihad and the term's relationship to violence. The voice of Karen Armstrong has been pioneering in this regard; in her book *Muhammad: Prophet for Our Time* (2006) she goes to considerable lengths to underscore Muhammad's essentially non-violent bias: 'his life was a jihad: as we shall see, this word does not mean "holy war," it means "struggle"'. Moreover, she writes,

'Muhammad used the term jahiliyyah to refer not to an historical era but to a state of mind that caused violence and terror in seventh-century Arabia'.[33] Armstrong stresses that the peaceable connotations of the word 'Islam' itself signify primarily 'surrender' to God, and certainly such an attitude is evident in Updike's Ahmad. And yet as Strawson argues in a different context,

> it is rather defensive to deny that Jihad has other meanings and uses . . . The assumption appears to be that once you accept that Jihad has military content at all, then September 11 becomes an example of Jihad and thus a Muslim holy war against the United States.[34]

In this way Armstrong's discourse on jihad becomes part of what Strawson identifies as 'a banal form of constructing the good or the bad Muslim', a polarized and reductive discussion in which he also includes political figures like Tony Blair.[35] Indeed, since 9/11, the search for the 'moderate Muslim' has led in the UK to a focus on the large Sufi population precisely because of Sufism's mystical emphasis—an emphasis that has come under fire from Islamist revivalist movements. And yet as Ron Geaves points out, the characterization of Sufism as tending largely towards the other-worldly belies the fact that 'historically the Sufi orders have been centres of resistance to colonial rule in Sudan, Algeria and the Caucasus' and share much of the Islamist critique of western decadence.[36] If the search for the 'moderate Muslim' is really about silencing dissent from western practices and policies then, as Strawson suggests, and as Updike's novel seems to illustrate, the initial search for 'the good Muslim' inevitably gives way to the discovery of the 'bad'. This is in large part because Islam does not on the whole observe the public/private distinction assumed by a secular (read: Christian) West.

Conclusion: Interrupting 'America'

As Strawson notes, all the conspirators that lure Ahmad into the terrorist plot 'are either foreigners or speak Arabic as their first language'; so 'despite Updike's portrayal of Ahmad as "American" . . . it is this very American "ness" that opens him to be manipulated by foreign influences'.[37] Ahmad himself feels out of place in Arab American living spaces—'these homes', we are told, 'affect Ahmad with uneasiness, as do the city neighborhoods where shops advertise in mixed Arab and English and mosques have been created by substituting a crescent for the cross on a deconsecrated Protestant church' (177). He thus occupies a peculiarly doubled position: sinister in that he cloaks his increasingly militant Muslim identity under the guise of American identity; innocent in that he is seduced from his American identity by a religious culture marked foreign. In this sense, as Strawson writes, 'there appears to be no other space for Muslims in post-September 11 America'.[38] And yet there is a caveat to be noted here. Towards the end of the novel, Charlie tells Ahmad:

'You can't do just you and God, Madman. He sent His Prophet, and the Prophet created a community. Without the *ummah*, the knowledge and practice of belonging to a righteous group, faith is a seed that bears no fruit' (231). I have tried to show that this attitude in *Terrorist* is problematically identified as a source of Islamic malaise. Yet it is significant that this position is most explicitly articulated by Charlie Chehab, one of the principal agents of Ahmad's 'radicalization', who turns out to be working not for Islamist ideology but rather for the CIA. While this is perhaps indicative of yet another attempt on Updike's part to rescue a 'true' Islam from the sinister tentacles of politics—and thus another example of the writer's failure to conceive of a religious culture that necessarily makes claims on the social world—it does register the possibility that Muslim hostility to the US has some political as well as cultural legitimacy. For this CIA agent, metonymically representing US political intervention on the world stage, acts as a midwife to Ahmad's reluctant turn to violent jihad.

This aspect of the plot points up the fact that the novel does include a critique of a specifically post-9/11 US nationalism. Most interestingly for the purposes of this discussion, at one point in *Terrorist* this critique is articulated via a biblical register. During his visit to the African American church, Ahmad listens to a particularly violent rendition of the Exodus narrative, in which the preacher identifies with the ancient Israelites as a 'chosen people'— as conquerors of a new 'promised land' that has been cleared of the native inhabitants of Canaan, whose eviction from the land is divinely ordained: '"The Lord is with us: fear them not"' (56). It is important to note that this story unfolds in an African American church, which belongs to a tradition that has long appropriated this biblical myth as a way of articulating its own deliverance from oppression. Yet in a novel that registers an awareness not only of Palestinian oppression in the Middle East but also of the genocide of Native Americans which cleared the way for the settlement of the United States, it is hard to avoid the conclusion that this rendition of Exodus points to a critique of national identity politics. In its bringing together of religious, national and ethnic forms of belonging, Exodus highlights a model of religious identity that potentially supports a 'blood, soil and land' variant of nationalism, one that strongly contrasts with the Islamic concept of the *ummah*—which notably transcends the boundaries of the nation-state and has consequently often found itself in conflict with various forms of particularly Arab nationalism. This has implications not only for Zionism, which is repeatedly referenced throughout the novel as source of Muslim anger, and which at various stages in its history has enlisted Judaism as religious sanction for its project of national founding. It also has implications for Protestantism, the religious model that Updike appears to privilege.

In contrast to Islam, Protestantism's historical conditions of possibility were inextricably tied to nationalist projects which sought to break away from the Christian 'ummah' of the Catholic church. The North American

context is a vivid illustration of the ways in which Protestantism has functioned as a potent vehicle both for western European nationalisms and
for their colonial twin. For a dominant US Protestantism has co-existed
with—and to a certain extent enabled—an American civil religion that lends
Christian themes and imagery to the nation in order to in effect deify the
state. This civil religion is arguably most vividly on display in presidential
speech-making—particularly on inauguration day—during which 'God' is
routinely called upon to bless the nation. And it experienced something of a
resurgence in the aftermath of 9/11. In *Terrorist*, the religious zeal with which
'America' was defended following the attacks is most clearly illustrated, and
satirized, through the character of Hermione, the paranoid and often hys-
terical assistant to the Secretary for Homeland Security, who evidences a
clear critique of those who, in the name of patriotic fervour, unthinkingly
vilify Islam as the preserve of 'fanatics'. In response to her boss's articulation of that now most American of questions—'why do they hate us?'—Hermione responds by combining Christian scripture with the Enlightenment
economy of darkness and light which, mapped onto notions of the irrational
and the rational, functioned as justification for western colonialism: 'They
hate the light', Hermione tells him loyally. 'Like cockroaches. Like bats. *The
light shone in darkness*', she quotes, knowing that Pennsylvania piety is a way
to his heart, '*and the darkness comprehended it not*' (48).

Though *Terrorist* undeniably and problematically singles Islam out for
its associations with violence, it also points to the fact that no Abrahamic
faith in its raw, scriptural form is, in John Shepherd's words, 'safe for human
consumption'.[39] Nowhere is this clearer than in the story of Abraham and
Isaac. Comparable to Kierkegaard's rendering of this story—which refuses
the synthesizing move that would reconcile religion to the social world—*Terrorist* exposes and interrupts America's post-9/11 attempt to seamlessly co-opt
religion for its variant of 'holy war'. For while *Terrorist* consistently posits
Ahmad's faith as incompatible with his American context—'*America wants to
take away my God*'—this incompatibility, the novel arguably suggests, derives
as much from a chauvinistic American civil religion as it does from an Islam
seemingly intolerant of 'unbelievers' (39). In this way the monolithic structures on which a 'clash of civilizations' thesis rely come crumbling down
in what Updike proposes is a 'Godless' antagonism between an ultimately
incoherent East and West.

Notes

1. See Edward Said, *Covering Islam* (London: Vintage, 1997).
2. See Edward Said, *Orientalism* (London: Penguin, 1995).
3. This is particularly the case in Said's *Culture and Imperialism* (London: Chatto &
    Windus, 1993).

4. Judith Butler, 'Is Judaism Zionism?', in Judith Butler, Jürgen Habermas, Charles Taylor and Cornel West, eds, *The Power of Religion in the Public Sphere* (New York: Columbia University Press, 2011), 70–91 (72).

5. Ronald L. Grimes, *Rite out of Place: Ritual, Media, and the Arts* (Oxford: Oxford University Press, 2006), 75.

6. John Strawson, 'Images of the Muslim Terrorist Five Years after September 11: Orientalism Today', presented at the 10th Annual Conference of the Association for the Study of Law, Culture and the Humanities, Georgetown University, 23–24 March 2007 (unpublished paper—cited with the permission of the author), 1–2.

7. John Updike, 'John Updike Explores Arab Immigrant Culture', interview with Steve Inskeep, *NPR* (Audio), 13 June 2006, http://www.npr.org/templates/story/story.php?storyId=5479128&ft=1&f=5482086 (accessed 26 April 2011).

8. John Updike, 'An Interview with John Updike: In "Terrorist," a Cautious Novelist Takes On a New Fear', Charles McGrath, *New York Times*, 31 May 2006, http://www.nytimes.com/2006/05/31/books/31updi.html?ex=1306728000&en=113b53291e0f3fc1&ei=5090&partner=rssuserland&emc=rss (accessed 26 April 2011).

9. Updike, Interview with Steve Inskeep.

10. John Updike, *Terrorist* (London: Hamish Hamilton, 2006), 3, 49. All subsequent references are to this edition.

11. John Updike, 'John Updike's "Terrorist"', interview with Tom Ashbrook, *On Point* (Audio), 13 June 2006, http://onpoint.wbur.org/2006/06/13/john-updikes-terrorist (accessed 26 April 2011).

12. Updike, Interview with Charles McGrath.

13. Marshall Boswell, 'Updike, Religion, and the Novel of Moral Debate', in Stacy Olster, ed., *The Cambridge Companion to John Updike* (Cambridge: Cambridge University Press, 2006), 43–57 (43).

14. Ibid., 46.

15. Karen Armstrong, *Muhammad: Prophet For Our Time* (London: HarperPress, 2006), 17.

16. For a discussion of the instructions left in Mohamed Atta's luggage on the morning of September 11, 2001, copies of which were also found in the effects of hijackers on other planes, see Bruce Lincoln's *Holy Terrors: Thinking about Religion after September 11*, 2nd edn. (Chicago: University of Chicago Press, 2006), 8–18.

17. Yvonne Yazbeck Haddad, *Not Quite American? The Shaping of Arab and Muslim Identity in the United States* (Waco, TX: Baylor University Press, 2004), 51.

18. Adam Zachary Newton, *The Fence and the Neighbor: Emmanuel Levinas, Yeshayahu Leibowitz, and Israel Among the Nations* (Albany: State University of New York Press, 2001), 173.

19. Clifford Geertz quoted by Bruce Lincoln, *Holy Terrors: Thinking about Religion after September 11* (Chicago: University of Chicago Press, 2006), 1.

20. Lincoln, *Holy Terrors*, 1–2.

21. See Charles Taylor, 'Why We Need a Radical Redefinition of Secularism', in Judith Butler et al., eds, *The Power of Religion in the Public Sphere*, 34–59.

22. See Talal Asad, *Formations of the Secular: Christianity, Islam, Modernity* (Stanford: Stanford University Press, 2003).

23. Lincoln, *Holy Terrors*, 3.
24. Ibid., 4.
25. Updike, Interview with Tom Ashbrook.
26. Updike, Interview with Steve Inskeep (emphasis added).
27. Updike, Interview with Tom Ashbrook.
28. Strawson, 'Images of the Muslim Terrorist', 1.
29. Ibid., 3, 1.
30. Ron Geaves, 'Who Defines Islam "Post"-September 11?', in Ron Geaves, Theodore Gabriel, Yvonne Haddad and Jane Idleman Smith, eds, *Islam and the West Post 9/11* (Aldershot: Ashgate, 2004), 62–74 (64).
31. Edward Said, *Orientalism* (London: Penguin, 1995), 1–28.
32. See 'Why Updike Delved into Suicide Killers' Psyches', *MSNBC*, 18 July 2006, http://today.msnbc.msn.com/id/13581725/ns/today-books/ (accessed 26 April 2011).
33. Armstrong, *Muhammad*, 19–20.
34. John Strawson, 'Holy War in the Media: Images of Jihad', in Steven Chermak, Frankie Y. Bailey and Michelle Brown, eds, *Media Representations of September 11* (Westport, CT: Praeger, 2003), 17–28 (23).
35. Strawson, 'Images of the Muslim Terrorist', 1; see also John Strawson, 'Islamic Law and the English Press', in *Law After Ground Zero*, ed. John Strawson (London: Glasshouse Press, 2002), 205–214.
36. Geaves, 'Who Defines Islam?', 67.
37. Strawson, 'Images of the Muslim Terrorist', 4.
38. Ibid.
39. John J. Shepherd, 'Self-Critical Children of Abraham? Roots of Violence and Extremism in Judaism, Christianity and Islam', in Ron Geaves *et al.*, eds, *Islam and the West Post 9/11*, 27–50 (42).

9 Invading Ideologies and the Politics of Terror

Framing Afghanistan in *The Kite Runner*

Kristy Butler

For centuries societies have turned to story to explain the unfamiliar. It was the ancients who first taught us to narrate the complexities and mysteries of the universe and in so doing provided a way for us to know ourselves amid an uncertain world. The contextualization that narrative presents is often comforting, because through language, a familiar and powerful tool, the storyteller creates worlds as much as he or she attempts to explain existing ones. Thus, narrative is not simply a self-fashioning apparatus but a means by which one can reimagine an enigmatic Other. However, there is a danger that in creating worlds and the heroes and villains who inhabit them, instead of finding understanding and knowledge, one can also construct agents of power and control. This is the story of ideology.

Indeed, ideology is not an endearing narrative. It has been interpreted by many critics and social scientists from Althusser to Gramsci. In the context of this essay, I will use the term as Paul Ricoeur does in *Memory, History, Forgetting* (2004) where he defines ideology as a legitimizing tool that fills 'the gap of credibility opened by all systems of authority'.[1] Similarly, Slavoj Žižek states in *Mapping Ideology* (1994) that what one must remember about ideology is that it is neither fact nor fiction but a complex system by which perspectives are relayed to the subject-audience by an individual or group in a position of power.[2] In many cases, these perspectives are embedded into the collective cultural consciousness covertly. In fact, ideology is most effective when it invades the spaces we consider safe from its grip. In his book, *Violence: Six Sideways Reflections* (2008), Žižek states that ideology exists undetected because many assume that its influence is strictly political and implemented only by political zealots.[3] However, ideology can surface just as easily in the realm of the ordinary to affirm individual attitudes. Indeed, through narrative ideology captures our attention, invades our perceptions and 'wins our hearts and minds'.

On September 11, 2001, many looked to the sky and trembled at the uncertainty of their world and turned once again to story to reimagine a world they thought they knew and to engage for the first time perhaps with one that was completely unknown. Thus, while military forces were literally invading its physical borders, Afghanistan was simultaneously invaded by a western public consciousness informed by popular fiction. One of the most successful of these new Afghan-set novels was one that granted access to the unfamiliar through both a narrator and an author well-versed in the language and ideology of the West. Khaled Hosseini's bestselling novel *The Kite Runner*,[4] published in 2003, presents the life of Amir, a young Afghan whose story of betrayal, family, friendship and redemption moves from the trials of youth in his native Kabul to his coming-of-age in America. The publication of the novel was timely and the response it elicited from an American audience can be seen as highly significant. Hosseini was born in Kabul but is now an American citizen and this arguably gives him an aura of 'authority' about the region for readers. That the book recycles western tropes of the East—as I will go on to show—further legitimizes the power of these perspectives. The stereotype that portrays Afghanistan as a den of violence and lawlessness helps establish the authority of the outsider's gaze, augmented as it is by the political authority through which certain modes of interventionist action can be justified. In other words, the pre-existing idea of Afghanistan is a convenient and readily available source of legitimacy for our beliefs about its culture and politics. When faced with uncertainty, ideology to some extent affirms assumed knowledge, not because it reflects reality but because it supports our preconceptions about *a* reality. Such ideology accounts for that which we cannot explain and thus provides an authority upon which we orient our own perspectives. Thus chaotic images of the Middle East in general gain credibility in *The Kite Runner* because they form part of a familiar construction that is affirmed by Hosseini, who serves as a voice for both East and West.

As the Twin Towers fell, America's perception of safety from a stereotypical violent Middle East was shattered. As Edward Said states in the 2003 Preface of his seminal work *Orientalism*, 'The suicide bombing phenomenon has appeared with all its hideous damage, none more lurid and apocalyptic of course than the events of September 11 and their aftermath in the wars against Afghanistan and Iraq'.[5] The extensive news coverage that persistently reported on marketplaces ablaze and the ever-present threat of an uprising among rival insurgent groups further contributed to the idea of a region riddled with violence and lawlessness. The *New York Times* has reported regularly on developments in Afghanistan since the US invasion in October of 2001. While the names and places of these accounts change, the image of Middle Eastern violence remains largely static. Appearing mostly in the opinion section, past headlines have included 'High Risks in Afghanistan', 'Losing Afghanistan' and 'Why are We in Iraq? (And Liberia? And Afghanistan?)'.[6] These articles emphasize the importance of success in Afghanistan to eliminate terrorist threats and to secure the region. In particular, 'Losing Afghanistan' states that the US must act quickly and effectively to establish a government that can counteract the corrupt police agencies and oppose the Taliban's brutal tactics if it is to defeat terrorism. This editorial is definitive in saying that the Afghan people cannot achieve this stability independently.[7]

Beyond anticipating the risks of political instability for Afghanis, these articles are emphatic about the link between this instability and the potential emergence of new terrorist regimes. For example, in 'High Risks in Afghanistan', the unnamed author states that 'Afghanistan is in danger of reverting to a deadly combination of rule by warlords and the Taliban, the allies and protectors of Osama bin Laden'.[8] Nitzan Ben-Shaul states that this message permeates visual media, and that while there is truth to the sensational elements of terrorist event coverage,

> not all terror events are treated equally . . . while the Middle Eastern terrorist acts are given extensive coverage, South American ones are hardly covered at all . . . Moreover, among reports on Middle East terror extensive coverage is variable and selective, following ideological directives.[9]

Out of this milieu emerged an explosive discourse that uses language to further legitimize the perception of a chaos-ridden Middle East.

After 9/11, the words 'Taliban' and 'jihad' took up residency in every home in the country. Kenneth Church, an assistant professor of US History at St Lawrence University, writes that the US government's successful engagement with semantics has persuaded its populous that 'jihad' is synonymous with 'terrorism' to mask the realities of the conflict.[10] The semantic, cultural and political impact of the phrase 'war on terror' resides in its imprecision. In developing a history of 9/11, it became increasingly important to use language in a way that precipitated action based upon emotion and a collective ideal rather than a denotative construction of the events as they unfolded. Barry Glassner, a professor of Sociology at the University of Southern California, argues that political administrations have become masters at exploiting public anxieties. Glassner supports his claims by citing the powerful commentary made by former US National Security Adviser, Zbigniew Brzezinski, who has suggested that the use of the vague phrase, 'war on terror', gained its authority because it 'stimulated the emergence of a culture of fear. Fear obscures reason'.[11] Thus, where actual knowledge of Afghanistan or of the Taliban as a political force, rogue or otherwise, was deficient, it was replaced by passion and intensity mobilized by fear. Stuart Croft explains in his book *Culture, Crisis and America's War on Terror* (2006) that language is a powerful tool in constructing reality regardless of its roots in the real:

> Particular descriptions become not only important in themselves, but also in terms of constituting an understanding of that which is under discussion . . . The analysis is not concerned with the validity of what

is said; but rather with understanding what is done through particular accounts . . . Words, ideas, language matter to the policy world.[12]

Indeed, political action in relation to the 'war on terror' is linked inextricably to the ideology of terror—how one is made to be afraid. If the invasion of Afghanistan both physically and culturally is a type of response to terror, then ideology dictates the motivations behind that response. There is nothing covert about the increasing availability of books, documentaries and editorials on Middle Eastern politics in the years immediately following 9/11. Certainly historians, social scientists, journalists and political strategists would have a great deal to contribute to the discussion of what has been called by Samuel P. Huntington, a 'clash of civilizations'.[13] However, what is interesting is the role fiction has played in the shaping of, and response to, the discourse of the Middle East. The popularity of novels preoccupied with the portrayal of modern Afghanistan suggests that the public sought additional sources of information on the region apart from mainstream media representations. In particular, while journalistic accounts focus largely on groups, novels often focus one's gaze on the individual. In this sense, many readers embraced the intimate reflections of complex characters concerned with familiar dilemmas such as parent-child relationships and coming-of-age experiences. One novel that captures this intimate portrait is *The Kite Runner*. Yet, the appeal of the novel also raises several questions: in reading *The Kite Runner* were readers looking to escape the raw representations of violence that permeate the media in an effort to gain a more palatable portrait of life in the Middle East? What elements of the novel particularly resonated with readers? And to what extent has this reading influenced their perspective on Afghanistan and its people? The answer to these questions lies, in part, in the words of the readers themselves.

Timothy Aubry writes in his 2009 essay, 'Afghanistan Meets the *Amazon*: Reading *The Kite Runner* in America', that the overwhelming response to the novel by readers posting reviews on Amazon.com was visceral, especially in response to the novel's portrayal of 'universal human themes, such as guilt, friendship, fatherhood, and forgiveness'. One reviewer wrote: 'It is foreign in language at times, in metaphor some of the time, and in detail of situation almost all the time. But at its core it is more deeply human than any book I've read this year'.[14] Aubry goes on to state that the central character,

> Amir enables readers to project themselves, through a combination of narcissism and dislocation into a foreign identity, facilitating their discovery of familiar values and feelings in what they perceive to be an extremely inhospitable context, as a test case for an idealistic hypothesis about human commonality.

Riddled throughout the reviews are words like 'connection', 'humanity' and 'universal'.[15] They imply a desire to empathize with the people of Afghanistan and the suffering they endure as portrayed in the novel. However, as the comments reveal, the force behind this connection is limited, for the most part, by the familiar. The reference to the novel's foreign nature in language and metaphor is superseded by its human qualities. Insight into the culture of Afghanistan in *The Kite Runner* is secondary to the comfort of what is known and shared. I am not suggesting that the novel is disingenuous in its ability to stir these emotions. It is a powerful novel with haunting imagery. However, one cannot ignore that, given the political and cultural climate at the time of publication, at least part of its American readership sought to contextualize the Middle East in its own familiar terms rather than to investigate objectively a foreign culture. The satisfaction found in reading *The Kite Runner* was often a consequence of its ability to reinforce particular feelings and attitudes in its reader rather than an opportunity to challenge preconceived ideas. Moreover, Aubry's primary aim in writing the essay is to investigate reader response to the popular novel, specifically analysing the 'desires, values, and expectations that shape the reception of "foreign" fiction among Americans'.[16] He discovers that the novel is used as a spur to introspection by the reader rather than as an examination of the foreign. There is, of course, a longstanding history to, and psychological comfort to be had in, domesticating, and hence taming, the strange. As Said states of Orientalism, it forms 'a considerable dimension of modern political-intellectual culture, and as such has less to do with the Orient than it does with "our" world'.[17] It should come as no surprise, then, that the popularity of the novel, based on Aubry's findings, has very little to do with Afghanistan or its people.

Aubry writes that many of the reviewers praised the supposedly apolitical nature of the novel. The fact that Assef, the primary villain in the story and a Taliban official, makes limited appearances throughout the novel

> suggests an unspoken frustration with, perhaps even repudiation of, the polarizing rhetoric that posits a conflict between Islam and the West and may reflect a desire to transcend ideological and ethnic divisions through an affective experience that underscores our shared, though culturally differentiated, humanity.[18]

Yet Assef plays a very particular ideological role in prompting a certain type of culturally-loaded empathy. In the novel, Amir fails to intervene when Assef rapes his friend, Hassan, and he is haunted by this betrayal years later and miles away in America. Upon his return to Kabul, however, Amir faces Assef again, this time in an effort to rescue Hassan's son from a similar fate. Hassan's rape and Sohrab's rescue are pinnacle moments of trauma in the novel. Thus, the emotional response so overwhelmingly expressed by the Amazon readership is inextricably linked to the character of Assef and the terror he instills in Amir, and consequently the reader. Amir is the catalyst for this catharsis. Thus, it is not merely the humanity of suffering and redemption that reverberated with readers; rather, it was a particular kind of trauma, a journey of mourning and a path of retribution that so many Americans found themselves travelling after 9/11.

David Holloway writes in his book *Cultures of the War on Terror: Empire, Ideology, and the Remaking of 9/11* (2008) that the literature published shortly after 9/11 concerns itself with tense familial relationships, and specifically scenarios where parents fail to protect their children. Holloway asserts that this reflected a milieu of cautious apprehension that carried with it a 'tendency to sublimate contemporary anxieties about state activity, and about the state's jeopardizing of the safety of its citizens'.[19] This sense of trepidation found its way into a vast array of cultural texts, including films, television series and fiction. Similarly, Aubry states that the link between *The Kite Runner* and the 'war on terror' is undeniable and insightfully notes that the victimization of the innocent in the novel stirs feelings of guilt and a sense of one's own humanity. He goes on to say that Amir, like many readers, is caught between the role of victim and victimizer through deeds done and left undone. Several Amazon reviewers expressed support for US foreign policy measures in the Middle East, particularly as a result of reading the depictions of modern life in Afghanistan and the portrayal of the Taliban. 'This book really made me realize what we are fighting for', wrote one reviewer. Similarly another claims that 'Anyone who doubts the need to stamp out terrorism should read this book'. Such comments were challenged by other Amazon reviews that saw the novel as offering justification for the invasion of Afghanistan while ignoring the consequences for Muslim Americans in the US who faced the backlash from such characterizations. One posting specifically called the book 'irresponsible' in its neglect of the impact September 11 had on Muslim Americans who were forced into hiding for fear of harassment, including physical threats. This same reviewer also challenges Hosseini's own motivations: 'I have to wonder, cynically, if he [Hosseini] purposely left this out because he knew how many of his American audience he would piss off if he appeared "un-American" and I just don't have much respect for that'.[20] In a novel that has been praised for its seemingly apolitical stance, the majority of those who felt compelled to post reviews about it not only perceived the political implications of the text, but also claimed that reading the novel encouraged them to take a firm position regarding the US policies in Afghanistan and the problem of terrorism.

Importantly, *The Kite Runner* has also facilitated discussions about the cultural and political issues raised by the topic of Afghanistan when it appears in American classrooms. Both Masood Ashraf Raja and Ruth R. Caillouet have written about their experiences teaching literature in a post-9/11 age.[21] Common to both accounts is the novel, *The Kite Runner*. While Raja and Caillouet write about their experiences in teaching the novel at different levels within the American educational system, at university and high school respectively, a common motivation exists between the educators. Both wish to expand the worldview of their students through literature about war, colonialism and foreign culture. For Raja's students, studying the novel was an opportunity to explore the political elements that facilitated the war in Afghanistan. The events of the novel became a pseudo-history and a catalyst for discussing how the actual conflict evolved. Raja's concluding remarks about the students' responses echo those of the Amazon.com message boards:

> Hence, while the novel evoked for us the human experiences of two estranged brothers and the narrator's struggles to redeem himself by rescuing his half-brother's son, the reading group's background research helped the class as a whole to understand the existential circumstances of the modern Afghan tragedy. After we discussed *The Kite Runner*, it was obvious that Afghanistan was no longer just another hostile place for my students, but rather a country that needed international help to survive the aftermath of a war in which all western powers had participated through their Afghan warlord proxies.[22]

While Raja and his students are to be commended for their initiative in exploring the historical and political acts that contributed to the war in Afghanistan, their efforts appear limited as the language of their interpretations reflects the prescribed attitudes at work in the novel. Raja states that he encourages his students to approach people that are different from them with understanding. He claims this practice develops a critical self-awareness that recognizes the need to change personal behaviours for the common good. However, Raja follows up this insight by stating that a successful pedagogy is one that does not threaten the identity of the student, even when the purpose of the lesson is a confrontation with another culture.[23] Raja's practice in the classroom seems to contradict his theory about non-threatening encounters with other perspectives and the challenge they represent to self-identification. Thus, *The Kite Runner* affirms ideology not only present in the text itself, but also in the teaching of it. Undoubtedly, the students were able to learn more about the culture and history of Afghanistan through secondary readings that informed the novel and vice versa. However, this educational epiphany is diminished when ideas are approached only through the lens of familiarity so as not to startle one's sense of self when confronted with an Other. While Raja importantly incorporated historical events that led up to the war in Afghanistan into the course, even those events that implicate the US and its allies, his reflection that students could now see Afghanistan as a country in need of western salvation seems to undermine one of the lessons they were meant to learn. The warning about the unforeseen dangers of interfering in complex political and social structures is eclipsed by the ever-familiar ideology that the West knows best how to implement law and order. For some, the role is one bound by duty and honour. Ruth R. Caillouet's curriculum review, entitled 'The Other Side of Terrorism and the Children of Afghanistan', is markedly influenced by her own son's tour of duty in Afghanistan. Poetically, she states that after September 11, she began 'teaching peace in times of war, of teaching hope in a world of unrest, of teaching about honor and fear, justice and outrage, service and protest'.[24] Moreover, September 11 would become for her son 'the day to define his generation, the day to spur him into action to join the armed services, toward making a choice of honor, bravery, loyalty, and all that he believed in'.[25] Caillouet acknowledges her 'conflicting emotions' surrounding the war and strives to negotiate them within the classroom along with her students. For her, engaging with the text(s) of Afghanistan is cathartic. She states, 'My son was in Afghanistan, and in my need to find a way to cope, I turned to literature and teaching'.[26] Yet the language of her catharsis reveals a prescribed attitude toward the conflict between East and West, one that, like her emotional response to the war, must be negotiated.

In particular, Caillouet's use of the words 'honor, bravery, loyalty' affirms a response to 9/11 in terms of military valour as a particular idea of heroism. Her subsequent evaluation of *The Kite Runner* reflects an acceptance of Afghan culture as portrayed by the novel's representations, underpinned by letters she would receive from her son while he was in active duty. Thus, in addition to her reading of the novel as an educator, hers is an interpretation that reflects a maternal need for familiarity amidst chaos. 'But *The Kite Runner* is not just the pleasant story of a young man in a foreign land', she asserts; 'It is also a tale of a boy wanting desperately to get his father's approval'.[27] While she also recognizes the story as one of hatred and violence, her language focuses on her preoccupations and allegiances in the war in Afghanistan. The 'young man in a foreign land' is Amir, whose foreign life begins in America, not in Kabul. However, for her, and for her students, he is the alien character that has suddenly appeared within their worldview. Secondly, her son is a soldier who is *her* young man in a land foreign to both of them, and who perhaps seeks the approval of his father, not to mention his fatherland—America.

Caillouet begins by asking her students to recall and to write about where they were on 9/11.[28] Thereafter, the course develops into more complex portrayals of war in general, primarily through the perspective of children. Especially noteworthy is the progression of the curriculum. It begins with the imagery of 9/11, the emotions tied to that day and the aftermath that followed. The presentation of the eastern culture of Afghanistan originates at home—from a familiar perspective. Instead of beginning with the history of war in general and its legacy throughout various texts, she chooses to begin at the end where these cultures collide, with raw images of a day that she asserts will define a generation. Thus, a whole nation and a culture will also be defined in the context of 9/11, seemingly lacking a history outside its shadow.

Caillouet further suggests that teachers who wish to emulate this module plan should consider, as she did, teaching only excerpts of *The Kite Runner* to their high school students because the language and content of the text may not be age-appropriate. This observation reflects practical pedagogic concerns. However, sanitizing the text and presenting a fragmented view of it compromises the goal of the lesson plan, which is to present to her students the complications of conflict; it might also work against the personal catharsis she claims to seek—to find understanding and a means of coping with the unfamiliar. Nevertheless, she concludes by stating that difficult circumstances and situations must be presented to students as realities of the war: 'We cannot choose to ignore that our nation is at war if we truly care for students and their role in deciding the future'.[29] As she believes her son was called to service, so she feels called, along with her fellow educators, to present the images of a post-9/11 battlefield. The war seemingly will be decided according to the story we tell ourselves about ourselves.

A close reading of *The Kite Runner* reveals that Amir, a self-proclaimed storyteller, appeals to an American audience because the story he tells is the narrative the West has long been telling itself based on an ideology of East versus West. Aside from his own coming-of-age tale and the portrayal of the immigrant experience in America, Amir acts as a legitimizing voice for the West. Whether as a Pashtun or an American, Amir's unique access to both cultures characterizes him as an ally for both. Yet regardless of which role he assumes, he is a member of a privileged class. In the novel, Amir explains that Hassan is illiterate but fascinated by language and stories. His fascination exists in spite of his inability to access formal education because of his lowly caste. Thus, Amir affirms his authority within society by using narrative as a weapon of privilege against Hassan: that is, until he realizes Hassan can solve the riddles he poses faster than he can himself. Amir states: 'I read him stories he couldn't read for himself . . . But despite his illiteracy, or maybe because of it, Hassan was drawn to the mystery of words, seduced by a secret world forbidden to him' (28). Arguably, Amir uses narrative against the reader in much the same way as he does against Hassan. America is largely illiterate in reading the culture of the Middle East. The western audience in general relies on both Hosseini and Amir to offer access to the riddle that is Afghanistan. Whether or not Amir believes the West can solve the riddle better than the Afghan people is difficult to determine for certain. His is a hybrid identity that must negotiate a position between East and West. Acting as a cultural translator, Amir must articulate the familiar amidst the unknown and forbidden. If the response on Amazon is any indication, he is a masterful interpreter.

The secret of his success is language. From the first pages of the novel, Amir discusses 'soccer', not football, and recalls trips to the cinema in Iran to watch westerns like *Rio Bravo,* starring America's hero, John Wayne. Amir recalls his surprise when he first learned that John Wayne didn't really speak Farsi. Hosseini cleverly constructs a secondary narrative that acts as a doubling of *The Kite Runner*; that is, in the novel, Amir narrates his experience in Afghanistan as a cultural insider, yet his ultimate portrayal of the region echoes western stereotypes partially framed by his hybrid Afghani American identity. Similarly, the John Wayne films, while dubbed with Middle Eastern voices, showcase distinctly American themes and attitudes that are stereotypical of the western film genre and the idea of justice in the 'wild west'. This is not to suggest that Hosseini is behind a contrived conspiracy to fool the reader or to promote a particular agenda. However, it does reveal the effect an Afghan narrator who idolizes American heroes and drinks Coca-Cola might have on an American audience. Contributing to this sense of the iconic, desirable West is Amir's portrayal of his fellow Afghans, which aligns with the time-honoured American narrative of the valiant cowboy amid the outlaws when he states, 'Afghans cherish custom but abhor rules' (52). In her book, *The Terror Dream: Fear and Fantasy in Post-9/11 America* (2007), Susan Faludi writes that after 9/11 there was a nostalgia for the figure of the cowboy and a spirit of vigilantism, quoting one *New York Post* columnist who asserted that '[w]e have to fight the terrorists as if there were no rules'.[30] To defeat the lawless, law must be set aside—but not justice. This is evidenced by a recurring, yet again familiar narrative that flows through *The Kite Runner*. Hassan's battle with Assef is reminiscent of the biblical tale of David and Goliath, a story that elevates the weak over the strong, the lowly over the tyrannical. The narrative strategy at work capitalizes on two narratives that are important to the heritage of America, both of which emphasize good over evil and the victory of the underdog. Amir recalls Hassan's intercession when Assef threatens Amir, brass knuckles in hand:

> There was a flurry of rapid movement behind me. Out of the corner of my eye, I saw Hassan bend down and stand up quickly. Assef's eyes flicked to something behind me and widened with surprise . . . I turned and came face to face with Hassan's slingshot. (42)

The connection Amir makes with western readers requires his assimilation to their narratives. Although he narrates his own experiences, cultural translation favours the texts and contexts of the West. Indeed, mimicry of western tropes is evident in the scene above as it mirrors the biblical account of David's defeat of Goliath not only in its positioning of the underdog against the powerful warrior, but also down to the detail of weaponry: the slingshot. In so doing, Assef is cast as villain and Hassan a valiant hero. Similarly, in traditional western plots, the cowboy dressed in white, signifying his goodness, duels the cowboy in black, who is most often an outlaw and bully. The cowboy's victory saves the town from the lawlessness that threatens to destroy its happy existence. In resurrecting these stories, characterizations of both 'good' and 'evil' emerge as culturally inflected and a system of power materializes.

Jacques Derrida's concept of hauntology concerns itself with this phenomenon. In fact, Derrida's theory of hauntology allows for an examination of the various discourses that dominate the public consciousness, causing repressed modes of thinking to haunt hegemony.[31] Hauntology is a 'dimension of performative interpretation, that is, of an interpretation that transforms the very thing it interprets'.[32] This essay has already explored how this can appear within the classroom. Such interpretation demonstrates the importance of perception in creating and recreating reality. To approach Afghanistan in narrative is to digest and recycle an active ideology. Any traces of the 'real' Afghanistan present in Hosseini's *The Kite Runner* are not mirrored in authentic cultural encounters, but rather reinforce the spectres of ideology that seek to blend fact and fiction. In so doing, the reader is encouraged to accept the historical events and accounts of life in Afghanistan alongside the fictional images of what that life *might* be like without any differentiation between these perspectives. Derrida states that engaging in this kind of blurring creates tension between 'the thing itself and its simulacrum'.[33] When the line between fact and fiction is uncertain, reality can be easily moulded or reshaped.

So it is for Amir, who produces his own version of the American story to help him construct a new identity, one free of the ghosts he tries to leave behind in Afghanistan. He celebrates Halloween and Thanksgiving, drives a Ford, and envies Americans who can marry for love. Although he remains loyal to the Afghan community that he and Baba find in California, including marrying within the culture and according to its rules, over time Amir is disconnected from his homeland, its physical spaces. The narrative of violence that has unfolded in Kabul during his absence finds him when he is reunited with Rahim Khan, Amir's childhood mentor and Baba's close friend. Amir tells Rahim of his life in America, Baba's illness and then asks about the rise of the Taliban: 'Is it as bad as I hear?' he asks. Rahim responds, 'Nay, it's worse. Much worse . . . They don't let you be human' (198). It is then that another ghost is resurrected by a letter from Hassan, which Rahim has faithfully delivered. The letter reads: 'Alas the Afghanistan of our youth is long dead. Kindness is gone from the land and you cannot escape the killings. In Kabul, fear is everywhere' (216). Painfully, Amir asks what has become of Hassan only to learn that his fears have been realized, that the larger violence which Hassan describes in his letter has become a personal tragedy. Both Hassan and his wife have been executed by the Taliban.

Up to this point, Amir has been a telescope through which the reader can view Afghanistan and its people. But what Amir knows of Afghanistan is limited to images of the past, memories of a childhood when the kites ran high in the sky and David could stand up to Goliath. However, as Amir returns to Kabul to find Hassan's orphaned son, Sohrab, he says 'I feel like a tourist in my own country' (231). A taxi driver informs him that as an Afghan who 'probably lived in a big two-or three story house with a nice backyard that [the] gardener filled with flowers and fruit trees . . . you've *always* been a tourist here, you just didn't know it' (232). Amir's moment of disillusionment is the reader's moment of enlightenment and further affirmation of the western narrative of Orientalism—the lawless Middle East that has seemingly *always* existed. The remainder of Amir's stay in Afghanistan is plagued by violence and poverty. He observes a man selling his leg on the street and in a packed stadium he witnesses the public stoning of a woman accused of adultery. Amid the mob, Amir spots an individual, a Talib, dressed in white whom he describes as a mixture of Jesus and John Lennon (271). Western interpretation again invades a scene of eastern violence. But this Talib is no prince of peace; rather, he is Goliath resurrected, Assef, with whom Amir must bargain for Sohrab's freedom.

Later meeting face-to-face, Amir is stunned into silence and Assef overtakes the narrative. He describes acts of mass murder: 'Door to door we went, calling for the men and the boys', he says, 'We'd shoot them right in front of their families'. The delight Assef conveys in his telling is chilling. Suddenly, Assef brings that same terror to a more familiar door asking Amir, 'You come from America? . . . How is that whore these days?' (277–278). In two questions, Assef has transplanted the trauma of the stoned woman in the stadium into the heart of the American reader. Just as the narrative of the cowboy and David and Goliath resurrects the West's fascination with the hero, the novel also rekindles its portrayal of the villain. Yet, although Osama Bin Laden became the face of terror following 9/11, it is not his visage that acts as a model of evil personified in Hosseini's novel. Instead, the face of evil is Adolf Hitler's. Assef, of both Afghan and German descent, is a hybrid of hatred, haunting both East and West.

Assef's national and political loyalties lie in his Pashtun heritage, one he inherits from his Afghan father. However, his physical form favours the German heritage of his mother. As such, Assef is a blond, blue-eyed tyrant who resurrects the legacy of Nazi Germany. He demonstrates an innate ability for political propaganda, and his tactics are recognizable to the western reader. Through Assef's imitation of Hitler and his language of violence, Afghanistan is offered as a parallel landscape of terror, power and genocide to 1940s Germany. Apart from such moments of familiarizing contextualization, Afghanistan and its people are outside the western reader's frame of reference.

So it is with Amir, who states that it was only when he learned the English term for Assef's pathology that he could verbalize and therefore contextualize what he was, a 'sociopath' (38). Amir's reliance on English to narrate his experience continues to grow at the semantic level. English fills the void created by a linguistic lack in his native tongue, Farsi. Similarly, Assef's employment of western words further characterizes him as a spectre of hate. He lauds Hitler as a leader and one whose vision he seeks to emulate, demonstrated by the mimicry of his poisonous language:

His blue eyes flicked to Hassan. 'Afghanistan is the land of Pashtuns. It always has been, always will be. We are the true Afghans, the pure Afghans, not this Flat-Nose here. His people pollute our homeland, our *watan.* They dirty our blood . . . Afghanistan for Pashtuns, I say. That's my vision.' (40)

What seems like a frightening plan for Afghanistan's future aligns with a terrifying reality that haunts the West's past. According to Derrida, hauntological dimensions refract time and space so that 'what seems to be out in front, the future, comes back in advance: from the past, from the back'.[34] Thus, as the reader witnesses Assef's imitation of Nazi propaganda, an uncanny future presents itself that is haunted by past horrors. The West cannot ignore this evil once it is identified. It is called to act, even if action lies only in naming it. Assef embodies a threat that the West has already defeated once. Not only does Assef mimic Hitler by resurrecting his propaganda, he recreates haunting images of door-to-door killings under cover of night that mirror those carried out by the Gestapo. The reader is invited to equate the regimes. And yet, because the terror of the unknown has been contextualized within the recognizable, it becomes somehow less threatening. Assef and the other Talibs transform into familiar foes in an act of performative interpretation. Regardless of the fear he instills, Assef and the danger he poses are contained within western narrative, a narrative that ultimately reassures us of the victory of good over evil.

So it is with great relief and a sense of justice that Assef is ultimately defeated, but not by Amir. Sohrab, like Hassan before him, intervenes on Amir's behalf. Slingshot in hand, he sends a brass ball into Assef's left eye, bringing the giant to his knees, shrieking in pain (290–291). Amir and the boy escape. But Sohrab, like Afghanistan, is not fully recovered. Instead he retreats to sleep: 'That's how children deal with terror', Amir explains, 'They fall asleep' (342). Amir vows to take him back to America. Forced to overcome many bureaucratic setbacks and Sohrab's suicide attempt, Amir finally keeps his promise. He and Sohrab return to California, a place Amir calls 'home' in August 2001. Yet the boy remains markedly silent as Amir, the storyteller, describes 9/11 in remarkably casual tones stating, 'One Tuesday morning last September, the Twin Towers came crumbling down and, overnight, the world had changed' (362). Amir, like Sohrab, like much of America after 9/11, experiences life-changing trauma as a memorialization, images of the past that require retelling, recalling and yet create spaces for acquiescence and despondency. Yet, amid the silence one must not assume that the ideological does not or cannot exist. Ideology's ability to anticipate and covertly shape our responses often results in a prescribed outcome rather than analysis of the process by which conclusions are drawn—a means to an end. Or as Amir states:

In Afghanistan, the ending was all that mattered. When Hassan and I came home after watching a Hindi film . . . what Ali, Rahim Khan, Baba, or the myriad of Baba's friends . . . wanted to know was this: Did

the Girl in the film find happiness? . . . Did the Guy in the film . . . fulfill
his dreams, or was he . . . doomed to wallow in failure? (357)

Amir's explanation sounds uncannily American as well; it could be said that
his self-conscious inability to provide an overtly consoling resolution is still
addressed to the western reader's desire for a happy ending. He continues to
parrot the story of the West to the West, concluding that if asked whether his
story and that of Hassan and Sohrab ends in happiness, he wouldn't know
how to answer. Perhaps he has no answers.

While fiction can be fertile ground for explorations of the foreign, offering
opportunities to begin dialogue in a seemingly safe, self-contained space, it can
also inhibit these opportunities by allowing readers to fall asleep in the comfort
of readily available cultural constructions so often supported in other contexts
and by other mediums. As we continue to look to storytellers for explana-
tions of an uncertain world, we must be careful not to confuse familiarity with
knowledge or to leave unexplored the motives of those who create heroes and
villains, nor to leave unchallenged the ideologies that reinforce these representations. While *The Kite Runner* is only one in an ever-growing list of novels that
have framed Afghanistan for a post-9/11 audience, if we truly desire a deeper
understanding of its culture and politics, we must expand our readings beyond
the frame of familiar western assumptions. The complexity of the world and
the experience of subjects within it, whose lives are often marked by the violence of antagonistic cultures, demand nothing less.

Notes

1. Paul Ricoeur, 'The Exercise of Memory', in *Memory, History, Forgetting*, trans.
    Kathleen Blamey and David Pellauer (Chicago and London: The University of
    Chicago Press, 2004), 56–92 (83).
2. Slavoj Žižek, 'Introduction: The Spectre of Ideology', in Slavoj Žižek, ed., *Map-
    ping Ideology* (London and New York: Verso, 1994), 1–21 (6).
3. Slavoj Žižek, *Violence: Six Sideways Reflections* (New York: Picador, 2008), 36.
4. Khaled Hosseini, *The Kite Runner* (New York: Penguin, 2003). Citations will be
    inserted in the text.
5. Edward Said, 'Preface', in *Orientalism* (London: Penguin, 2003), xiii.
6. 'Why Are We In Iraq? (And Liberia? And Afghanistan?)', *New York Times*, 7
    September 2003.
7. 'Losing Afghanistan', *New York Times*, 26 August 2006.
8. 'High Risks In Afghanistan', *New York Times*, 17 November 2003.
9. Nitzan Ben-Shaul, *A Violent World: TV News Images of Middle Eastern Terror and
    War* (Lanham, Maryland: Rowman & Littlefield, 2006), 40.
10. Kenneth Church, 'Jihad', in John Collins and Ross Glover, eds, *Collateral Lan-
    guage* (New York: New York University Press, 2002), 109–124 (109).
11. Barry Glassner, *The Culture of Fear: Why Americans are Afraid of the Wrong Things*,
    Tenth Anniversary Edition (New York: Basic Books, 2009), xii.

12. Stuart Croft, *Culture, Crisis and America's War on Terror* (Cambridge: Cambridge University Press, 2006), 43.
13. Samuel P. Huntington, *The Clash of Civilizations and the Remaking of World Order* (New York: Touchstone, 1997).
14. Timothy Aubry, 'Afghanistan Meets the *Amazon*: Reading *The Kite Runner* in America', *PMLA: Publications of the Modern Language Association of America* 124.1 (2009): 25–43 (27, 25).
15. Ibid., 32.
16. Ibid., 25–26.
17. Edward Said, 'Introduction', in *Orientalism* (London: Penguin, 2003), 1–28 (12).
18. Aubry, 'Afghanistan Meets the *Amazon*', 36.
19. David Holloway, *Cultures of the War on Terror: Empire, Ideology, and the Remaking of 9/11* (Montreal, Kingston and Ithaca: McGill-Queen's University Press, 2008), 108.
20. Aubry, 'Afghanistan Meets the *Amazon*', 27, 32–33, 35.
21. Masood Ashraf Raja, 'The Postcolonial Student: Learning the Ethics of Global Solidarity in an English Classroom', *Radical Teacher* 82 (2008): 32–37. Project Muse: http://muse.jhu.edu/journals/radical_teacher/v082/82.raja.html (accessed 30 August 2010); Ruth R. Caillouet, 'The Other Side of Terrorism and the Children of Afghanistan', *The English Journal* 96.2 (November 2006): 28–33. JSTOR: http://www.jstor/or/stable/30047124 (accessed 13 September 2010).
22. Raja, 'The Postcolonial Student', 36.
23. Ibid., 33.
24. Caillouet, 'The Other Side of Terrorism', 28.
25. Ibid.
26. Ibid., 29.
27. Ibid., 31–32.
28. Ibid., 29.
29. Ibid., 32.
30. Susan Faludi, *The Terror Dream: Fear and Fantasy in Post-9/11 America* (New York: Metropolitan Books, 2007), 4, 155.
31. Jacques Derrida, *Specters of Marx: The State of Debt, The Work of the Mourning, and the New International*, trans. Peggy Kamuf (New York and London: Routledge, 1994), 38.
32. Ibid., 51.
33. Ibid., 10.
34. Ibid.

10 Representation and Realism

Monica Ali's *Brick Lane*

Sara Upstone

In the political domain, we can speak of parliamentary, diplomatic, or union representation. In the aesthetic domain, we can speak of representation in the sense of mimetic substitution, notably in the so-called plastic arts, but, in a more problematic manner, of a theatrical representation in a sense which is not necessarily or uniquely reproductive or repetitive but in order to name in this case a presentation (*Darstellung*), an exhibition, a performance . . . If the noun 'representation,' the adjectives 'representing,' 'representable,' 'representative,' the verbs 'represent' or 'represent oneself' are not only the grammatical modulations of a single and identical meaning, if kernels of different meanings are present, at work in or produced by these grammatical modes of the idiom, then the lexicologist, the semanticist, indeed the philosopher who would try to classify different varieties of 'representation' and of 'representing,' to give account of the variables or the divergences from the identity of an invariant meaning, is going to have a rough time of it.

–Jacques Derrida, 'Sending: On Representation', 299–300

Introduction

Monica Ali's *Brick Lane* (2003) is perhaps the most well-known work by a British Muslim author since Hanif Kureishi's *The Buddha of Suburbia* (1990); like Kureishi's work, Ali's fiction has been subject to cinematic adaptation, which has brought it to the mainstream. At the same time, it is also the most controversial work of fiction to be published since Salman Rushdie's *The Satanic Verses* (1988), something which the film version also precipitated. When British Muslims based in Brick Lane, with their ancestry in the Sylheti region of Bangladesh, objected to the novel's presentation of their community, there were obvious resonances with the Rushdie Affair.[1] Published only two years after the events of 9/11, the novel exposed an already vulnerable community to further scrutiny, highlighting the ways in which anti-Muslim and Islamophobic discourses had made South Asian Muslims intensely sensitive to any potential denigration of their culture.

This context for the novel's reception dominated early critical approaches. In this chapter, however, I want to return to the novel—more than seven years on—to consider how its function beyond and outside this controversy has important implications for approaching the relationship between fiction and community politics. At the same time, returning with this critical distance allows a more nuanced understanding of the novel's reception, and the reasons for its infamy, both in terms of the post-adaptation furore and early reviews which similarly offer a definite position on the novel's content. *Brick Lane*, I argue, is mired in debates surrounding representation and correlative concerns for realism and authenticity, from both those who criticize the novel on cultural grounds and those who challenge its literary quality. Such readings, I suggest, overlook the more strategic intervention into the politics of representation—the *utopian realism*—which makes Ali's novel so significant for any concern with post-9/11 attitudes to British Muslim communities and the impact of these attitudes on those communities.

Brick Lane as Realist 'Failure'

Criticisms of *Brick Lane* focus overwhelmingly upon associating it with a realist discourse that has somehow 'failed'; they identify the novel as a declaration by Ali of a real-world correspondence, cemented by the novel's title, its reference to real-world events such as 9/11 and the Oldham riots, and the author's referencing of sociological studies such as Naila Kabeer's *The Power to Choose* (2000) in her acknowledgments. For Sylheti protestors, the novel was not a realistic portrayal of their East London community. In this context, criticisms of Ali's novel are situated within longstanding debates over the 'burden of representation' placed on ethnic writers specifically.[2]

Negative reactions by literary critics focus not so much on the potential misrepresentation of the Sylheti community, but rather on the novel's 'unrealistic' conclusion. The celebratory ending, in which Nazneen, the protagonist, seemingly assimilates with ease into mainstream British culture as she goes ice-skating in a sari, whilst her close friend Razia declares 'This is England . . . You can do whatever you like',[3] is identified as jarring with the majority of the novel, in which Nazneen is alienated by her position as a Muslim woman in Britain, trapped within the dual oppressions of Bangladeshi patriarchal and English racist discourses cemented by the socio-economic deprivation faced by being part of one of the most disadvantaged communities in Britain. So for the literary critic Yasmin Hussain the novel is 'trying to represent the concerns of Bangladeshi women' but 'fails to achieve this due to Ali's lack of familiarity with the issues she is discussing'; the novel is declared weak because it fails to convey 'the atmosphere and experience of Bangladeshi culture from "within"'.[4] For James Procter, Nazneen's agency 'has little to offer in the way of political alternatives'.[5] This academic response is echoed in newspaper reviews; for Natasha Walter the ending 'felt as if Ali was trying for a more definite fictional closure than, by that time, her complicated characters can bear', whilst for Delia Falconer there is an 'overdetermined plotline which seems . . . to push the narrative in a feel-good feminist direction', and for Michael Gorra a conclusion that is 'squishily affirmative'.[6]

Whilst these two types of criticism may be different in focus, they are not different in their essential character. In both cases, it is the intersection of cultural concerns with Ali's chosen literary form—English realism—that provoked such strong reactions. It is largely unproblematic to declare that in general terms Ali's novel is realist—it fulfils the commitment to the location of characters within identifiable historical context, everyday reality, and the focus on individuals from mundane social backgrounds that are the features of the realist novel as outlined in Auerbach's *Mimesis* (1953), and widely adopted even to the present day.[7] If negative reactions to the novel rely upon a particular definition of realism—one in which Brick Lane promises a reliable representation of the East London Muslim community—then they return to a way of conceptualizing literature undoubtedly rejected long ago by literary criticism, which now overwhelmingly accepts the comparable artistic reworkings of different approaches such as realism, modernism and postmodernism, and the universal distancing between verisimilitude and the 'real' world. Nevertheless, whilst the connection between realism and reliability might now seem outdated within the realms of literary criticism, it is alive and well in criticisms originating from interested readers and observers within the British Muslim community. The idea of realism as presenting 'a concrete, individualized figure embedded in the context of a particular place at a particular time', with a concern for 'fidelity to life', is what drove British Muslim complaints: this was their place, and their time, they announced, and Ali had been unfaithful in her representation of both.[8]

In this respect, British Muslims and those who supported their criticisms returned to unproblematized assumptions of the correlation between realism and reality woven into early nineteenth-century definitions of the form: the concept of '*la literature du vrai*' which only with Henry James gave way to the looser and now accepted definition of verisimilitude.[9] Their assertions also resonated with later Marxist celebrations of social realism popularized most famously by Georg Lukacs. For Lukacs, a great realist 'will, without an instant's hesitation, set aside these his own prejudices and convictions and describe what he really sees, not what he would prefer to see'. Under this definition, according to the British Muslim complainants, Ali is rather a 'second-rater', one of those classified as 'bringing their own *Weltanschauung* into "harmony" with reality, that is forcing a falsified or distorted picture of reality into the shape of their own world-view'.[10] According to criticisms, Ali reflects what Lukacs describes as the writer's desire to 'direct the evolution of his characters at will', one which not only prevents one from being a great realist, but also a true realist, or even a good writer.[11]

For Lukacs, this desire not only means a failure of realism, of course, but consequently also of realism's political function. Lukacs here would draw from those earlier nineteenth-century definitions of realism—what Louis-Edmond Duranty in 1856 points to as the social responsibility of realism, as a form 'reproducing the things affecting the lives of the greatest number'.[12] Ali, in this context, fails the British Muslim as a community—her choice to focus, allegedly, on the humorous qualities of the Sylheti community does not do justice to their social hardship and suffering.

Turn, likewise, to critics' complaints and we see a similar reliance. Literary critics, one might think, should be above recourse to outmoded definitions of realism. As noted earlier, whilst the majority of the novel was lauded as a triumph, its seeming movement away from realism in its final pages was the target of negative appraisal by most critics. The ending in these terms defies the 'marked redundancy and foreseeability of its content' that for Philippe Hamon characterizes realist discourse.[13] Hamon's movement towards monosemesis, 'utopian language as nomenclature, of the transparent message', is adhered to in *Brick Lane*, as the novel's conclusion speaks obviously to the possibility of multicultural Britain. The transparent message which emerges in these terms, however, is not one which critics see as adhering to the obvious, expected conclusion that one should be able to foresee in realist fiction.[14] Nazneen does not crumble. She does not buckle under the weight of either South Asian patriarchy or British post-9/11 Islamophobia, or even under the combination of these pressures. Yet this is what popular reporting and dominant media discourse would prescribe for her, and it is what critics, therefore, expect.

Of course, no one can say definitively that the world of *Brick Lane* is 'real' or not. This is largely a matter of reader response. Yet both literary and parochial critics, in their own way, felt that *Brick Lane* was *not real* in a sense which alienated them from a fiction they felt was promising to *be real*. Here it is useful to consider Damian Grant's perception of two kinds of realist truth: the coherent, and the correspondent. The latter is a matter of evidence and documentation. The former, however, is a matter rather of perception, and of belief:

> In the coherence theory, on the other hand, the epistemological process is accelerated or elided by intuitive perception. Truth is not earned by the labour of documentation and analysis but coined, a ready synthesis, and made current—as is any currency—by confidence, 'the confidence of truth'. Evidence is replaced by self-evidence.[15]

Whilst correspondence announces documentary realism, coherence is driven towards the possibility of language (and literature therefore) as generating its own 'truth':

> The coherence theory of realism, on the other hand, is the conscious-
> ness of literature: its self-awareness, its realization of its own ontologi-
> cal status. Here realism is achieved not by imitation, but by creation; a
> creation which, working with the materials of life, absolves these by the
> intercession of the imagination from mere factuality and translates them
> to a higher order.[16]

This sense of reality as created by the artist, rather than as existing *a priori*,
is not just a mark of now widely accepted theories of verisimilitude, but also
something that has been further developed in the wake of the poststructuralist literary criticism that infuses Grant's ideas. Whilst critics of *Brick Lane*'s
ending focus on 'correspondence', they neglect the 'coherence' of the novel
and the fact that both elements must exist within a realist fiction, but also the
important tension between these two modes of truth.

Brick Lane, then, is not the conscientious realism of the nineteenth century
which Grant identifies, with its suspicion of the imagination and commitment
to exact social reproduction. *Brick Lane* does not represent the deference to a
simple—itself problematically defined—nineteenth-century realism that many
critics identify (and therefore see as failing in the novel's final pages). In
poststructuralist terms, the concern over the novel's ending foregrounds what
the majority of literary critics have accepted for a long time: that reality is a
fiction the author creates, rather than something *a priori*. And in this context,
what Ali creates is a novel playing upon the tension between overt realist
form and a more postmodernist reality. What emerges from this tension, as
I shall outline in the next section, is a powerful utopianism representing the
claims of British Muslims to British citizenship and the 'return' of this right
in a post-9/11 context, and marking the text as far more radical than both
British Muslim and literary complainants recognize.

Brick Lane's Utopian Realism

The 'coherent' realism, then, of *Brick Lane*, creates a world which may not
seem realist either to some British Muslims or to reviewers and some literary critics. The threat of the novel perceived by British Muslims relies upon
the assumption that 'fictional worlds can seem to us to be almost as "real"
as the real one is, even though we know perfectly well that they are not'.[17]
Yet this awareness, I would suggest, has a benefit overlooked in such criticism. *Brick Lane* makes the reader believe that the world it offers *does* exist,
with politically powerful results. Whilst this has little impact in terms of
stereotypes that critics from within the British Muslim community perceive
in the novel, it has considerable effect in evaluating the reservations of literary critics.

What Ali succeeds in doing runs counter to Lukacs's vision of political realism, in that it is precisely this 'failure' of representation—at least in

Lukacs's terms—that makes Ali's novel so politically powerful: a potency, indeed, that the majority of critics overlook in criticism of the novel's ending and adherence to privileging strictly realist modes of representation. *Brick Lane* offers, instead, a *utopian realism*, the power of which lies in an ability to gesture beyond, rather than simply reflect, the prevailing social and material existence for many British Muslims.

Lukacs himself identifies negatively the movement away from strict realism as a utopian moment. In his analysis of Balzac he frames the discussion thus:

> What makes Balzac a great man is the inexorable veracity with which he depicted reality even if that reality ran counter to his own personal opinions, hopes and wishes. Had he succeeded in deceiving himself, had he been able to take his own Utopian fantasies for facts, had he presented as reality what was merely his own wishful thinking, he would now be of interest to none and would be as deservedly forgotten as the innumerable legitimist pamphleteers and glorifiers of feudalism who had been his contemporaries.[18]

Yet, in a Black British context, this ability to pursue the utopian moment is critically transformed. Postcolonial critic John McLeod, most notably, identifies the power of utopianism in Black British writer Caryl Phillips.[19] For McLeod, popular contemporary writers such as Zadie Smith have been falsely identified as offering 'celebratory' narratives; Phillips offers an alternative to such discourse in a 'progressive utopianism' that is hopeful and yet non-idealized in acknowledgement of past struggles and present tensions. I would contend, in fact, that this utopianism is the defining feature of dominant Black British and British Asian writers active in Britain today, and that Ali's use of such form—alongside Phillips's already identified preference— only situates her writing as a particularly high-profile example of a much larger trend.[20] McLeod's discussion opens up a useful possibility to consider the role literary form must play in such strategies. Whilst his analysis focuses largely upon the content of Phillips's later work, one must also consider how such utopianism transforms and reworks the English realist tradition, something McLeod himself hints at in his suggestion that what he refers to as 'innovative thought' is not 'as remote from the "grim prose" of . . . subaltern lives' as some postcolonial critics assume.[21] As McLeod identifies, celebratory utopianism 'can never progressively contribute to social transformation as it remains detached from and blissfully unaware of the material world'.[22] To represent a more politically powerful utopianism, therefore, writers must address tensions between the rooting of utopia in unreality—an etymology which means literally 'nowhere'—and the need for identifiable time and place to make social comment. Realism, then, must be central to ethnic fictions if they are to posit political interventions. To be hopeful in the wake of this announces a realism with utopian undertones.

Whereas McLeod, however, critiques the idealized as less powerful than the work of Phillips with its glimpses of possibility yet still 'predominately still and sobering tone' (the former most notable for him not in fiction but in the work of cultural critic Paul Gilroy), a novel such as *Brick Lane* opens up possibilities for political power to be retained in fiction where this emphasis has been reversed: where the tone is predominately optimistic, yet rooted in sober reality and with full acknowledgment of past and current challenges.[23] This is not to question McLeod's argument on the limitations of idealism, but rather to point to how writers who have emerged after Phillips (who first began writing in the 1980s) have placed greater emphasis on the utopian to make more radical points about the need to construct a different future for British society and to, perhaps, draw readers' attention to this need more starkly than to remind them of past failures.

For Lukacs, shattering utopian illusions is central to realism's role in exposing the realities of human existence, particularly in terms of the proletariat. A fiction such as Ali's, in contrast, functions in an alternative cultural-historical context in which realism itself must be transformed to be politically significant. *Brick Lane* thus draws attention to the evolving nature of realist writing as an ethical and social force, in the twenty-first-century context of multimedia discourse. Whilst the early part of Ali's novel may draw attention—in classical realist form—to the harsh reality of ethnic minority life on London's inner city estates, particularly for its female inhabitants, these realities may be equally—and more obviously—exposed by mass communication forms such as newspapers, television, cinema and electronic media. The role of the novel therefore becomes to gesture beyond reportage: to speak specifically to communities that might do most to in fact change this reality. Such communities are two-fold: on the one hand, they consist of those educated readers who might be motivated to challenge government policy or influence public affairs through their own employment or social influence; on the other hand, they consist more specifically of ethnic readers who might take action within their own communities, although of course there is significant overlap between these two groups of readers, with many potentially finding the novel speaking to them simultaneously on both these levels. At the centre of this debate is the nature of representation itself, and the need—particularly in a postcolonial context—to question the transparency of representation as a conceptual parameter for judging works of fiction. Recent scholarship on Jacques Derrida, drawing attention to the consequences of the philosopher's concern for representation for literary interpretation, is particularly useful here. Shane Weller, for example, argues that

> the essence of the literary event would lie in its resistance to the question of essence. And yet, this resistance does not entail the mere disappearance of literature. Rather, it is literature's very chance. There remains for Derrida 'something irreducible in poetic or literary experience', but this

irreducibility lies precisely in literature's singular capacity to suspend (rather than simply annul or free from itself) 'thetic referentiality'.[24]

At the heart of literature, in these terms, is the resistance of essences such as those privileged by Lukacs. That such resistance is 'literature's very chance' points to the potential offered which exceeds the reportage of other non-fiction sources. It is a 'singular capacity': not to be replicated in other forms.

Most powerful here is Weller's emphasis on the suspension of thetic referentiality in literature, as opposed to an annulment of or freedom from prescriptive prose. It is this suspension which utopian realism embodies. As for my argument, so for Weller this potential identifies literature as more powerful than other modes of discourse:

> Indeed, the literary event becomes the privileged form of resistance in 'our historical situation' to the brutality of nihilism defined as that force which would close down all possibility of the future as the 'to come' (*à venir*). As the 'nothing-ing of nothing', the literary event is that non-programmable and singular 'good violence' which acts in the interests of the other in its value.[25]

Realism is always engaged in the project of producing 'a work of art' that is to 'induce the reader to believe that it is an image of reality'.[26] But in *Brick Lane* the utopian aspect of this realism comes from utilizing the realist form to convince the reader of a reality that *is not*, at least in the context of the specific, realist temporality and spatiality of post-9/11 Britain. It is about declaring *what can be*. So *Brick Lane* is filled with declarative and performative structures: not just Razia's final pronouncement, but also Nazneen's commitment to meetings ('that was before I knew what I could do') (407), to a rural England that 'she *would* visit' (366, emphasis added), and to a future where '*I will say what happens to me*' (337); her recognition of the fact that '*Anything is possible* . . . See what *I can* do' (50, second emphasis added), and the estate mothers' awareness that their children, wanting to direct their own course, '*will* do that' (404, emphasis added).

Indeed, the novel as a whole speaks to this declarative confidence. This is exemplified in the book's underlying theme—the concern for whether our lives are pre-destined or dictated by our own agency. Such a debate opens the novel with Ali's choice of epigraphs, and is woven into the story of Nazneen's 'fateful' birth, which teaches her that 'since nothing could be changed, everything would have to be borne' (11). By the novel's conclusion, Nazneen's daughters declare this story, so well-told, as 'boring'. Nazneen, rather than ignoring their conclusion, accepts its relevance—'True', she declares, and then, in response to the request for a story, 'I'll tell you a better one' (405). What this 'story' is, the narrative does not reveal; Nazneen's declaration remains tentative and yet full of promise, a glimpse of a future in which she will define her own destiny rather than accept her 'fate' or, indeed, the social constraints placed on her by others (which this 'fate', in reality, is revealed to be).

Postmodernist deconstruction offers the possibility to expose the text as being 'in fact quite other than what it appears to be'.[27] For Derrida, this means questioning the notion of representation itself. Yet Derrida's work should not be taken simply to uphold the limits of seeing writing as representative, however useful this is within the context of the burden of representation. In fact, in his essay 'Sending: On Representation' Derrida argues explicitly for the retention of the concept:

> Today there is a great deal of thought against representation. In a more or less articulated or rigorous way, this judgment is easily arrived at: representation is bad. And this without being able to assign, in the final analysis, the place and the necessity of that evaluation. We should ask ourselves what is this place and above all what may be the various risks (in particular political ones) of such a prevalent evaluation.[28]

For Derrida, however, such retention must act against representation as a passive form: something we merely represent. Instead, it must be appreciated for its dynamic, and resistive, potential.

Derrida does much here to draw attention to the connection between representation as a political process—the act of speaking for an individual, group or community—and representation in the aesthetic realm: the act of replicating. Whilst the present age, he tells us, has become obsessed by the truth of representation—its accuracy in terms of what it represents—what is also needed is appreciation of the role of representation 'as delegation', including political delegation.[29] The value of representation, and its authority, thus centres not simply on being realistic, although this is important, but on the act of representing the Other, and in doing so politically speaking as an envoy of that other ('Not only someone who sends himself or gives himself objects but who is sent (*est l'envoye de*) by something else or by the other'.).[30]

To be an envoy is quite different from the kind of 'speaking for' voice that Gayatri Spivak critiques. For Spivak, there are two types of representation—'"speaking for," as in politics, and representation as "re-presentation" as in art or philosophy'.[31] Ali, like Rushdie before her, however, has been disadvantaged by the synthesis of these two definitions—Ali engages principally, as a novelist, in 're-presentation', and yet is held accountable as responsible for representation: identified not simply as offering a presentation of the real, but also as speaking for those who fall within the scope of this presentation. Whilst for Spivak these two terms are 'related but irreducibly discontinuous', for critics of Ali they are easily conflated. There is little recognition of the singularity of these differing aims: that an author might succeed in 're-presentation' outside the accurate voicing of the community they choose to artistically present.

To be an envoy, however, is to explicitly position oneself outside—not to speak for, but to act as one who is sent by that other. This subtle difference is important, and it points to the political potential of *Brick Lane* even as it functions most specifically as a text of re-presentation.

Brick Lane announces itself as a realist novel concerned with the act of replicating a particular culture and locality. Yet it also, in its function as a British Asian novel within the context of 9/11 and the persecution of British Muslims, speaks for this community in a politicized context. If one sees—as I do—Ali's voice as being the envoy not of Brick Lane Muslims specifically, but of the British Muslim community more broadly, with a membership that is both geographically and socially heterogeneous, it is possible to argue in favour of a Derridean function, one which successfully manages to speak as an envoy for the other, *without speaking for.*[32] In these terms, criticism of the novel's ending can be reconsidered: the re-presentation (in aesthetic terms) of *Brick Lane* gives way only in service of the need for representation (in political terms) that the novel gestures towards.

It is less important, therefore, that *Brick Lane* speaks from within the community or ends realistically in limited terms, and more significant that it offers, in utopian spirit, a coherent vision of what British Muslim identity might be, or indeed had the potential to be before the events of 9/11. Ali's conclusion locates a simultaneously mental and physical 'thirdspace' maintaining the possibility of religious devotion *within* secularized Britain. Such possibility lies not within the confines of narrow definitions of either multiculturalism or community cohesion, and therefore posits an alternative to existing government discourses. This utopian need to announce British Muslims as rightful claimants to British citizenship must take precedence over the need to maintain an uncomplicated realism. Utopian realism becomes a re-presentation of reality which serves political representation rather than mimetic realism. Here, then, Ali's representation is about the 'making-present' which Derrida positions as central to representational concerns.[33] For Derrida, this making-present is two-fold: firstly a bringing into being; secondly, an allowing to return: a re-presentation. In the linear chronology Ali employs, this is indeed what *Brick Lane* indicates. Abuse of Muslims post-9/11 is an anathema: a temporary aberration consigned to a specific and non-generalizable place in history. It is not, the novel suggests, that no progress is made from the 1980s to the twenty-first century, but rather that 9/11 and reactions to it stall this progress.

To appreciate this locates why the end of the novel is utopian, but not fantastical. It is an allowance of return: Nazneen and her daughters almost join Chanu in Bangladesh, yet in their final decision to remain in Britain this more traditional migrant's 'return' is forgone for the more radical 'return' to the place in British society which their presence has afforded them and which they are entitled to claim as right. Their actions make them present, but also mark their return to a citizenship eroded by post-9/11 discourse.

Interestingly, the novel's racial dynamics here work alongside its feminist credentials and its place as intra-community critique—Nazneen and her daughters equally are claiming their presence within the context of male patriarchal Bangladeshi culture, and marking a return of voices silenced by that culture, so powerfully represented in the novel by both Nazneen's sister and her mother.

Ali's approach here is usefully compared to what J. Hillis Miller identifies as Charles Dickens's strategic realism in his *Sketches by Boz*.[34] For Miller, it is limited to see Dickens's work as offering a simple correlation to any external reality. *Sketches*, instead, needs to be read as a 'journalistic' text, full of metonymy and synecdoche, actively constructed to encourage the reader to take 'as mimesis solidly based on an extra-literary world a work which is in fact fiction and which contains the linguistic clues allowing the reader to recognize that it is fiction'.[35] In a text dominated by themes of play acting and deception, both in terms of class identity and more literal theatrical performance, Dickens highlights society as a space of illusion and disillusionment. Freedom comes only through role-playing, through playing the game rather than departing from it.[36]

Brick Lane is similarly revealing of its own realistic limits, and of the power of performativity. It is naïve to assume that Nazneen unproblematically assimilates. Like Dickens's characters, her freedom comes by strategically performing or learning the game of Britishness—and intelligently choosing to manipulate its rules for her own purpose. This may seem less powerful than outright rebellion, and is indeed what some critics object to. But to object is to refuse the possibility that British Muslims might dwell within a thirdspace that is both Muslim and British. Nazneen's confidence at the novel's conclusion proves the reality of her British citizenship. It is a mistake to read this as assimilationist discourse when, in fact, it speaks to the promise of successful multiculturalism—Nazneen's skating in a sari or dancing to Lulu with the same garment tucked up into her underskirt, her daughter Shahana's sandwiches of cream cheese spread and mango pickle and Dairylea Triangles in chapattis, all of these are cultural markers of the possibility of retaining one's cultural affiliations and yet at the same time incorporating western practices. If critics of the novel desire a dire conclusion, they miss the fact that, throughout, *Brick Lane* draws attention to the limitations of such negative readings of British Muslim identities—the clash of cultures as Chanu describes in verbose detail is silenced by a simple 'Crap!' (92).

As has been argued elsewhere, this vision is not the levelling out of difference sometimes implied in concepts of hybridity, but rather a contingent adaptation sensitive to the need to retain, in particular, religious identity.[37] Nazneen's continual return to Islam as the ethical core of her life privileges the importance of undiluted belief structures within the more fluid possibilities of hybrid cross-cultural encounter. Nazneen's agency is one guided by scripture; her rejection of fate and assertion that '*I will say what happens to me*' is in favour not of liberal free-will but of a more considered religious life, so that her decision about whether to go to Dhaka with her husband is made via prayer; the novel itself represents this fusion as page by page it oscillates between expressions of agency and their tempering by religious dictate (337–338). Significantly, this knowledge comes not from British liberalism, but from the lessons Nazneen learns in the village as a child, from the women who teach her that 'Everything is within you, where God put it' (52). As the Quran teaches of future glory, so the novel takes this awareness and—in befitting multicultural form—transforms it into a future hope for similar social transformation in the present life (45).

In this sense, *Brick Lane* might be seen to hopefully offer the promise of a renewed multiculturalism, what Tariq Modood refers to as a dialogue which promotes integration rather than simply toleration or accommodation, or what the Commission on the Future of Multi-Ethnic Britain referred to in 2000 as a 'community of communities'.[38] Multiculturalism in these terms is radical—evidence of 'the challenging, the dismantling and the remaking of cultural identities' rather than their stagnation or isolationism. Moreover, it is a complement to national identity rather than in opposition to it.[39] So Razia may celebrate England as a place where you can 'do whatever you like', may wear her Union Jack sweatshirt and declare her Britishness, precisely because to do so is not to assimilate but to celebrate a multiculture which, if adopted properly, should allow Nazneen, equally, to assert her Muslim identity. In the context of recent critiques of multiculturalism as an isolationist practice which may have played a part in the rise of so-called 'home-grown terrorists'—as evidenced in the 7/7 London tube and bus bombings—such an intervention is particularly timely.[40] It speaks not in favour of government alternatives to multiculturalism—the policy of community cohesion, with its emphasis on assimilation and the dilution of specific cultural practices—but rather to the potential for a revised post-9/11 multiculturalism which exists precisely in the context of liberal politics rather than in opposition to it: evidence of Modood's belief that 'multiculturalism could not get off the ground if one truly repudiated liberalism; but neither could it do so if liberalism marked the limits of one's politics'.[41]

Here, the ending of *Brick Lane* becomes an invitation to performativity on the part of the reader, who should not be identified as incapable of engaging with such complex shifts in representation and their political potential. Lilian Furst suggests that we can see 'the world of the fiction as adjacent to that of reality, and as producing its own fictional truths, to which readers are persuaded to subscribe through their capacity to enter believingly into the created realm'.[42] In this analysis, realism depends on a conscious willingness to accept a representation at odds with lived experience, especially in the action of characters. *Brick Lane* manipulates realism to persuade of an ending which is *untruth* but which might become *truth*; in doing so readers show their ability to creatively reimagine reality, but also—in the context of British cultural politics—to reimagine a multicultural society. Here *Brick Lane* is a potent example of Walton's suggestion that '*psychological* interaction between worlds is possible'.[43] Acceptance of Nazneen's actions does not represent an oversight of the harshness of post-9/11 society and the persistence of Islamophobia; rather it illustrates a willingness to accept a reality in which her actions *might* be possible, and a commitment to working towards this aim. Just as the novel's later pages point to future social change—the fact that 'after the riot, everything was going to change' (405), a 'Tower Hamlets Task Force' that will report in two years' time (406)—so it speaks more generally to what might be, rather than what is already. The possibility of Nazneen, therefore, also speaks to a wider possibility—that society might go beyond the limits of the current situation as regards attitudes towards British Muslim and, by extension, other religious and racial groups. The novel's productive tension, between the harsh reality of lives for migrant women and what might be possible for these same women, is most exposed when we see Nazneen reaching beyond the role which might stereotypically be assigned to her. For example, when Nazneen negotiates the East London streets searching for her daughter in the midst of the riots, her own lack of knowledge jars with the accurate geography the author offers to describe the journey—'Down Bethnal Green Road. Turned at Vallance Road. Jogged down New Road. Stitch in her side on Cannon Street'.[44] Nazneen herself might not be able to yet describe her journey in these detailed terms, with the urban familiarity they indicate, and yet Ali's own ability to do so speaks to the possibility of this as the eventual outcome of Nazneen's increasing public presence.[45] The author herself provides the rationale for optimism—evidence of a utopian promise realized which may not yet be available to less socially advantaged women such as Nazneen, but which is not, nevertheless, permanently beyond their reach. It is in this context that Nazneen's eventual hopefulness is so significant; it is she, and not British-born Muslims such as her lover Karim, or patriarchs such as her husband Chanu, who finds the possibility of happiness in Britain. This marks the potential of such multicultural inclusion for *all;* for if an individual disadvantaged in terms of gender, race, religion and class can find such positivity the question must be asked, *who cannot?*

Conclusion

Comparisons with Dickens draw attention to the fact that to reread Ali in such terms is not to draw her writing away from influences most commonly identified in her fiction. *Brick Lane's* success does rely upon the attraction of an earlier nineteenth-century form, reworked in a twenty-first-century context. Yet such realism has never been the transparent representation which critics of the novel identify. Indeed, the Derridean project is one which only resurrects the voices of other nineteenth-century writers. Take, for example, Guy de Maupassant's comments on the realist novel:

The realist, if he is an artist, will seek not to show us the banal photograph of life, but to give it a more complete, more striking, more probing vision of reality itself . . . I conclude from this that the talented realists ought rather to call themselves Illusionists.[46]

Utopian realism, then, has a history. It might be linked to terms such as ideal realism, optimistic realism and visionary realism, which are amongst the twenty-six sub-types of the form identified in Damian Grant's influential guide.[47] Postmodern or nineteenth-century verisimilitude, the emergent fiction is less simplistic than existing criticism might initially suggest.

One of the questions naturally emerging from such a rereading of *Brick Lane* is whether, several years on, the novel's vision has become more realistic, or more utopian. The answer to this question has consequences not only for how we read Ali's novel, but also for how it constructs a dialogue allowing us to read the state of community relations in contemporary Britain. In some ways, the situation is bleaker and the novel thus more utopian, as the rise in race hate crime, Islamophobia and media hostility towards religious communities more generally seem to indicate.[48] Yet, despite these failures, in 2007 Modood felt optimistic enough to declare that 'Simultaneously respecting difference and inculcating Britishness is not a naive hope but something that is happening'.[49] This suggests, in contrast, that the hopefulness of *Brick Lane* might actually have become more 'real' in the past five years. This can be seen to be the case not simply in terms of the novel's optimistic position on multiculturalism, but also in terms of the rise in Britain of a socially progressive and more inclusive Islam—with vocal youth and female members—and a broader agenda for social justice as has been evident more recently in large-scale demonstrations and social activism. This is the novel's promise, and—it would be heartening to think—its prescience: a re-presentation that declares a commitment to a reality where, in Karim's words, 'We want everyone to be represented' (193).

Notes

1. The offensive passage comes on page 21, where Chanu insinuates that Sylhetis are 'dirty little monkeys'. Of course, Chanu is established throughout as a figure without authority; his prejudices should not be confused with the attitudes of the author.
2. See Kobena Mercer and Isaac Julien, 'Introduction: De Margin and de Centre', *Screen* 29.4 (1988): 2–10.
3. Monica Ali, *Brick Lane* (London: Doubleday, 2003), 413. Subsequent references are given parenthetically.
4. Yasmin Hussain, *Writing Diaspora: South Asian Women, Culture and Ethnicity* (Aldershot: Ashgate, 2005), 17, 109.
5. James Procter, 'New Ethnicities, the Novel, and the Burdens of Representation', in James F. English, ed., *A Concise Companion to Contemporary British Fiction* (Cambridge: Blackwell, 2006), 101–120 (8).

6. Natasha Walter, 'Citrus Scent of Inexorable Desire', *Guardian* online, 14 June 2003, http://books.guardian.co.uk/bookerprize2003/story/0,13819,1019773,00. html; Delia Falconer, 'Brick Lane', *Sydney Morning Herald* online, 2 August 2003, www.smh.com.au/articles/2003/08/01/1059480538023.html; Michael Gorra, 'East Enders', *The New York Times* online, 7 September 2003, http://query. nytimes.com/gst/fullpage.html?res=9C01E6DB1E39F934#A3575AC0A9659 C8B63 (accessed 10 April 2010).
7. Eric Auerbach, *Mimesis: The Representation of Reality in Western Literature*, trans. Willard R. Trask (Princeton: Princeton University Press, 1953), 491.
8. Lilian Furst, 'Introduction', in Lilian L. Furst, ed., *Realism* (London: Longman, 1992), 1–23 (6).
9. Ibid., 2.
10. Georg Lukacs, *Studies in European Realism* (London: Merlin, 1972 [1950]), 11.
11. Ibid.
12. Louis-Edmond Duranty, *Le Realisme* 2 (15 December 1856); reprinted in Furst, 31–32 (31).
13. Philippe Hamon, 'Un discours contraint', *Poetique* 16 (1973): 411–445; reprinted in Furst, trans. Lillian Furst and Seán Hand (1991), 166–185 (173).
14. Hamon, 'Un Discours contraint', 181.
15. Damian Grant, *Realism* (London: Methuen, 1970), 9.
16. Ibid., 15.
17. Kendall L. Walton, 'Appreciating Fiction: Suspending Disbelief or Pretending Belief?', *Disposito* 5 (1983): 1–18; reprinted in Furst, 218–238 (233).
18. Lukacs, *Realism*, 22.
19. John McLeod, 'Diaspora and Utopia: Reading the Recent Work of Paul Gilroy and Caryl Phillips', in Mark Shackleton, ed., *Diasporic Literature and Theory: Where Now?* (Newcastle: Cambridge Scholars Publishing, 2008), 2–17.
20. For example, Meera Syal, Zadie Smith, Andrea Levy and Hanif Kureishi can all be seen to engage with alternative realisms professing the positivity of race relations in Britain.
21. McLeod, 'Diaspora and Utopia', 4.
22. Ibid.
23. Ibid., 9.
24. Shane Weller, '"Rather than Nothing": Derrida, Literature, and the Resistance of Nihilism', in Simon Morgan Wortham and Allison Weiner, eds, *Encountering Derrida: Legacies and Futures of Deconstruction* (New York and London: Continuum, 2007), 21–32 (29–30).
25. Ibid., 31.
26. Furst, 'Introduction', 15.
27. Furst, 'Introduction', 18.
28. Derrida, 'Sending: On Representation', trans. Peter Caws and Mary Ann Caws, *Social Research* 49.2 (1982): 295–326 (304).
29. Ibid., 317.
30. Ibid., 316.
31. Gayatri Chakravorty Spivak, 'Can the Subaltern Speak?', in Cary Nelson and Lawrence Grossberg, eds, *Marxism and the Interpretation of Culture* (Illinois: University of Illinois Press, 1988), 271–313 (275).

32. I am not suggesting here that the Brick Lane Muslim population is singular or easily identified. Rather, there is a concept of this population as identified by Ali and by critics as having a particular character—largely working-class and of Bangladeshi heritage—which contrasts with the diversity of Islam as represented in contemporary Britain as a whole. Indeed, criticisms of Ali, such as those made by Hussain, often identify her position as 'outside' of this population as limiting the novel's authenticity, thus equally revealing the prevalence of a particular image of this community which is somewhat narrowly defined.
33. Derrida, 'Sending', 308.
34. J. Hillis Miller, 'The Fiction of Realism: Sketches by Boz, Oliver Twist, and Cruikshank's Illustrations', in Ada Nisbet and Blake Nevius, eds, *Dickens Centennial Essays* (Berkeley: University of California Press, 1971); reprinted in Furst, 287–318.
35. Ibid., 302.
36. Ibid., 313.
37. See my discussion of Ali's 'contingent hybridity', *British Asian Fiction: Twenty-First-Century Voices* (Manchester: Manchester University Press, 2010), 179–182.
38. See Tariq Modood, *Multicultural Politics: Racism, Ethnicity and Muslims in Britain* (Edinburgh: Edinburgh University Press, 2005), 174, and *Multiculturalism: A Civic Idea* (Cambridge: Polity, 2007), 48; Commission on the Future of Multi-Ethnic Britain, *The Future of Multi-Ethnic Britain* (London: Profile Books, 2000), paragraph 4.19.
39. Modood, *Multiculturalism*, 43, 146.
40. For a summary of such criticisms of multiculturalism see Modood, *Multiculturalism*, 10–14.
41. Modood, *Multiculturalism*, 8.
42. Furst, *Realism*, 205.
43. Ibid., 223.
44. Ibid., 390.
45. A similar argument can be made for Ali's accurate mapping of Nazneen's tube journey on pages 374–375, or Razia and Nazneen's shopping journey on pages 325–326.
46. Guy de Maupassant, 'The Novel', Preface to *Pierre et Jean* (1888); reprinted in Furst, 45–47 (45).
47. Grant, *Realism*, 47–63.
48. In 2006 it was widely reported that race hate crimes rose by 28 per cent. The website *Islamophobia Watch* documents continued incidences of anti-Muslim action: http://www.islamophobia-watch.com/islamophobia-watch/2011/4/13/islamophobia-on-the-rise.html (accessed 10 October 2010).
49. Modood, *Multiculturalism*, 150.

Part IV
Culture, Politics and Religion

11 From 'the Politics of Recognition' to 'the Policing of Recognition'

Writing Islam in Hanif Kureishi and Mohsin Hamid

Bart Moore-Gilbert

Introduction

This chapter will explore aspects of the representation of Islam either side of the watershed of 9/11, associated attacks on the West and reactions to them, notably the ongoing interventions in Iraq and Afghanistan. This aim will be pursued with reference to Hanif Kureishi's *The Black Album* (1995) and Mohsin Hamid's *The Reluctant Fundamentalist* (2007), two works by secularist writers of Pakistani-Muslim heritage. More specifically, I intend to examine how the two authors deploy the issue of 'Islamic fundamentalism' as a means to frame their analysis of the situation of Muslims, whether considered as a transnational global community, as national formations or as minorities within particular western nation-states. Equally, the chapter will explore the implications of such representations for dominant western conceptions of the axes of *inter-* and *intra*-national community relations in the period immediately prior to the attacks on the Twin Towers.

In the decade or so before 9/11, one set of discourses embracing both these axes centred around 'the politics of recognition'. In terms of *inter*-national relations, perhaps the most celebrated example was Francis Fukuyama's 'The End of History', published in article form in 1989 and as a book in 1992. This foretold the imminent 'end of history', understood as Man's age-old struggle for adequate 'recognition', by which Fukuyama meant the demand 'to be recognized as a *human being*, that is, as a being with a certain worth or dignity'.[1] Following Hegel, this demand was presented as the determining motor of human history: 'The desire for recognition, and the accompanying emotions of anger, shame, and pride . . . are what drives the whole historical process'.[2] According to Fukuyama, it is this unsatisfied demand, rather than class conflict, ideology or a struggle for resources and territory, which explains the countless 'local' conflicts in human history, two world wars, even the possibility of humanity's annihilation during the decades-long stand off between the United States and the Soviet Union.

However, Fukuyama prophesied that the fall of the Berlin Wall in 1989 and the ending of the Cold War which this symbolized were to usher in a new, more productive, era of 'recognition', which he extrapolated from the model of the western secular, liberal-democratic nation-state: 'Liberal democracy replaces the irrational desire to be recognized as greater than others with a rational desire to be recognized as equal'.[3] As a social system which allegedly could not be improved upon, it was supposedly destined—at least in the long-term—to spread across the world. Consequently, nations with sometimes radically different cultural histories and values would be able to co-operate with progressively greater facility on the basis of proper 'recognition' of each other's legitimacy and integrity, making redundant the rivalries which had stoked the conflicts of the past. Particularly germane to the work of postcolonial writers, including Kureishi and Hamid, is the claim that the dawning era of 'recognition' on the liberal-democratic model augurs 'the end of imperialism, and with it, a decrease in the likelihood of war based on imperialism'.[4]

With the qualified exception of class relations, Fukuyama has little to say about the struggle for 'recognition' amongst groups *within* nation-states. This is because, in the West, at least, the problem has allegedly been solved by a model of 'universal and reciprocal recognition, where every citizen recognizes the dignity and humanity of every other citizen, and where that dignity is recognized in turn by the state through the granting of *rights*'.[5] A very different reading of this problematic is offered by Charles Taylor's 'The Politics of Recognition', also published in book form in 1992. Like Fukuyama, Taylor sees 'recognition' as a cornerstone of human development: 'Nonrecognition or misrecognition can inflict harm, can be a form of oppression, imprisoning someone in a false, distorted, and reduced mode of being . . . Due recognition', he went on, 'is a vital human need'.[6] In strong contrast to Fukuyama, however, Taylor challenged the idea that the problem had been solved *within* western liberal-democratic societies, which were becoming increasingly multicultural as a consequence of migration from the non-western world in the wake of globalization.

In this conjuncture, Taylor argued, the terms on which 'recognition' had hitherto been framed—at least implicitly—in models like Fukuyama's (though the essay doesn't mention his colleague) might potentially lead to new kinds of social tension and forms of exclusion. Such models were based on what Taylor calls 'the principle of equal respect [which] requires that we treat people in a difference-blind fashion'.[7] This emphasis on the rights of the individual, which Taylor terms 'procedural' liberalism, however, generates resistance from minorities which see themselves as having distinctive *group* identities and conferring these on their individual members. For some such communities, 'procedural' liberalism 'negates identity by forcing people into a homogeneous mold that is untrue to them . . . The claim is that the supposedly neutral set of difference-blind principles of the politics of equal dignity is in fact a reflection of one hegemonic culture'.[8] Taylor acknowledged that 'recognition' of the rights of minorities *as groups*, in other words as positing an identity or value-system 'that is not universally shared',[9] potentially conflicted with the principle of equality of individuals before a uniformly applicable system of law. Consequently, he called for a new, more 'hospitable' form of liberal society 'willing to weigh the importance of certain forms of uniform treatment against the importance of cultural survival [of minorities *as minorities*], and opt sometimes in favour of the latter'.[10]

Influential though both theories undoubtedly proved, they have come to seem increasingly vulnerable since 9/11 and its aftermaths. Perhaps the most signal empirical oversight in both philosophers' work was the absence of any substantial 'recognition' of the challenges increasingly posed by Muslim religious identities for the dynamics of both international relations and the internal cohesion of western liberal-secular societies. Thus while acknowledging the phenomenon of Muslim 'fundamentalism', which he described as bearing 'a more than superficial resemblance to European fascism', Fukuyama confidently states that Islam 'cannot challenge liberal democracy . . . on the level of ideas' and 'has no resonance for young people in Berlin, Tokyo, or Moscow'.[11] Despite temporary local victories over western values, then, not even a religion embracing a fifth of the world's population can finally resist the Hegelian juggernaut of historical unfolding in which the world is 'progressively' reshaped in the image of western secular, liberal-democratic, capitalist society. Islam is therefore strikingly absent from the list of major challenges which the West has overcome in the past or is likely to encounter in the future.[12]

Taylor's engagement with Islam is scarcely less limited. The issues posed by Muslim immigration to the West elicit a single paragraph in the essay, in the course of which Taylor refers to the Rushdie Affair and comments:

> The awkwardness arises from the fact that there are substantial numbers of people who are citizens and also belong to the culture that calls into question our philosophical boundaries. The challenge is to deal with their sense of marginalization without compromising our basic political principles.[13]

The essay's faith in the efficacy of a more 'hospitable' variant of the 'politics of recognition' to deal with this challenge may be explained in large measure by the fact that the normative horizons within which Taylor's theory operates are generated from the context of debate about relations between Quebec and the rest of Canada. Given that there were barely a quarter of a million Muslims in the whole of Canada at the time of his essay,[14] it is perhaps unsurprising that Taylor does not address in detail the 'problems' posed by Muslim identity for his conception of 'the politics of recognition'. By contrast, Kureishi and Hamid address contexts in which they are central and inescapable. The London of *The Black Album* already boasted a population of 250,000 Muslims in 1991 (with more than 1.7 million in Britain as a whole).[15] *The Reluctant Fundamentalist*, in turn, explores how such—often substantial—minorities based in the West articulate with larger national and transnational Muslim communities to bring into question the nation-state, the primary building-block in Fukuyama's vision of a new, more harmonious, international order. To different degrees and in different ways, the work of each writer both endorses and critiques the philosophical premises and strategic political arguments associated with the two influential formulations of 'the politics of recognition' summarized above. However, the thrust of their respective engagements with 'the politics of recognition' is often very different, a fact which can be attributed in substantial measure to the cataclysmic effects of 9/11 and its aftermaths.

The Black Album

Kureishi's novel addresses in far greater depth than Taylor what was perhaps the first instance of 'Islamic fundamentalism' in the West to widely impact on public perception—the riots and book-burnings in British cities in the wake of the fatwa pronounced on Salman Rushdie in 1989. While oddly coy about the actual title of the book which Riaz and his cell set fire to at the end of the novel, the reader is clearly invited to draw parallels with the burnings of *Satanic Verses* in Bradford and London in 1989–1990. Kureishi draws on such events to explore the role and predicament of Muslim communities within Britain at the time, and their implications for received understandings of national belonging and multiculturalism in western societies of the kind Fukuyama strenuously champions as the template for the emergent 'new world order'. In doing so, he offers a complex engagement with 'the politics of recognition'.

To a considerable extent, Kureishi endorses Taylor's thesis about the necessity for greater 'recognition' of minority individuals and culture if liberal-democratic societies are to function harmoniously. This problematic is approached initially through Shahid's early obsession with his 'invisibility'.[16] Like *Invisible Man* (1952) by Ralph Ellison, one of the protagonist's favourite authors, Kureishi's text pulls no punches in identifying the barriers to adequate 'recognition' of the ethnically-marked subject and, more particularly, those of Muslim heritage. Though British-born and middle-class, Shahid regularly experiences first-hand modes of objectification and Othering which are rampant even in the multiethnic city-space of London. Further, *The Black Album* suggests that the dominant ethnicity increasingly identifies Muslims as the most potent threat to its traditional (self-)identifications. Thus Jump, despite being Zulma's lover, warns that 'they are entering France through Marseilles and Italy through the south. Soon they will be sweeping through the weakened Communist regions, into the heart of civilized Europe' (159). Such attitudes have their depressing material analogue in the violent harassment suffered on an almost daily basis by the Muslim family which Riaz's group seek to protect on the 'sink' housing estate in East London. As a consequence, his militant demands for greater 'recognition' of the community he represents, with to some degree a different value-system to the social dominant, are initially treated with sympathy. Indeed they are implicitly compared with the struggle for group civil rights in America which Shahid studies so enthusiastically at college.

To this degree, the novel also endorses Taylor's scepticism about the limitations of 'procedural' liberalism. However, Kureishi also calls into question the Canadian philosopher's more 'hospitable' version of multicultural relations. *The Black Album* is particularly concerned by how apparently positive 'recognition' of *group*-cultural difference may have negative consequences. For example, the protagonist is deeply ambivalent about the experimental multicultural curriculum at the institution he attends (and it's worth remembering that at the time of Taylor's essay, issues surrounding the 'politics of recognition' were perhaps most immediately in evidence in relation to 'the canon wars' in the western academy). For Shahid, a syllabus designed to reflect in a 'relevant' way the ethnic diversity of the student body—as well as his tutor Deedee Osgood's own particular interests—does not necessarily constitute a liberating acknowledgement of the equal value of different cultural histories. Rather, it may represent a new form of exclusion, denying him access to the 'great tradition' of the metropolitan culture to which he belongs as a second-generation migrant. The latter, by implication, remains reserved for white students at more exclusive educational establishments.

At the personal level, moreover, Shahid experiences apparently positive 'recognition' of his ethnic difference as coercive. Thus from Deedee, he encounters a fashionable, consumerist demand for 'authenticity' which threatens to fix him in an identity he is keen to complicate and experiment with at every opportunity. The text suggests that one of the most grievous aspects of what Chili calls the 'brown man's burden' is to be forced to be representative of his ethnicity and supposed cultural roots, even as he strives to evade the tendency of the dominant culture, 'liberal' or otherwise, to see minority individuals in typological terms. Deedee's obsession with his 'café-au-lait' (175) skin makes Shahid feel 'as if he were being hired for a job, the specifications of which she had prepared already' (102): to this extent, for much of the novel, the 'recognition' of difference which his mentor offers aligns her with the woman on the estate who prizes Shahid as a 'darlin' darkie' (113). This mode of 'recognition' reaches its nadir when Strapper complains that Shahid is getting 'too fucking Westernized. You all wanna be just like us now' (162).

The Black Album is particularly concerned by the characteristic unidirectionality of 'recognition' implied even in Taylor's more 'hospitable' model. The latter certainly acknowledged Frantz Fanon's insistence in *The Wretched of the Earth* (1961) that 'the major weapon of the colonizers was the imposition of their image of the colonized on the subjugated people. These latter, in order to be free, must first of all purge themselves of these depreciating self-images'.[17] Yet in his own argument, 'recognition' remains something which is conferred primarily by the dominant rather than achieved by the subordinate. Fanon's earlier text, *Black Skin, White Masks* (1952), exposes the problems with this dynamic. As much indebted as Taylor would later be to Hegel's elaboration of the 'master-bondsman' relationship in *The Phenomenology of Mind* (1807), *Black Skin* anatomizes a number of moments when the Black man is 'recognized' by the (former) master, including by radical anti-racists like Jean-Paul Sartre, only to dismiss each in turn as insufficient. For Fanon, 'recognition' cannot simply be conferred by the dominant without its authority being thereby reconfirmed: as *Black Skin* puts it, 'the white man, *in the capacity of master*, said to the Negro, "From now on you are free."'[18] Instead, Fanon argues, the bondsman must force recognition on his own terms, by violence if necessary, as the messianic language of both *Black Skin* and *The Wretched of the Earth* proclaims.

Something similar might be inferred from the evident inadequacy of the top-down 'gift of recognition' offered in *The Black Album* by ethnically dominant 'liberals' and 'radicals' alike, although—as will be seen—Kureishi severely circumscribes the terms on which the subordinate may legitimately demand fuller satisfaction of its needs. From the Labour politician George Rudder, to the ethical/ethnic tourist Brownlow, the 'group rights' of the minority Muslim community are insisted upon by a variety of figures in the text. However, such figures are represented as being primarily, if sometimes unwittingly, interested in shoring up the authority, political and cultural, of the ethnic centre to which they belong, by acting as 'referee' between competing marginalized groups, including the ethnic British 'underclass'. Thus Rudder interests himself in the predicament of the Bangladeshi family and pays lip-service to the revelation associated with the aubergine. But in both cases, this is primarily a means to securing the Asian vote and thereby his own political power. Brownlow is equally compromised by his patronizing Orientalist attitudes. These include his attitude of unmistakable lewdness towards Tahira and his literal misrecognition of Shahid, whom he twice confuses with Tariq. Reinforcing a commonplace racial stereotype, the 'ethnic subject' always looks the same to Brownlow and, *pace* his investments in 'difference', he is unable to recognize it at the most basic individual level. Like her husband, whose fruity voice is the kind which 'put down mutinous colonies', Deedee sometimes betrays a 'colonial mentality' towards minority group rights, persistently 'translating' their travails into a traditional (ethnicity-free) dialectic of class struggle (77, 181).

Yet by exploring further axes of 'recognition' not discussed by Taylor, Kureishi paradoxically returns to a substantial reaffirmation of key arguments in 'The Politics of Recognition' and, indeed, 'The End of History'. The first involves the relationship between different marginalized groups.

The London of *The Black Album* involves a far more complex diversity of (sub-)cultures than Taylor entertains, posing severe obstacles to achieving the greater 'hospitality' of 'recognition' that he advocates. While the city is represented as tending towards increased polarization of minority groups, Kureishi's focus in this regard is on relations between the Muslim minority and other disadvantaged formations which are not defined even in part by ethnicity. In the first place, he explores the conflict between the competing rights of women as a group and those of Riaz's community. The tension is clearest in Deedee's intervention on behalf of two young Asian women whom she hides in her house to shield them from patriarchal coercion by their culture of origin. Equally problematic is Riaz's attitude towards gays, which is uncompromisingly hostile and threatening. Thus Kureishi suggests that greater 'recognition' of an individual minority's 'group rights' is not necessarily the panacea for social disharmony but may rather, in a broader perspective, actually exacerbate the disadvantages of other sections of society.

The second such axis operates between the minority community to which Taylor is keen to extend greater 'recognition' and the individuals which comprise it. Thus, baffled by the host community's refusal to grant him meaningful 'recognition', Shahid understandably turns for support to the Muslim group at college. However, while pleased that someone is taking an interest, it is soon apparent that he will only be 'recognized' in this context at the price of surrendering crucial aspects of his (self-)identifications. A prime example concerns his investment in pop music, signifying Shahid's partial accession to the dominant culture and, for Kureishi, a potent symbol of the possibilities of an empowering, globalized, cross-culturalism. The more coercive his new associates become in their demands that he abjure such identifications, the more Shahid experiences a comparable lack of 'recognition' to what he suffers at the hands of mainstream society.

The failure of Riaz's group is perhaps most grievous in respect of the third axis, the gaze of the subordinate community on the dominant one. While legitimately demanding greater 'recognition', Riaz's circle refuses to 'recognize' what are represented as the entirely legitimate group-cultural rights of the majority culture. Thus the quasi-Fanonian form of violent resistance it offers Deedee and the book-burning alike imply a demand that the rights of a relatively small minority should override the democratically-agreed ones of the community as a whole. The more that Riaz's group advances this idea, both in words and action, the more it loses the authority initially conferred by its conception of Islam as a genuine and more flexible alternative to the flawed multiculturalism of mainstream society. It could be argued that Shahid's escape from London at the end of the novel implies a desire to evade altogether the problematic of 'recognition', in so far as this involves his identification as a member of an ethnic minority group. Indeed, one might infer that for much of the narrative what makes him a martyr (*shahid*) is precisely the dynamics of 'recognition', whether the gaze falling on him is that of the social dominant or the Muslim community claiming him.

Yet this ending in fact suggests an affirmation of the 'procedural' liberal model of social relations, whereby the rights of the individual are privileged over those of communities *as groups*. For example, the right of the writer, and Salman Rushdie more particularly, to absolute freedom of expression, clearly weighs more heavily in the text than Riaz's demands for 'respect' for his community's values. Thus Kureishi endorses Taylor's position that 'compromise is close to impossible'[19] on such points of principle. Indeed, in certain respects, *The Black Album* also endorses Fukuyama's vision of 'Islamic fundamentalism' as being akin to fascism. Riaz is an increasingly authoritarian figure, demanding absolute obedience from his followers, who are prepared to use threats to keep wavering recruits like Shahid in line. However, Kureishi goes further than Fukuyama in implicitly ridiculing the epistemology of Islam. The 'divine aubergine' phenomenon discredits those Muslims who see in it evidence of revelation and, by inference, the idea of revelation itself. Aside from its association with irrationality and despotism, neo-Orientalist stereotyping in *The Black Album* is evident in its 'framing' of Islam in terms of its humourlessness, philistinism and 'backward' conception of gender relations.

Kureishi's vision of a clear 'inside' and 'outside' in regard to who or what should be 'recognized' in western liberal societies has its correlates in the form he employs, a mode of comic realism with a clear *hierarchy* of narrative voices and spaces. While primarily focalized through Shahid, there is an omniscient narrator whose ironic distance from his protagonist diminishes as the latter increasingly approximates to the authorial vision of what is appropriate to the identity and identifications he constructs for himself. Around Shahid, at the centre of the novel, we have a number of more or less 'realist' characters, notably Deedee, who have relatively complex interiorities. By contrast, almost all the 'Muslim fanatics' exist in the discursively marginalizing mode of two-dimensional caricature. Consonant with its conventions, they are identifiable in the first instance by external markers—beards, veils, *kurtas* and speech mannerisms.

As its description of the bustling multicultural London mosque suggests, Kureishi's text certainly challenges Fukuyama's argument that Islam has little purchase in the West and that the problem of 'recognition' has been solved within the societies Fukuyama champions. Nonetheless, the predominantly comic register of *The Black Album* expresses its author's perception that the threat of 'fundamentalism' is minimal and that its exponents are primarily ridiculous and self-deluded rather than evil or, indeed, *rational* actors. (Thus Chad harms himself as much as mainstream society by his violence at the end). However, aside from expressing the complacency of the pre-9/11 era, such comedic conventions—with their moral-discursive demarcation of different *orders* of character/characterization—also demonstrate how any 'politics of recognition' almost inevitably segues into the 'policing of recognition'.

The inescapable inference to be drawn from *The Black Album* is that the more complexly-drawn ('liberal') characters are more fully human, as well as being more worthy citizens, than their 'fundamentalist' antagonists. If the latter are not necessarily 'bondsmen' in the Hegelian sense, their humanity is, in Fukuyama's formulation, 'as yet incomplete'.[20]

The Reluctant Fundamentalist

Judith Butler argues that such structures of discrimination are intrinsic to the dynamics of 'the politics of recognition' derived by Fukuyama and Taylor alike from *The Phenomenology of Mind*. She suggests that Hegel,

> misses a couple of important points. The terms by which we are recognized as human are socially articulated and changeable. And sometimes the very terms that confer 'humanness' on some individuals are those that deprive certain other individuals of the possibility of achieving that status . . . These norms have far-reaching consequences for how we understand the model of the human entitled to rights or included in the participatory sphere of political deliberation.[21]

It is these very 'norms' and the boundaries constituting them which Hamid's text complicates to such telling and chilling effect. He thereby suggests the infinitely more problematic nature of both effectively promoting the 'politics of recognition' according to 'liberal' models and of 'policing' it in the wake of 9/11, associated events like 7/7 in London, and the West's reactions to them.

This is partly a function of the greater global reach of *The Reluctant Fundamentalist* compared with *The Black Album*'s focus on one small corner of London. There are certainly hints of a link between Riaz and 'the Iranians' and acknowledgement that the worldwide predicament of Muslims plays some role in his anger. There is also evidence of identification with a newly-reconfigured *ummah* in Chad's insistence: 'No more Paki. Me a Muslim' (107). However, such transnational affiliations are central to Hamid's vision. Extending from Pakistan to New York and from Chile to the Philippines, the novella addresses the emergence of a new class of mobile, global citizens who, in Rushdie-esque fashion, defy the 'gravity' of traditional, territorialized belongings. Indeed, until 9/11 shatters the protagonist's complacency, one might be persuaded that Fukuyama's vision of a beneficently pluralized 'new world order' is well on the way to being realized.

Equally, the first part of *The Reluctant Fundamentalist* seems to suggest that 'recognition' is no longer a problem *within* western liberal democracies. Thus the economic system represented by Underwood Samson (as its initials suggest, a metonym for the 'US') welcomes workers irrespective of ethnicity or geographical origin, to the point that Changez soon feels 'completely comfortable' as 'a young New Yorker with the city at my feet'.[22] The Pak-Punjab Deli and Burmese restaurant which Changez frequents represent a dynamic of seemingly relaxed demographic, commodity and cultural exchange through which hybridity is increasingly 'recognized' as a defining characteristic of the West.

Yet even before the 9/11 attacks, Hamid's protagonist expresses reservations about the 'recognition' of the non-western subject afforded in the United States, the model from which Fukuyama extrapolates much of his argument. When compared to Kureishi's London, the terms on which it is offered, even to selected, privileged members of the migrant New York community—let alone the underclass which frequents the Pak-Punjab—are sometimes faulty or partial. Thus to some extent, Changez's initial success rests on rendering his 'Pakistaniness' invisible. He allows Jim to project onto him his own history of escape from white, working-class roots, so that his boss realizes too late the importance of his subordinate's Pakistani identity—notably the fact that, like Kureishi's Zulma, Changez is from the postcolonial elite. Most egregiously, he allows Erica, the allegorical figure of Am*erica*, to construct him in the image of her former lover Chris, symbolically turning the new immigrant Other into a version of the Same. On the other hand, like Shahid, Changez also suffers from moments when his difference is fetishized or essentialized. During the Greek vacation, the protagonist suspects he is 'well-liked as an exotic acquaintance' (17). Erica, meanwhile, at times overvalues the 'authenticity' of her Asian lover, being ravished by his Lahori clothes and treating him as a desirable accessory at the gallery-opening (compare Deedee's treatment of Shahid at 'The White Room'.)

After the 9/11 attacks, the existing regime of 'recognition' is shown to retract much too easily into a concern with 'policing' difference based on external signifiers like skin colour, rather than extending 'hospitality' towards non-western and, especially, Muslim, subjects. Changez has already found himself becoming annoyed at Erica's father's Orientalist stereotyping of Pakistan and it is the instantaneous generalization of such thinking in public discourse which generates the enormous apparatus of surveillance brought to bear in the wake of 9/11. This ranges from enhanced airport security to the everyday street-level harassment of American Muslims and greater difficulty in the job market. Even the hitherto privileged Changez becomes increasingly liable to the cruder forms of racist exclusion, most notably when he is misrecognized as a 'fucking Arab' during his mission to New Jersey. The 'recognition' he has thus far earned is progressively withdrawn, even in Underwood Samson, once he rebels against the new dispensation by the simple measure of growing a beard.

However, the text suggests that increasing globalization and transnational mobility in the period since the Fall of the Berlin Wall and the Rushdie Affair have made much more difficult the resurrection of traditional forms of 'policing recognition', symbolized during the Greek vacation by the redundant fortifications dividing West and East in Rhodes. The difficulty is announced from the very beginning of the text, as Changez and his unnamed interlocutor circle warily around each other. Is the narrator a 'terrorist' intent on having an American agent killed, or an amiable Lahori explaining his city to an innocent tourist—or some combination of such possibilities? Despite the foreboding built up through a series of successively more ominous hints, these key issues remain unresolved at the end. Is Changez leading the American back to the safety of his hotel or into an ambush? Or will he himself become 'collateral damage' in the 'war on terror', assassinated by a shadowy assailant who has 'misrecognized' him 'fundamentally'? The unsettling irresolution of such questions lends *The Reluctant Fundamentalist* much of its dramatic power. But it is also key to the text's central cultural-political concern, to make the reader re-*cognize* the term 'fundamentalism' contrary to how it is generally deployed in the West. As a property only of 'crazed and destitute radicals' (102), it is seductively easy to assume it to be identifiable for 'policing'.

In Hamid's text, 'fundamentalism' is much more difficult to 'recognize' and therefore 'police' for three principal reasons. Firstly, consonant with the profiles of the real-life 9/11 attackers, Hamid hints that the prime threat to the West lies in precisely the well-educated, upwardly and geographically mobile migrant constituency represented by Changez and, to a lesser degree, by Shahid in *The Black Album*. Whereas the latter's engagement with 'fundamentalism' is no more than a flirtation leading to clear affirmation of the 'procedural' liberal values of mainstream society, Changez's trajectory takes him in the opposite direction, towards the project of 'stopping' America—the supreme object of desire, by contrast, for Kureishi's secular Asian British characters like Chili. What now becomes dangerous to the West are precisely the hybrid qualities which have enabled Changez to take his place amongst the global captains of industry, whose transnational corporations have helped make traditional national boundaries so porous. It is his deterritorialized identity which makes Changez such an elusive target for the reader and, by implication, the putative American agent. His very name, with its echo of 'changes', suggests a chameleon-like protagonist whose affiliations—and loyalties—are impossible to fix with any certainty.

'Fundamentalism' is further difficult to 'recognize' and therefore 'police' because to this degree it is also seen as a function of globalization rather than simply a form of irredentist, reactionary anti-modernism of the kind associated with the group led by Riaz (who, like most of his semi-literate constituents, comes from village Pakistan). Changez is entirely at home in the world of laptops, the internet and GPS phones. Globalized communications systems fuel his increasing discontent with America and allow him to flit between continents to spread the message which has perhaps brought him to the attention of his unnamed interlocutor. Indeed, *The Reluctant Fundamentalist* reverses the teleologies within which 'fundamentalism' is stereotypically framed. It is the West which clings to 'traditional' conceptions of boundaries, both literal and symbolic, thereby making itself increasingly vulnerable to attack. Indeed, the forces it sends out to counter the threat to its hegemony are described as being almost medieval. This symbolizes the West's failure to 'recognize' the new kinds of opposition made available by the very forces of globalization it has unleashed on the rest of the world. Erica's regret for the certainties and securities of the vanished world associated with Chris (who is himself associated with the 'Old World') is allegorical of a whole culture's fatal nostalgia for 'a sort of *classical* period that had come and gone' (117). As Changez observes, 'it is not always possible to restore one's boundaries after they have been blurred . . . we cannot reconstitute ourselves as the autonomous beings we previously imagined ourselves to be' (173–174).

A third difficulty arises because of the way that Hamid links 'fundamentalism' to forms of principled and *rationally*-framed anti-colonial resistance. For example, Changez's disaffection is partly stimulated by well-established traditions of 'Third World' nationalism. Already troubled by the invasion of Iraq, and well-aware since his visit to the Philippines of the dishonourable history of US interventions in Asia, notably Vietnam, the protagonist is dismayed by the extension of the 'war on terror' to Afghanistan. However, it is only when his homeland of Pakistan comes under direct threat, notably from America's regional proxy India, that he begins to consider severing his material links with the West. It is at this point that Changez decides he cannot be away from home. In this respect it is important to 'recognize' that Changez's political activism is henceforth centred on an attempt to have Pakistan disengage from an increasingly 'bondsman'-like relationship with its American 'master', a trajectory which has countless precedents in anti-colonial history and literature.

Further, Changez's resistance is linked to the long tradition of leftist pursuit of social and political justice. In contrast to both Fukuyama and Kureishi, Hamid's text suggests that it may be premature to dismiss left politics, particularly as a locus of opposition to American-led globalization and its analogues, notably 'the war on terror'. The aggressive nature of contemporary US capitalism is suggested by the military imagery with which it is consistently represented. Thus Changez's unnamed interlocutor is seen, interchangeably, as a businessman/special agent. As a new 'recruit' to Underwood Samson, Changez 'reports for duty' to a boss called Sherman, invoking the standard American tank of World War II, and Jim more than once praises his subordinate's 'warrior' qualities. The protagonist's blinders about the colonial nature of globalization first come off when he is 'recognized' as an agent of empire in the Philippines, a process repeated in Chile, where he has an epiphany after visiting the home of the socialist and anti-colonialist Nobel Laureate poet, Pablo Neruda. Such moments are not framed in terms of religious awakening but as the product of rational weighing of empirical evidence. This leads Changez to a 'recognition' of the effects of unremitting pursuit of profit, primarily at the expense of the non-western world but also, importantly, at home—as in his New Jersey operation. This ruthless ethos is reflected in the corporate maxim of Underwood Samson, 'focus on the fundamentals' (98). Thus the title of Hamid's text may refer as much to Changez's growing disillusion with global capitalism, increasingly represented as the greatest threat to the world, as to any incipient attachment to 'Islamic fundamentalism'.

Indeed, 'Islamic fundamentalism' as habitually conceived in western public discourse ostensibly plays little part in Changez's growing disaffection. Until he grows a beard, he has none of the visible markers of the stereotypical 'Muslim fanatic' found in *The Black Album*. Indeed, unlike Shahid, we never even see him in a mosque, or even at prayer. However, consonant with his hybrid identifications, the protagonist retains many characteristics of a 'cultural Muslim' in America. His politeness, charitableness, deference to elders, as well as his continuing interest in Islamic culture as represented by Mughal miniatures, for example, are all symptoms of his formation in Lahore. On his first flight back to Pakistan, Changez's discomfort with his fellow passenger is not because the latter prays in the aisle, but on account of his fatalistic views about nuclear annihilation. Thus it is little surprise that the protagonist's political awakening is partly motivated by his sense of 'kinship' with Muslim Afghanistan or that the demonstration he organizes against the US in Lahore is attended by 'religious literalists' (100, 179). The conjuncture of such activists with transnational subjects like Changez, as well as 'communists, capitalists, feminists' (179), suggests the emergence of a rainbow coalition of opponents to American imperialism (or globalization) impossible to manage effectively by conventional forms of 'policing', material or discursive.

That Hamid's analysis of both 'fundamentalism' and the dynamics of the 'politics of recognition' is so much more troubling than Kureishi's is also attributable to his choice of form. Cast in the form of first-person dramatic monologue, his novella enforces the argument that there is no 'inside' or 'outside' to the problematic of 'recognition', as might be inferred from the omniscient narrative and comedic conventions of *The Black Album*. Changez's western guest never speaks directly and everything is reported through a narrator whose account, he himself hints, should not necessarily be taken at face value. This reinforces the claustrophobic nature of the reading experience, aligning the reader with the American, making him/her struggle to gain sufficient distance to make decisions about whether Changez is, indeed, a 'fundamentalist' and, if so, of what kind. However, consonant with the protagonist's investment in cultural hybridity, the difficulty of achieving 'perspective' on such issues may owe something to the narrative template of the 'Mughal miniature', which is cited more than once. Hamid perhaps draws most obviously on its characteristic techniques of compression but it is also significant that such work does not conform to the perspectival conventions of post-Renaissance visual representation in the West. Consequently, the challenge for the viewer/reader to grasp the relationships between different aspects of the work in question is significantly greater than in a perspectivally 'realist' work like Kureishi's.

Hamid's text can easily be read as much darker in tone than *The Black Album*. Globalization is viewed as a dispensation characterized not by the more or less harmonious extension of 'recognition', whether within western liberal societies or across the world, but of increasing tension and conflict based on a binaristic vision of the Other. This is something more akin to 'the clash of civilizations' envisaged by Samuel Huntington in his celebrated riposte to Fukuyama.[23] Nonetheless, *The Reluctant Fundamentalist* is also, paradoxically, perhaps more hopeful than Kureishi's text. The dissolution of old boundaries and the impossibility of restoring them speaks to a 'third space' of common ground between the global antagonists. Thus while 'fundamentalists' of all kinds in both texts retreat to a more or less black-and-white vision of intercultural relations, Changez retains his 'in-between' location to a significant degree. Professing at the outset of the text that he remains a 'lover' of America, the protagonist's continuing deep immersion in western culture is signified by his argot, allusions to Hollywood films and citation of western literary texts, notably Conrad's *The Secret Sharer* and *Heart of Darkness*.[24] Indeed, the fact that he aligns himself with Kurtz, the dissident *westerner*, rather than any of the native rebels of postcolonial literature, is further symptomatic of the ambiguous zone from within which he troubles the traditional dynamics of 'recognition'.

Conclusion

Hamid has argued that the flipside of the insecurity brought upon the West by the 9/11 attacks is a radical insecurity in the Islamic world, as every Muslim country wonders anxiously whether it will be the next to be invaded or bombed.[25] Contrary to American exceptionalist myths of 'difference', this suggests that the 'pain' which apparently *divides* the West and the Islamic world is also, paradoxically, 'shared'. If this was *mutually* 'recognized', the text implies, it might provide the basis of negotiations towards a more productive future relationship between the two sides.

However, it could nonetheless be argued in turn that Hamid himself does not altogether solve the problem of normativity in his questioning of the frameworks within which Fukuyama, Taylor and Kureishi operate respectively. *The Reluctant Fundamentalist* certainly persuades the reader that his protagonist is no sociopath by emphasizing the moral conflicts he experiences and attempts to solve by rational ethical means. Perhaps the most 'subversive' and challenging aspect of the book is thereby to impart, by association, some measure of rational political calculation and moral energy to the 9/11 attackers.

However, to 'translate' the phenomenon of 'fundamentalism' into the honourable and, above all, secular, tropes of an older tradition of leftist anti-colonialism or Third World nationalism is to risk *re*-presenting resistance to American-led globalization in terms which can be more or less comfortably 'recognized' by the liberal metropolitan reader. To this degree, the issue of the representability of 'Islamic fundamentalism' *per se* is not fully 'solved' within either text under discussion here. Indeed, one might ask whether it can ever be represented adequately in the current climate of vexed relations between the West and certain Muslim formations or whether the phenomenon is 'unwritable' in the sense that its subject is doomed, to adapt Fukuyama's formulation, to remain '[unrecognizable] as a *human being*, that is, as a being with a certain worth or dignity'.[26]

Taylor's call for a more 'hospitable' form of liberal society seems to have fallen by the wayside in the face of the rise of new political groupings in the West of a specifically anti-Muslim character—from the English Defence League, to Holland's Freedom Party and the Sweden Democrats, the latter two organizations having now gained significant electoral power. But the difficulties are equally apparent in the current wholesale rush in mainstream western political thinking back towards 'assimilation' as the appropriate mode of engagement with minorities of non-western provenance, especially Muslim ones, rather than further elaboration of the Taylorian 'mosaic' model, based on the principle of a pluralistic respect for difference.[27]

Thus the conditions within which the Muslim religious subject, let alone 'Islamic fundamentalism', might be addressed more adequately than Kureishi manages, or Hamid attempts, appear to be as far off as ever. Given that the novel is a space for *novel* imaginings *par excellence*, this does not bode well for the emergence of the kind of regime of 'recognition' which will be necessary to end the standoff between parts of the West and some of its Muslim antagonists. If they are ever to be constituted, then, as Judith Butler has also argued, a new kind of social imagination is needed. This might perhaps involve shifting the emphasis within 'the politics of recognition' towards the acknowledgement of what is new, even unprecedented, rather than confirmation of what is already known. This is not a call, in Butler's words, 'to celebrate difference as such but to establish more inclusive conditions for sheltering and maintaining life that resists [sic] models of assimilation'. It involves, as she goes on to argue, a willingness

> in the name of the human, to allow the human to become something other than what it is traditionally assumed to be . . . we must learn to live and to embrace the destruction and rearticulation of the human in the name of a more capacious and, finally, less violent world, not knowing in advance what precise form our humanness does and will take.[28]

Notes

1. Francis Fukuyama, *The End of History and The Last Man* (London: Penguin, 1992), xvi.
2. Ibid., xvii.

3.　Ibid., xx.

4.　Ibid., 245.

5.　Ibid., xviii.

6.　Charles Taylor, 'The Politics of Recognition', in Amy Gutmann, ed., *Multicultur-alism: Examining the Politics of Recognition* (Princeton: Princeton University Press, 1994), 25–26.

7.　Ibid., 43.

8.　Ibid.

9.　Ibid., 39.

10.　Ibid., 61.

11.　Fukuyama, *End of History*, 236, 46.

12.　Ibid., xi, 284.

13.　Taylor, 'Politics,' 63.

14.　http://en.wikipedia.org/wiki/Islam_in_Canada (accessed 10 June 2011). Tay-lor's more recent work, by comparison, is inflected by much greater awareness of 'substantive communities of Muslims' in the West for his thinking. See, for example, 'Why We Need a Radical Redefinition of Secularism', in Eduardo Mendieta and Jonathan Vanatwerpen, eds, *The Power of Religion in the Public Sphere* (New York: Columbia University Press, 2011), 36.

15.　http://www.mcb.org.uk/library/statistics.php#1 (accessed 10 June 2011).

16.　Hanif Kureishi, *The Black Album* (London: Faber, 1995), 5. All subsequent refer-ences are to this edition.

17.　Taylor, 'Politics', 65.

18.　Frantz Fanon, *Black Skin, White Masks*, trans. C. L. Markmann (London: Pluto, 1986 [1952]), 220 (emphasis added).

19.　Taylor, 'Politics', 63.

20.　Fukuyama, *End of History*, xvii.

21.　Judith Butler, *Undoing Gender* (London: Routledge, 2004), 2. Compare Butler, *Excitable Speech: A Politics of the Performative* (New York: Routledge, 1997), 5.

22.　Mohsin Hamid, *The Reluctant Fundamentalist* (London: Hamish Hamilton, 2007), 48, 45. All subsequent references are to this edition.

23.　Samuel Huntington, *The Clash of Civilizations and the Remaking of World Order* (New York: Simon and Schuster, 1996).

24.　There isn't space to explore these intertexts on the present occasion; however, the formal as well as thematic parallels between the former work and Hamid's are particularly striking.

25.　At a reading at Senate House, University of London, 9 October 2007. The podcast of this interview is available at http://www.framingmuslims.org/event-archive.html?start=16 (accessed 10 June 2011).

26.　Kureishi's film script *My Son the Fanatic* (1997) represents a significant improve-ment on *The Black Album* in this respect. However, the efforts of *novels* like John Updike's *Terrorist* (2006) 'to get inside the mind' of 'Islamic fundamentalists' have proved largely unconvincing.

27.　See, for example, then Prime Minister Gordon Brown's 'The Future of British-ness' (2006), http://www.fabians.org.uk/events/speeches/the-future-of-britishness; compare German Chancellor Angela Merkel's critique of German multicultur-alism in October 2010, http://www.bbc.co.uk/news/world-europe-11559451; and David Cameron's attack on 'state multiculturalism' in February 2011, http://

www.bbc.co.uk/news/uk-politics-12371994. This was endorsed by the leaders of both the British National Party and the French *Front National*: http://www.guardian.co.uk/commentisfree/2011/feb/09/cameron-scapegoating-muslims-toxic-impact?intcmp=239; and http://www.guardian.co.uk/world/2011/feb/10/marine-le-pen-cameron-multiculturalism. All accessed 10 June 2011.

28. Butler, *Undoing Gender*, 4, 35.

12 Resistance and Religion in the Work of Kamila Shamsie

Ruvani Ranasinha

This essay explores the work of Pakistani author Kamila Shamsie (b. 1973) who grew up in Karachi, was partially educated in the US and is now based in London. As the daughter of the literary critic Muneeza Shamsie, and the grand-niece of the author Attia Hosain, Shamsie pays homage to the three generations of women writers in her family: 'while I grew up in the harsh world of a misogynist military government in 1980s Pakistan—where women's freedom was severely threatened—my familial legacy enabled me to imagine, without pressure or expectation, a life centred around writing'.[1] Shamsie's first novel *In the City by the Sea* (1998) was short-listed for the John Llewellyn Rhys and *Mail on Sunday* Prize and awarded Pakistan's Prime Minister's Award for Literature. Explorations of Karachi and Pakistani cultural identity followed in *Salt and Saffron* (2000) and *Kartography* (2002). This essay seeks to examine Shamsie's engagement with the politics of representation and counter-representation of Islam and Muslim identities, with a particular focus on the overlapping parameters of gender, religion, secularism and female emancipation. It explores her more recent work, notably her fourth novel *Broken Verses* (2005), and her Orange Prize-nominee novel *Burnt Shadows* (2009) which traverses Japan, Pakistan, the US and Afghanistan, alongside her collection of essays *Offence: The Muslim Case* (2009) published as part of a series in association with *Index on Censorship*.

As a Pakistani female author from an elite, westernized, avowedly secular background who distinguishes between Islam as a religion (of *taqwa*) and a culture, Shamsie's fiction and non-fiction needs to be considered in terms of three related contexts. First, Shamsie belongs to a new generation of Anglophone Pakistani authors trying to bring the predicament of their country to an international audience that is fixated by its turbulent political situation. Contemporary geopolitical shifts have changed the world's awareness of the nuclear-armed Pakistani nation (of 170 million) and its tenuous grip on democracy. Seen as under grave threat from Islamic extremists, Pakistan is often headlined as 'the most dangerous place in the world', or in the former British Prime Minister Gordon Brown's words during a visit to Pakistan as 'a crucible of terror'.[2] The anxiety that Pakistan and religious fundamentalism

arouses in post-9/11 North America and Western Europe is brilliantly articulated in Mohsin Hamid's Man Booker Prize short-listed novel *The Reluctant
Fundamentalist* (2007). Although writing for over a decade, Shamsie, alongside others of her generation, has only come to the fore in recent years, eclipsing the Indian writers who dominated the 1990s, because of this confluence
of literary and political interests. News coverage and a media boom have
helped these writers win both acclaim and readerships hungry for stories
beyond the headlines and the bombs, and from less well-known parts of the
Indian subcontinent.

Secondly, Shamsie belongs to a particular generation of writers from Pakistan's small English-speaking elite who had been able to live an insulated
lifestyle up to the 1980s, and whose coming of age under the oppressive
dictatorship of General Zia ul-Haq was a dramatic wrenching change that
created a fertile ground for writers.[3] Shamsie's fascination with writing fictional lives set against a backdrop of politics is fuelled by her experiences
growing up under a censoring dictatorship. Rushdie's novel *Shame* (1982)
was, she recalls,

> the first clear indication that fiction was a place of truth, more trustwor-
> thy than the news. Given this strange disconnect between the factual yet
> inaccurate picture created by censored news, and the fictional yet true
> worlds of novels, it's hardly surprising that for many of us who grew up
> in states of censorship one of the most compelling urges in our fiction is
> to tell those stories that have been suppressed.[4]

These 'stories' include Mohammed Hanif's debut novel long-listed for the
2008 Man Booker Prize *A Case of Exploding Mangoes*—a dark comedy about
the Islamic fundamentalist rule of General Zia ul-Haq in the 1980s—Nadeem
Aslam's *The Wasted Vigil* (2008) which is set in modern Afghanistan (Aslam's
father was exiled under Zia ul-Haq) and Ali Sethi's *The Wish Maker* (2009).

Thirdly, Shamsie's fiction and her journalism/essays are in dialogue with
the increasing number of fictional and non-fictional representations of Islam
and Muslims by Muslim and non-Muslim authors and commentators. Her
work connects to both public and political discourses with regards to political realignments since the Cold War, the Rushdie Affair, the ongoing effect
of international suspicion and demonization of Muslim identities after the
9/11 attacks, the inception of the so-called 'war on terror', the London bombings of 2005, and the negative effects of contemporary discourses of Islamophobia. These responses include increasingly reductive views of Islam and
Islamic fundamentalism, and a more pronounced dichotomy between Islam
and the West. Shamsie comments wryly on the absence of 'stone-throwing
fundamentalists'[5] in her novels, alluding perhaps to Hanif Kureishi's narrow
representations (particularly in his novel *The Black Album* (1995)) of Muslim
identity that define Islam exclusively in terms of a violent, repressive form of

fundamentalism that evokes many well-worn stereotypes of Muslims in the western media.[6] Unlike British-born writers Monica Ali, Zadie Smith and Kureishi, Shamsie is less concerned to explore why Islam is so appealing to some second- and third-generation British-born Muslims. Instead her focus is on the minutiae of lived experience in Pakistan amongst a predominantly elite and cosmopolitan class. Countering simple demonizations of Islam, Shamsie's early fictional texts—*In the City by the Sea* (1998), *Salt and Saffron* (2000), *Kartography* (2002) and *Broken Verses* (2005)—delineate instead, the political manipulation of religion by all parties and governments through Pakistan's history. Her writings collectively question those who argue Pakistan's religious right problem began with the rule of Zia ul-Haq in 1977, by drawing attention to both Zulfikar Ali Bhutto, and subsequently Benazir Bhutto's capitulation to the hardliners despite campaigning on a secular, socialist platform.[7] Nevertheless, it is the ruthless Islamization of Pakistan by Zia ul-Haq (1977–1988) and the hijacking of Islam under his military dictatorship that come under the most scrutiny in her oeuvre: 'but it was the General in the wings who decided to show everyone how Islamization was really done'.[8] Thus, Shamsie's engagement with questions of gender, religion and secularism needs to be examined in relation to the burden of representation in the reception and circulation of the fictional and non-fictional works of a new generation of women writers from Muslim backgrounds writing in the context of discourses that fix Islam as inherently patriarchal, alongside hegemonic representations of Muslim women as victims within Islamic societies.

While numerous male commentators articulate such hegemonic views of Islam, I am interested in assessing Shamsie's intervention in this regard in relation to the recent trend evident in novels such as Azar Nafisi's bestseller *Reading Lolita in Tehran* (2004), which reconstruct 'authentic' female Muslim voices for western audiences. Such texts, as Mitra Rastegar has argued, are liberation narratives 'that reconstitute Orientalist attitudes toward Islamic societies'.[9] Furthermore, such female-authored texts often enact a means of demarcating the female author's own 'progressive' distance from Islam.[10] So, in contrast to Ayaan Hirsi Ali's conceptualization of misogyny (alongside violent anti-Semitism) at the heart of Islam rather than just at its militant periphery in her memoir *Infidel: My Life* (2007), how do Shamsie's novels situate themselves differently within debates surrounding Muslim women? I want to begin by delineating Shamsie's engagement with hegemonic constructions of Islam as inherently antithetical to women's rights. To what extent does she explore female oppression, interleave issues of Islamic culture and female emancipation and counter views of Muslim women as victims in her novel *Broken Verses* (2005)?

This family mystery concerns thirty-year-old protagonist Aasmaani, a researcher for a Karachi TV station who has never dealt with the feelings of betrayal when her activist mother, the inspirational feminist icon Samina Akram, disappeared fourteen years ago. Unable to cope with the imprisonment and eventual murder of her dissident lover ('The Poet', Aasmaani's 'step-father') whose work was critical of the excesses of Pakistan's military regime, Samina goes missing and is presumed drowned. This familial narrative is embedded within a larger story of the resistance to the rise of the Islamic right, Zia ul-Haq's military dictatorship and oppression of women, notably, the Hudood Ordinances: rape victims were accused of adultery and stoned to death, and rape could only be proved in a court of law if there were four pious male Muslim adults willing to give eye-witness testimony; the Islamic law of evidence decreed in legal matters the evidence of two women equalled that of a man.[11]

Broken Verses deconstructs ideas of Islam as inherently patriarchal by individualizing Zia's particular brand of Islam as a misogynist deployment of religion to assert control over women: 'This move towards theocracy [Zia's announcement that Sharia law would be supreme] sent violent tremors down the spine of the women's movement, which knew that Zia's Islam concerned itself primarily with striking down the rights of women and befriending fundamentalists' (*BV* 138). The novel argues that the exegesis of the Quran influenced by certain cultural norms of the era oppresses women, rather than the teachings of the Quran itself. The novel reiterates the patriarchal interpretation of Quran, and the role of human agency in Islamic jurisprudence through the Poet and Samina, who despite their flaws remain the moral compass of the novel as touchstones for democracy, accountability and justice: '"How can words be used for such indignity?" the Poet said, when he heard the details of the [Hudood] laws being passed in the name of Islam' (*BV* 91). Significantly, critique is not the preserve of the secular atheists: Aasmaani's grandfather 'the most gentle and pious of men, wept himself to death over it' (*BV* 91). The gap between patriarchal interpretation and the actual teachings of the Quran is foregrounded throughout. We learn Samina 'went to Egypt to work with women's groups and discovered the feminist traditions within Islam which would allow her to battle the hard-liners on their own turf' (*BV* 94). We witness her public debate with the Maulana where she contends that the laws of the Quran do not enjoin women to cover their head in public. The Maulana insists 'what is relevant is the commonly accepted usage' (*BV* 283).

While Shamsie's fiction depicts Pakistan as a deeply patriarchal country, she is equally concerned to map the thriving women's movements that have campaigned against the social and legal strictures against women: 'in the wake of the Hudood Ordinance the women's movement in Pakistan began to assert itself . . . it went into high gear with the formation of the Women's Action Forum in 1981' (*BV* 91). This preoccupation originates in her debut novel *In the City by the Sea* (1998). A fusion of a lyrical Bildungsroman of eleven-year-old Hasan (whose uncle Salman is charged with treason and imprisoned) with a powerful study of life under a military dictatorship in a high-spirited, liberal household in Karachi, it depicts a local feminist campaign for illegally dispossessed widows.

To what extent does this emphasis on resistance counter still persistent stereotypical representations of women in Islamic societies as archetypal victims? Constructed around real events, *Broken Verses* offers a measured assessment of the feminist gains of the dissident movements of Aasmaani's mother's generation. The novel gives its non-Pakistani/western implied reader a potted history of the 'astonishing bravery' of the women activists taking on the military government, interleaved through Aasmaani's recollections of the harrowing days of her mother and the Poet's experience of 'prison, protest and exile' (*BV* 95). The novel's arguments are refracted through its protagonist's interior debate. Aasmaani's memory of the 'headiness at the centre of all the anti-government activity' is counter-pointed with her recall of the *lathi*-inflicted 'vicious bruises on mother' (*BV* 95), as well as her eventual understanding of the brutal circumstance of the Poet's murder when he paid for his integrity with 'every shattered bone' of his body (*BV* 215).

The actual achievements of the Women's Action Forum are spelt out: 'the Islamic law of evidence was amended to pertain only to financial matters. Safia Bibi, the blind rape victim sentenced for adultery was acquitted. The Ansari Commisson's recommendation that women be barred from high office never became law' (*BV* 94–95). Yet, the evaluation of feminist gains is mediated through the anguish of the adult daughter who struggles to come to terms with her mother's suicide after the Poet's death. In the face of the continued stranglehold of Pakistan's military regime on the novel's present, Aasmaani initially believes her 'mother's life as an activist, brave as it had been, was a lesson in futility' (*BV* 287). The novel's narrative arc traces Aasmaani's gradual acceptance of her mother's own appraisal of their achievements unearthed from a recording made before her death:

> it's not about the ultimate victory . . . True in concrete battles the tyrants may have the upper hand in terms of tactics, weapons and ruthlessness. What our means of protest attempt to do is move the battles towards abstract space. Force tyranny to defend itself in language . . . remember history outlives you. (*BV* 335, 338)

Aasmaani confronts the demons of her own past and of her country's recent history. The novel traces her growing respect for, and understanding of the choices Samina made during her childhood, 'going out to fight laws which say rape victims can be found guilty of adultery' rather then staying home to help with her homework (*BV* 257). Aasmaani resents having to defend her mother's political activism in a society that dictates 'that a woman's actions are only of value if they can be linked to maternal instincts' (*BV* 254). This is part of the novel's broader commentary on the arbitrariness of gender binaries, the associated dilemmas of educated women in contemporary Pakistan and the tensions experienced by women between the demands of children and their own lives and work. Samina's politicized activism and questionable maternal and sexually transgressive nature contest fixed pre-defined female subjectivities, provide a subversive female national icon and reconstruct the larger narrative of the nation and of women's roles within it, undermining patriarchal nationalist paradigms such as the 'woman as nation trope'.[12] Samina's participation in public debates and protests seeks an alternative form of nation where women are not subject to discriminatory laws and underlines the porous boundaries between domestic private and public spheres. *Broken Verses* emphasizes the performance and the manipulation of gender identities by revealing the construction as well as the dissolution of identity. At moments of trauma the novel reveals the fictive nature of identity itself: unravelled by grief 'Samina unbecame the woman she had been for so long' (*BV* 272–273). It is the marginal character, Samina's best friend, the lesbian actress Shehnaz Saeed, who most successfully articulates the radical displacement of gender and sexual norms, whilst also reinforcing a secular feminist critique of patriarchal interpretations of Islam, and contributing to the novel's dominant mocking, irreverent and comedic tone:

> already the mullahs in the Frontier are saying, 'Of course women can work, but only according to the guidelines of Islam.' What guidelines? There are no such guidelines! Maybe that's another reason for coming out of retirement. I don't want to be one of those women the beards approve of, the ones that sit at home and cook dinner. (*BV* 59)

Nevertheless, how does Shamsie's portrayal of both these secular Pakistani feminist activists impinge on her interleaving of Islam/Islamic culture and female emancipation? How does *Broken Verses* engage with the gendered parameters of the conflict between piety and secularism? The novel dramatizes the clash between the government and the activists as that of Islamic jurisprudence versus secular jurisprudence. Samina 'saw that her own belief in secular jurisprudence was not sufficient to take on a government intent on claiming its laws were God-ordained' (*BV* 93). The novel advances a liberal vision of secular pluralism. Towards the end of the novel, alluding to the blasphemy laws invoked against religious minorities, Samina summarizes their fight as 'expanding people's notions of what it means to be Pakistani' (*BV* 335). In this way the novel mirrors the explicitly secular stance that the actual Women's Action Forum had at its apex: one that deepened the divide between Islam and the secular. Since the death of Zia ul-Haq, the Women's Action Forum recognized its class bias, responded to critiques of the link between its secularism and the class background of its members and reassessed its hostile stance towards Islam, moving towards textually-based critiques of the Quran.[13] The novel reflects the class divide between westernized elite Cambridge-educated activists like Samina, and the disempowered maid imprisoned and unpaid by her employer, whose suicide acts as catalyst for Samina's active role in politics: 'it took an illiterate village woman's bloodied end to draw all those political ideals away from the abstract margins of her life and place them front-and-centre' (*BV* 87). The plight of this unnamed woman marks the limits of Shamsie's attempt to give voice to the suppressed, overlooked subaltern women. Samina 'goes from city to city, and often to smaller towns talking about the need to politicise women, to bring them together, to do something' (*BV* 93). Samina's debate with the Maulana enacts the shift towards the Women's Action Forum's feminist critique of the Quran. Expressing surprise at Samina's familiarity with the Quran, the Maulana deliberately assumes 'Shakespeare of West might carry more weight with you' and attempts to position Samina and the feminism she represents as something imported, 'westernised' and external to Pakistan (*BV* 285). This is an assumption the novelist challenges more fully in *Burnt Shadows*, in its suggestion that contemporary Pakistani notions of gender equality are not the imposition of western gender norms upon Muslim culture.

At the same time, the novel reflects Samina's generation of secular Pakistani feminists' discomfort with Islam and Islamic rituals. While we learn that Samina 'never fasted', in contrast, Aasmaani's younger generation find comfort in the rituals of cultural Islam, with religion playing a habitual role: 'Year after year, Eid in Dad and Beema's house followed a pattern as unvarying and comforting as the progression of the moon from sliver to sphere' (*BV* 223). The text celebrates the communal: Aasmani explains 'This was one of the chief joys of Ramzan—this evidence of everyone engaged in eating before daybreak, the transformation of that solitary hour into something communal' (*BV* 133). Again, this contrasts with Kureishi's representations of British Muslims where there is no representation of the communal that is not fundamentalist. Furthermore, unlike Kureishi, Shamsie tries to maintain a notion of secularism that is communal.[14]

This mixing of the sacred and the secular upturns entrenched conceptions of the two as discrete categories. The narrative presents Aasmaani and her cousins' younger generation as a new social formation: their ease with Islamic culture is not some reactionary throwback to prescribed gender roles as their mocking of the older aunt's admonition to the defiantly single, wisecracking Aasmaani not to 'die a virgin' makes clear (*BV* 226). By the close of the novel, having come to terms with her mother's suicide, Aasmaani, part of this new formation, moves away from her generation's characteristic disenchantment with and apathy towards political activism. She adopts a more activist role 'as a researcher for a documentary about the women's movement in Pakistan, to be broadcast in time for the twentieth anniversary of the Hudood Ordinances . . . a direct assault on the religious parties on the Frontier' (*BV* 335).

A further means by which the novel complicates binary notions of religion versus the secular is in the portrayal of the Poet who although resolutely opposed to 'organised religion' is immersed in the mystical Sufi tradition of Islam.[15] He describes the Sufi version of Lucifer and Adam's expulsion from

Eden (*Iblis aur Aadam*) as 'the first and final love story . . . we are just players in that great story Iblis and Allah' (*BV* 212). Aasmaani's recollections of the Poet's acolytes, 'all those poets in love with God', underscore the plurality of interpretations of Islam that flourished in Pakistan, that are now under threat more than a decade later in the novel's present. Aasmaani's admonition to the poet Mirza who now no longer thinks of Him because 'God has become the most dangerous subject of all' makes clear what is at stake if Mirza chooses to then leave God 'in the hands of the extremists' (*BV* 216). Aasmaani's sister Rabia reinforces this point: 'If you boycott religion because of them you only strengthen their claim to be the guardians and interpreters of that religion' (*BV* 133). Once again, Shamsie broadens Kureishi's rigidly dualistic approach by showing individuals opposed to fundamentalism can still be religious.

Although the novel complicates what Tariq Modood has described as perceptions that 'religion divides, the secular unites . . . Religion is "backward", secularism is progressive', it explicitly endorses the secularist positioning of piety and faith within the private and not public sphere.[16] This is articulated through the Poet's expressions of outrage:

> 'They're out there,' he had rallied once, walking up and down my mother's dining room, waving his finger in the air. 'They're out there, those men of war and politics, shouting about their God, insisting everyone own up to their relationship with Him, declare your devotion down on your knees, in Arabic, for all the world to see. It's an obscenity to make love so public'. (*BV* 213)

Condemning the performativity of faith in public and the pushing of 'internal, intimate belief' into 'something increasingly represented outwardly', *Broken Verses* privileges an avowedly secularist stance (*O* 56–57). *Burnt Shadows* reinforces the separation of public and private spheres that underpins conceptions of secularism in almost exactly the same terms: its protagonist Sajjad, settled in 1980s Karachi, similarly

> cursed the government, which kept trying to force religion into everything public. His mother, with her most intimate relationship with Allah, would have . . . told the President he should have more shame than to ask all citizens to conduct their love affair with the Almighty out in the open. (*BS* 147)

Thus both texts sanction a western model of democracy that separates 'church' from state, and privilege conceptions of religion faith as individualistic.

As we will see, Shamsie's subsequent novel *Burnt Shadows* (2009) develops some of the insights and representations of Islam delineated in *Broken Verses*. At first sight, *Burnt Shadows*' epic transnational articulations of Islam, and geographical imaginary on a global scale—with its depiction of intercultural bonds between two families across three generations of world conflict within the sweep of a violent century—contrast with the apparently Karachi-centric focus of *Broken Verses* and Shamsie's earlier fiction. However, many of the weighty questions of terrorism and its causes that Shamsie explores in the broader, sweeping canvas of *Burnt Shadows*, first emerge in a more distilled form in *Broken Verses*.

Broken Verses maps the wider circuitry of the rise of the religious right in Pakistan. It underscores the global politics that impinge on Pakistan especially in relation to the western nations that supported the religious fundamentalists, and failed to take a stand against the military dictatorship because of the Soviet invasion of Afghanistan. A stance satirized within the narrative when the Poet is told not to bother applying to America for asylum: 'Freedom of speech was all very well, but there was no need to exercise it against a government that was helping in the fight against communism' (*BV* 53). The novel critiques the human cost of emerging fundamentalist pan-Islamic notions of citizenship. In their debate, Samina excoriates the Maulana:

> You take a *territorial* issue of Afghanistan and you make it into a matter of religious duty—you and your unlikely bedfellows in the West. You spout phrases like unity of ummah as you hand . . . young, idealistic confused, angry, devout ready to be brain-washed boys . . . from Jordan, Syria, Sudan, Algeria, Egypt . . . the most sophisticated weapons . . . and tell them to get the infidel Soviets of Muslim soil. (*BV* 285–286, emphasis added)

Samina's insistence that 'Soil has no religion, Maulana' anticipates some of the arguments that appear in Shamsie's long essay *Offence*. Here Shamsie rejects conceptions of Islam in terms of deterrorialized space, and formulations that produce deterritorialized forms of religious identity that cannot be categorized within national frameworks, and appears to conceptualize the *ummah* as a politically regressive concept.[17]

Samina's anticipation of the bloodshed to come is poignant:

> What happens after Afghanistan, have you considered that? Where do they go next, those global guerrillas with their allegiance to a common cause and their belief in violence as the most effective way to take on the enemy? Do you and your American friends ever sit down to talk about that? (*BV* 286)

Samina's insistent reminder of America's unscrupulous global interventions form the subject of *Burnt Shadows*, which dramatizes (within a broader historical context) how American and British colonialism unleashed the spectre of 'Islamic' terrorism and today's violence. *Burnt Shadows* moves from Nagasaki in August 1945 to Delhi on the eve of Partition where Hiroko, a heart-broken survivor of the atom bomb that kills her German fiancé Konrad Weiss, flees to the home of his sister, Ilse Weiss, and her English husband, James Burton. Hiroko marries the Burton's Muslim employee Sajjad Ashraf and they leave India to raise their son Raza in the new country of Pakistan. The narrative fast-forwards to the 1980s where their lives become fatally entangled with anti-Soviet *mujahideen*, the Taliban and the CIA, where James and Ilse's son, Harry Burton, a covert CIA operative in Cold War Pakistan and his interpreter Raza have joined forces in a private security firm. The final section alternates between New York in the aftermath of 9/11 and Afghanistan in the wake of the ensuing bombing campaign, and hurtles towards a dramatic close with Raza waiting to be shipped off to prison in Guantánamo Bay.

With its broader historical sweep revealing the impact of shared transnational histories and perspectives through repeated echoes and patterns, *Burnt Shadows* reconfigures views of suicide bombers and militant assertions of radical Islam as unique and unprecedented. Hiroko recalls Japanese boys 'who dreamed of kamikaze' as forgotten precursors of the 'new wave of aggressive religion' amongst her students in Karachi in the 1980s, compared to whom 'these Karachi boys with their strange fervour for a world of rigidity were posturing youths'.[18]

The passages where Raza runs away with the militant Afghan Abdullah (whose 'brother died winning *their* Cold War') to a *mujahideen* camp in the 'vast, thrilling playground' of northern Pakistan with tragic consequences, recall Samina's fear about 'what happens after Afghanistan' (*BS* 352, emphasis added). The legacy of CIA backing for the anti-Soviet *mujahideen*'s resistance war, and abandonment of them once the Soviet army withdrew, is now replayed in 'Jihadi blowback'. Nevertheless, *Burnt Shadows* is not a 'three-generational tale of white oppression' as the *Washington Post* review claims.[19] Shamsie places responsibility for the rise of religious extremism on both the Americans and Pakistanis: the emergence of the Taliban is equally what Pakistan has done to itself. *Burnt Shadows* articulates a forceful, unequivocal condemnation of the 'Black-turbaned men who had banned everything of joy, blasted ancient prophets out of mountain faces . . . as the work of infidels' and who indoctrinate the young men into an intolerance of women: 'Abdullah at fourteen knew exactly what a woman's place was, and it was nothing that . . . Raza could understand' (*BS* 261).

Similarly, *Burnt Shadows* goes beyond *Broken Verses'* contestation of hegemonic, oversimplified representations of Islam as inherently oppressive to women, by articulating perceptions of some Muslim women's co-operation in their own subordination: Hiroko is puzzled by the veiled women on a Karachi beach 'who allowed their lives to be changed by Islamisation even as everyone recognised it as a political tool of a dictator' (*BS* 182). Such an 'interpretation' of these women's veiling enacts the fault-lines within contemporary discourses of feminism and the need for an alternative framework to conceive Pakistani women beyond the totalizing conceptual categories of both 'Islam' and 'feminism'. Shamsie appears to want to have it both ways here. With a nod to libertarian feminists who fail to ascribe agency to women who wear the veil, the phrase 'allowed their lives' ascribes a degree of individual choice. Yet the implicit assumption that any woman who wears a veil is oppressed by the logic of secular reason remains.

At the same time, *Burnt Shadows* goes further in its attempt to complicate the gendered parameters of the conflict between piety and secularism. Where *Broken Verses* broadly confined itself to depicting secular elite Pakistani feminists, *Burnt Shadows* attempts to offer at least a glimpse into the consciousness of pious, practising Muslim women in the characterization of Sajjad Ashraf's mother Khadija in pre-Partition Delhi. Khadija insists that piety and agency are not incompatible: 'I have a strong will. It doesn't make my dupatta fall off my head' (*BS* 52). With her 'talent for finding comfort through conversing with God as though He were a recalcitrant lover', Khadija couples piety with feminist instincts (*BS* 235). Sajjad attributes his desire for a modern wife to the stories his mother told him as a child 'of Rani of Jhansi and [significantly the less well-known Muslim] Razia of the Mamluk dynasty . . . powerful women who led troops and sat in council with the men, [that] made him fall in love with those images of womanhood' (*BS* 52). This reminder of the pre-colonial emancipated position of women questions the linear narrative of imperial progress that says the British were responsible for emancipation of Indian women. In this way, animated by the theoretical insights of 'Third World' feminist and postcolonial feminist scholarship, the novel interleaves issues of Islamic culture and female emancipation by suggesting that Muslim women have agency in non-obvious ways, and derive a feminist political theory specifically from their own cultural histories, background and experience.[20]

Ultimately the novel foregrounds an emphatically secularist position that co-exists with cultural Islam: for Sajjad 'religion had never been more than a constant background hum' (*BS* 235). Hiroko, the novel's strong moral compass, embodies secular liberal 'tolerance' of faith: 'religion was baffling, it seemed to defy all reason, and yet she would never be the one to attempt to wrestle the comfort of illusory order away from someone else' (*BS* 329). Yet, in the exploration of Islamophobia and the politics of representation of Muslim identities in a post-9/11 world, both *Burnt Shadows* and *Broken Verses* convey the power to self-identify as a secular Pakistani as nothing compared to the global media's power to associate one's identity with Islam. In *Broken Verses* Shehnaz Saeed's son Ed returns to Karachi where he works with Aasmaani, having left a previously idyllic life in New York, when after 9/11 he 'stopped being an individual and started being an entire religion' (*BV* 45). He recounts his realization to Aasmaani: 'now history will happen and I can do nothing but be caught up in it' (*BV* 46). Although Aasmaani counters Ed's internalization of Euro American myopic self-centredness, 'Extraordinary, that someone who'd grown up in Pakistan could say a thing like that . . . as if history hadn't been breathing down our necks all our lives' (*BV* 46), Shamsie makes the point that for Ed and others the choice to reject Muslim identification does not exist following 9/11.[21] This idea is reinforced in Abdullah's observation in *Burnt Shadows*: 'Everyone just wants to tell you what they know about Islam, how they know so much more than you do, what do you know, you've just been a Muslim your whole life?' (*BS* 352). But here the evils of stereotyping have tragic consequences: Harry's daughter Kim mistakenly assumes Abdullah's involvement in her father's assassination, and calls the police to arrest him, leading to Raza's internment.

Shamsie continues her hard-hitting critiques of Euro American politics in the context of the 'war on terror', writing journalistic essays 'with a different hat on' in *Index on Censorship*, *The Guardian* and in several Pakistani and Bangladeshi newspapers.[22] This essay closes with a discussion of the more restricted, nation-state structured focus on Pakistan in her volume of essays *Offence: The Muslim Case* (2009) where she argues that Islam must be located in the 'nation'. This stands in marked contrast to the reconfiguration of religion under 'cross-national' articulations and global concerns of *Burnt Shadows*. In *Offence*, through a consideration of Pakistan, Shamsie seeks to place the recent surge in extremist Islam within the framework of the nation-state, and expose the myth of Islam as a static global temporal entity. Shamsie examines the figure of the offended Muslim, and productively dispels the entrenched notion that offence is encountered in the Muslim world only when it clashes with the West: 'in Pakistan the name of Islam is invoked over a range of perceived offences, most of them entirely without reference to the non-Muslim world' (*O* 3). In this way her essays distil some of the arguments implicit in her fiction. As we have seen, *Broken Verses* and *Burnt Shadows* dramatize the idea that offence is a more political, intra-religious agenda. Routed in patriarchal politicization, Islam is invoked against women and religious minorities.

In contrast to the fictional snapshots offered in her stories that shift between past and present, Shamsie's extended essay chronologically traces the roots of 'the interplay of national politics and religious ideology in Pakistan' (*O* 15) through the long lens of history. She focuses particularly on the moment post-Partition when with nation achieved and the majority community no longer an issue, Pakistan needed 'some other glue to hold the nation together' (*O* 31). The investment in the idea of a Muslim nation contrasts with Jinnah's secular vision for Pakistan. She argues that the culture of intolerance was one fostered in terms of the nation's political identity. Shamsie goes on to question the idea of the unity of the *ummah*, citing the violent bloodshed of the civil war of 1971 that resulted in the violent birth of Bangladesh: 'any group . . . that really cared about Offence to Islam would have raised its voice in horror at the Muslim-on-Muslim rape and murder the army carried out in East Pakistan' (*O* 40). Shamsie recounts she is often asked, 'Why don't Muslims who aren't part of the Violently Offended stage their own protests rallies against those who spread the image of Islam as a religion of violence?'(*O* 75). She offers a measure of clarity in her response that there is no coherent opposition to the rising extremists because there is no class or group within Pakistani society which is not deeply conflicted about engaging against them: 'The feeling that "the West" deliberately chooses to insult Islam and then uses protests against those insults as an occasion to brand all Muslims "fanatics" makes a great many people uneasy about standing up on the side of "the West"' (*O* 76).

While Shamsie's essays reject 'the rhetoric of a Clash of Civilisations' between Islam and the West, and while she undermines this dialectic in her fiction,[23] one might question the extent to which the clash of civilizations really remains the accepted discourse in the West today? Shamsie's analysis in *Offence* is further weakened by her somewhat simplistic take on the faultlines within Islam. Her argument that we recast the matter as 'religious hardliners versus anti-hardliners' by separating those who advocate violence in the name of religion from those who do not, serves to collapse the hardliners with violence against 'the rest' (*O* 6). Moreover, her conclusion that 'the only way out of this vicious circle is for both sides to take a closer look at each other' seems somewhat trite and meaningless. We might look to her fiction, particularly *Burnt Shadows*, as a more powerful means of articulating the tragic consequences and dangers of stereotyping. Shamsie has argued for the ability of fiction to 'convey emotional truths, more revelatory about a time and place than any series of facts'.[24] This is certainly true of her own work. It is her novels peopled with Aasmaani's politically motivated mother, gentle father, the enlightened Poet and gay Mirza that communicate, as she states in *Offence*, that 'Muslims are not a monolith . . . placed on one side of a divide, lobbing grenades at the West' (*O* 15).

To conclude, Shamsie is not ambivalent about gender equality. The thematic focus of *Broken Verses*, in particular, dramatizes how issues of gendered oppression and violence require a universal conception of women's rights that is legally enforced. However, emphasizing Samina's connections to 'Third World' feminists, *Broken Verses* attempts to gesture towards a range of progressive gender possibilities framed within a discourse of human rights that transcends discourses of cultural imperialism. In its acknowledgement of radical teachings of equality within Islamic traditions, Shamsie's fiction is in dialogue with the insights of Muslim feminists such as Sara Ahmed and Leila Ahmed. In touching on the disparity between elite and poor women in Pakistan, Shamsie offers a glimpse (albeit fleeting) into the fissures in female identity that class produces, thus framing her analysis of gender inequality within the context of class and poverty, rather than religious traditions alone. In this way, Shamsie's disavowal of violence against women legitimized through discourses of Islamic tradition is quite different to Ayaan Hirsi Ali's suggestion that repressive roles for women are inherent to Islamic culture and Islam.

If Shamsie's liberal discourse of gender includes a belief in the superiority of western secular gender norms, she moves away from the concomitant demonization of non-western cultures that promotes a narrative of western intervention in non-western cultures on the grounds of gender equality. Shamsie's fiction details the tensions between the secular and the sacred with a noticeable leaning towards the secular in her book of essays. However, while her fiction advances a secular worldview, it also shows the limits of this worldview by revealing how important Islam remains to individual Muslims. Islam itself is depicted as gentle, spiritual, poetic and most importantly individualistic, and is thus de-Othered.

Notes

1. Kamila Shamsie, 'A Long, Loving Literary Line', *Guardian*, 1 May 2009, 16.
2. Lee Glendinning, 'Is Pakistan in a State of War?', *Guardian*, 4 March 2009, 30.
3. Kamila Shamsie, 'More Honest than the Facts', *Guardian*, 3 July 2007, 30.
4. Ibid.
5. Ibid.
6. Ruvani Ranasinha, *Hanif Kureishi: Writers and their Work* (Plymouth: Northcote House, 2002).
7. Shamsie undermines the polarity set up between Bhutto and Haq in Rushdie's novel *Shame*.
8. Kamila Shamsie, *Broken Verses* (London: Bloomsbury, 2005), 91. Hereafter *BV* pagination will be given in the main body of the text.
9. Mitra Rastegar, 'Reading Nafisi in the West: Authenticity, Orientalism and Liberating Iranian Women', *Women's Studies Quarterly* 34.1 (2006): 108–128 (116).
10. See also Sara Ahmed's critique of the way Islamic feminism is examined in relation to its proximity to 'real' (read Euro American) feminism. Sara Ahmed, *Strange Encounters: Embodied Others in Post-Coloniality* (London: Routledge, 2000).
11. Kamila Shamsie, *Offence: The Muslim Case* (London: Seagull Books, 2009), 48–49. Hereafter *O* pagination will be given in the main body of the text. The Ordinances were revised as the Women's Protection Bill in 2006 but still remain controversial.
12. Elleke Boehmer, *Stories of Women: Gender and Narrative in the Postcolonial Nation* (Manchester: Manchester University Press, 2005), 5.
13. Kamala Bhasin, Ritu Menon and Nighat Said Khan, eds, *Against All Odds: Essays on Women, Religion and Development from India and Pakistan* (New Delhi: Kali for Women, 1996).
14. Like both Ziauddin Sardar and Akbar S. Ahmed in another context, Shamsie conceives of Muslim identity in terms of inherited cultural tradition.
15. However, in contrast to Nadeem Aslam in his novel *Maps for Lost Lovers* (2004) Shamsie does not emphasize that gender equality is as much part of the Islamic Sufi tradition as of modern western discourse.
16. Tariq Modood, *Not Easy Being British: Colour, Culture and Citizenship* (London: Trentham Books, 1992), 87.
17. For different views on this subject, see Olivier Roy, *Global Islam: In Search of the New Ummah* (New York: Columbia University Press, 2004); and Bobby S.

Sayyid, *A Fundamental Fear: Eurocentrism and the Emergence of Islamism* (London: Zed Books, 2003).

18. Kamila Shamsie, *Burnt Shadows* (London: Bloomsbury, 2009), 142. Hereafter *BS* pagination will be given in the main body of the text.

19. Carolyn See, 'A Flawed Argument', *Washington Post*, 15 May 2009, CO9.

20. For an example of such scholarship, see Chandra Talpade Mohanty, *Feminism without Borders: Decolonizing Theory, Practicing Solidarity* (Durham, NC: Duke University Press, 2003), 51.

21. Shamsie's point is that following 9/11 Muslim identification is not simply a matter of individual choice as Kureishi delineates in his pre-9/11 novel *The Black Album* (1995).

22. Shamsie, 'A Long, Loving Literary Line', 16.

23. In *Broken Verses* the Poet observes 'if only we could view the motion of currents as metaphors for the gyres of history . . . we'd know the absurdity of declaring the world is divided into East and West' (*BV* 24). In *Burnt Shadows* Weiss is an idealistic German artist and scholar whose work attempts to discover how eastern and western civilizations might learn to live in harmony.

24. Shamsie, 'More Honest than the Facts', 30.

13 Mourning Becomes Kashmira

Islam, Melancholia and the Evacuation of Politics in Salman Rushdie's *Shalimar the Clown*

Peter Morey

Salman Rushdie has more reason than most to be hostile to Islamic militancy. A decade living under sentence of death might be expected to make anyone sanguine about the combination of politics and fundamentalist religion. Indeed, even before the fatwa the author was well-known for preferring a moderate brand of tolerant Islam, as personified by his Kashmiri maternal grandfather with whom he recalls having friendly theological disagreements, to tub-thumping brands with designs on state control and international violent jihad.[1] The theme of the different available varieties of Islam informs almost all Rushdie's work, from *Midnight's Children* (1981) and *Shame* (1983), with their tolerant believers and ambitious opportunists, to *The Enchantress of Florence* (2008), which pits the Emperor Akbar's idealistic *Hanafi* pluralism against the forces of religious authoritarianism. Rushdie's post-9/11 essays also take up this theme, albeit with a stronger aversion to religion in the public sphere. Indeed, it becomes an article of Rushdie's secularist faith that the privatization of religion is one of the distinguishing features of modernity. Moreover, there is what might be described as incredulity that faith alone can motivate action in the world: it must be tainted or manipulated by the agendas of self-seeking individuals. This causes Rushdie to fall back on more familiar novelistic staples when trying to describe seismic geopolitical shifts. Whereas in novels such as *Midnight's Children* and *The Moor's Last Sigh* (1995), central characters become allegorical participants in the fate of the nation, in his first post-9/11 novel, *Shalimar the Clown* (2005), Rushdie tends rather to make his characters the local, *symbolic equivalents* for national and international tensions and dilemmas. The cost of this shift of emphasis is an evacuation of the political dimension where the national anxieties characters emblematize shrink to become purely the motor for personal stories of defeated idealism, lost love, betrayal and revenge. Using Abraham and Torok's revision of Freud's distinction between mourning and melancholia, this essay argues that, in place of an engagement with the political causes of violence and fundamentalism, *Shalimar* offers repeated instances of the incorporation of lost love objects—mothers, lovers, even Kashmir itself—in the form of memory, spectres and dream visitors from the past. These lost loves are incorporated into the ego structures of characters, preventing them from working through the experiences of loss they undergo. Moreover, this process is replicated in the narrating voice, whose insistent pastoral nostalgia for Kashmir in the first half of the novel results in a breakdown in the ability of language to articulate subsequent experiences of loss that are actually the product of competing ideologies.

Shalimar the Clown presents the story of the communalization of the disputed Indian province of Kashmir since Partition through the experiences of a set of characters from the fictional village of Pachigam, most notably Shalimar, the Muslim tightrope walker with the village's entertainment troop, and Boonyi, the beautiful Hindu dancer.[2] Their marriage, and its subsequent breakdown as a result of Boonyi's infidelity with the American ambassador Max Ophuls—a liaison which leads to the birth of a daughter, India/Kashmira—comes to symbolize the fading possibilities for intercommunal co-existence as the forces of religiously-fired extremism take hold. People become embodiments of those places with which they are closely identified, and personal and national histories are run together and international trans-historical connections sought, as the novel sweeps back and forth across the political landscape of the last two-thirds of the twentieth century, incorporating the rise of Nazism, World War II, Vietnam and the deteriorating state of Indo-Pakistan relations as the century closes.

Indeed, *Shalimar the Clown* is a looping epic, beginning with the assassination of Ambassador Max Ophuls by his driver, Shalimar, in Los Angeles in 1991, before tracking back to fill in the gaps in what becomes a kind of postcolonial 'whydunit'. In the process, we witness the participants' involvement in some of the major historical upheavals of the twentieth century: including Max's heroic resistance work against the Nazis in World War II, and his legendary flight to freedom when all seems lost; the Partition of India which is to prove so fateful for the province of Kashmir; the Indo-Pakistan War of 1965; the Russian invasion of Afghanistan in 1979 and America's subsequent cultivation of an Islamic fighting force, the *mujahideen*; through the LA riots of 1991; and on to the book's climax at the turn of millennium, as India and Pakistan come to the brink of nuclear war and Kashmira Ophuls encounters Shalimar the Clown, the murderer of her father, in a final showdown. In tracing this circular course the narrative is measured and digressive, pausing in the early parts to describe the minutiae of daily life in Pachigam and to fill in the background of key figures. One of the novel's central questions is whether character is destiny, or whether more contingent (and violent) forces are in charge of events.

On one level, *Shalimar* appears to be Rushdie's most overtly political novel for some time. Moral themes such as good and evil and the grey areas between them find a more suitable vehicle in the story of the fate of Kashmir, which Rushdie ties to the broader history of the twentieth century, than in his previous works, *The Ground Beneath Her Feet* (1999) and *Fury* (2001), with their fascination with celebrity, penchant for lists and name-dropping. Throughout his career, it has been evident that Rushdie's creative intelligence is of the kind that accumulates facts and turns them into images, rather than one that inhabits character and experience. However, this tendency is less pronounced in *Shalimar*, particularly in the 'Boonyi' section, a kind of postcolonial pastoral of life in pre-communalist Kashmir, where the writing—while still infused with the magical realist quality allowed for by a non-industrialized setting and folkloric cosmology—introduces us with affection and without satire to the rural way of life of the Pachigam villagers and the deep bonds that unite them.

In particular, there is a close correspondence between people and places. Characters come almost to embody certain locales. This is partly to emphasize the deep roots of the non-sectarian Kashmiri community into whose world we are drawn, but who will eventually experience division and destruction. The central female character is originally called Bhoomi, meaning earth, but changes her name to Boonyi, after the local chinar tree. Later, after her elopement with Max, the American ambassador, she develops a code language in which her forsaken husband, Shalimar, personifies Kashmir itself—just as he does for her daughter, many years later, when he takes on the job as Max's driver, the better to carry out his plan of assassination. Boonyi's own sense of self is inextricably tied to her abandoned homeland; she begins to decline physically while in the 'gilded cage' of her concubinage and longs for the life-giving topography of home. The female child of her liaison is named Kashmira, but has her name changed to India by her adopted mother, Max's estranged wife. It is only later, when she discovers her true lineage, that she readopts the name that unites her with the lost valley of her mother. On her plane journey east to uncover her roots, the erstwhile India Ophuls proclaims, 'There is no India . . . There is only Kashmira. There is only Kashmir . . . She would not be India in India. She would be her mother's child' (356).

Thus, identity shadows place. Rushdie's technique in the novel involves constructing close correspondences between people and locations, but also between personal and regional histories. Echoing the famous device from *Midnight's Children*, Shalimar is born at the moment of Indian Independence in 1947: also, of course, the moment that calcified the arrangement originally set in place by the British in the mid-nineteenth century by which Muslim majority Kashmir was delivered up to a Hindu Dogra ruling house, and thereafter to independent India rather than her rival across the border.[3] Rushdie's treatment of the resulting political upheaval is scrupulously even-handed. In an essay entitled 'June 1999: Kashmir', penned at the time of the Kargil dispute which brought India and Pakistan to the brink of nuclear war, he makes clear his view that the essentially peace-loving Kashmiris are victims of the self-interested machinations of these regional rivals, and ventures that 'the present day growth of terrorism in Kashmir has roots in India's treatment of Kashmiris, but also in Pakistan's interest in subversion'.[4] In the novel he evinces the same disgust at the vicious crackdowns of the Indian security forces against anyone suspected of harbouring Pakistani sympathies as he does at the murderous indoctrination of Islamist demagogues. Yet, the terrors of the outside world are at first slow to impact on the cyclical and seasonal rhythms of Pachigam life. Local skirmishes are restricted to tussles between bands of entertainers and caterers and, despite the doom-laden prophesies of the local soothsayer, events such as the cross-communal betrothal of the childhood sweethearts, the Hindu Boonyi and the Muslim Shalimar, testify to harmony. It is not until the arrival of sectarian agitators and the incursion of a national television service that the populace begins to think of itself as marked by religious differences. Shalimar's brother is one of the first to abscond to join the anti-government insurgency, declaring—in a phrase that might sum up Rushdie's fusion of the personal and political—that 'the boundary, the ceasefire line, between private life and the public arena no longer existed. "Everything is politics now"' (220).

It seems that we are here, once again, in the realms of what Fredric Jameson called 'National Allegory', a mode of understanding postcolonial writing that has been taken as particularly apposite for Rushdie's work. Jameson famously (or infamously) declared that in 'Third World' writing, 'the story of the private individual destiny is always an allegory of the embattled situation of the public third world culture and society',[5] and there are certainly a number of points in the text where we seem to be invited to read the relation between the personal, national and international as one of direct, unvarnished symbolic correspondence. So, in an aside on the political fallout from the discovery of Boonyi and Max's scandalous relationship we are told: 'And that was how it came about that a faithless woman from the village of the *bhand pather* began to influence, to complicate and even to shape, American diplomatic activity regarding the vexed matter of Kashmir' (194). Max's ambassadorial impartiality on Kashmir is fatally compromised by his philandering, and his views on India's conduct come to be shaped by his infatuation. Most importantly for the novel, Shalimar's desire to kill Max, although at first understood in the context of the Kashmiri insurgency and the rise of Islamist terrorism, really turns out to be based solely on overriding personal motives of jealousy and revenge.

Yet, in *Shalimar* such personal-national correspondences are not of a piece with the celebrated entwining of, for example, Saleem Sinai and the political story of postcolonial India one sees in *Midnight's Children*. In the earlier novel, the allegorical dimension is integrated into the story and its telling; consider the multiple voices of the Midnight's Children's Conference, or the comfortable, middle-class Methwold Estate in which Saleem grows up, surrounded by friends who embody the diverse communities of India, in a house bequeathed by a departing personification of the Raj. It even finds itself inscribed on the knobbly, battered body of the central protagonist which, as the book ends, is beginning to crack and split apart, just as Indira Gandhi's suspension of democracy in the State of Emergency (1977–1980) threatens to break India's secular democratic consensus. In *Shalimar*, by contrast, the protagonists operate as *symbolic equivalents* for national and international tensions. To be sure, they experience the impact of macro-politics themselves—never more movingly than when the Pachigam villagers are rounded up and killed in a brutal crackdown by the Indian Army. However, the inflation of Max and Boonyi's somewhat tawdry affair, based on desperation and unrestrained appetite respectively, into a comic explanation for the tidal wave of anti-American youth protest that eventually helped end the Vietnam War, or for Indira Gandhi's authoritarian impulses, seems somewhat strained. Politicians speak out and the international news media goes into frenzy as Ambassador Max's increasingly partisan statements are exposed as a result of his having taken up with, and then cast off, a poor Indian girl from the country. Yet this typically playful Rushdiean expansion of the trivial into the global, serves to condense, and therefore simplify, a host of geopolitical factors. As with the irrelevant (and unexplained) appearance of the legendary fugitive Lord Lucan in a later part of the book set in early 1970s London, the device offers only a flimsy and unpersuasive relationship between the local and those larger events to which it is symbolically yoked. What is carved into the body of Salem Sinai in *Midnight's Children* is here piped round the world courtesy of the news media, the scandal sheets and the protest songs of Joan Baez. The private travails of the characters have unfortunate knock-on effects on world history in the 1960s, but no necessary integral relation to it.

In the same way, the breakdown of Shalimar and Boonyi's marriage is made to symbolize the decline of the possibilities for intercommunal understanding in Kashmir. Yet their respective motivations—Boonyi longs for a greater freedom than her traditional gender roles allow; Shalimar is motivated by an obsessive and murderous concern for his 'honour'—in reality have little bearing on the global forces with which they are metaphorically coupled. They exist alongside these bigger forces but are not really shaped by them. Their promptings are too general and too personal to serve as an adequate correlative to the story of the subjugation of Kashmir, first under the Raj and then as a part of independent India. And this points to something else about Rushdie's treatment of history in the novel: that it ignores the specific traces of historical process in favour of a generalized humanistic empathy with the victims of its remorseless march.

Instead, what Rushdie offers are parallels between different moments in history he takes to have similarities in terms of the human experiences of displacement and oppression. So direct comparisons are made between pre-War Strasbourg, the home of Max's family of Jewish printers, in the disputed Franco-German territory of Alsace-Lorraine, and the predicament of post-Partition Kashmir. In part, this comes through the somewhat hubristic reflections of Max himself, who remarks of these two contested frontier spaces: 'Could any two places have been more different? . . . Could any two places have been more the same? Human nature, the great constant, surely persisted in spite of all surface differences' (180). However, if we are expected to view Max's deliberations somewhat sceptically after his use and cruel desertion of Boonyi, it is not so easy to dismiss the insistence with which the narrative itself promotes such comparisons. The assassination of Max by Shalimar is at first understood as a latter-day replaying of the assassination of Lieutenant Governor O'Dwyer, instigator of the 1919 Amritsar massacre, by the avenging Udham Singh (30). Then there is Rushdie's account of what he terms 'the pogrom of the pandits', burned out of their homes by Muslim mobs, recalling the earlier fate of the Jews under Nazi rule (296). Yet such transhistorical comparisons only really work on the level of shared human suffering and—to use a cliché—man's inhumanity to man. As historical events they belong to entirely different spheres of causality. The Indian government cannot be a symbolic equivalent to the Nazis, even if in the period being described the influence of extreme right-wing Hindu nationalism was a rising factor. Likewise, Muslim insurgents do not work as stand-ins for those fighting tyranny in Europe sixty years before. A clue to Rushdie's interest and technique comes in an interview, quoted by Florian Stadtler, in which Rushdie justifies these anachronistic juxtapositions:

> In *Shalimar*, the character of Max Ophuls is a resistance hero during World War Two. The resistance, which we think of as heroic, was what we would now call an insurgency in a time of occupation. Now we live in a time where there are other insurgencies that we don't call heroic— that we call terrorist . . . I wanted to say: that happened then, this is happening now, this story includes both these things, just look how they sit together.[6]

However, the respective historical circumstances are so different as to make the comparison meaningless anywhere other than in the imagination of the novelist. In their juxtaposition Rushdie really offers the reader no more than a humanist experiential relativism. More telling is the use of the pronoun 'we' in this passage. Rushdie presupposes a literate, liberal western addressee who will be familiar with the politically tendentious language of 'terror' and 'insurgency', and prepared to think connectively across time about different historical phenomena. Yet, this is not the same as thinking historically. Rushdie is fully aware of the sequence of events that led to the rise of the Third Reich, and also those that resulted in a communalization of politics in Kashmir; indeed he gives quite a detailed account of the latter. However, to offer a transhistorical analysis through what is essentially a story of love, betrayal and revenge, must inevitably involve a simplification, a flattening out of complex factors as the novelist seeks to find allegorical equivalents for them in his story.

Of course, it can be objected that this is what all historical novels do. However, in Rushdie's text the evacuation of the political by the personal has particular implications for that larger struggle which marks this out as a post-9/11 novel: that between the values of liberal humanism as enshrined in the novel form, and those of the brainwashing religio-political cult of Islamic terrorism.

In his polemical essay from November 2001 entitled 'Not About Islam', Rushdie rejects contemporary responses to 9/11 which sought to claim that the attacks had nothing to do with Islam. He gives such suggestions short shrift, arguing that, for the majority of its adherents, Islam stands for a jumbled corpus of half-digested opinions, habitual customs and unexamined prejudices, linked only by a loathing of modern society and westernization. This is the Islam that constantly seeks to evade responsibility for actions committed in its name: 'This paranoid Islam, which blames outsiders, "infidels" for all the ills of Muslim societies, and whose proposed remedy is the closing of those societies to *the rival project of modernity*, is presently the fastest-growing version of Islam in the world'.[7] Here, by contrast, the benevolently religious are too busy tending the garden of the spirit to become embroiled in politics. Indeed, the confinement of religion to the private realm becomes, in the piece, the definitive test of whether societies are modern. Rushdie writes,

> the restoration of religion to the sphere of the personal, its depoliticization, is the nettle that all Muslim societies must grasp in order to become modern . . . If terrorism is to be defeated, the world of Islam must take on board the secular-humanist principles on which modernity is based, and without which their countries' freedom will remain a distant dream.[8]

These are sentiments likely to find favour in the political centres of the West, where religion in the public realm is either strictly abjured or treated as an embarrassing throwback to less 'ecumenical' times. However, the argument that the Muslim world—especially in its militant political incarnation—is less modern than the West and that secularism is actually the litmus test of modernity, is tendentious, disputable and highly ideological.

For example, at the same time that Rushdie was parroting this supposed truism, favoured by right-wing politicians and commentators alike, John Gray, in his perspicacious treatise, *Al Qaeda and What it Means to be Modern*, was pointing out that the distinction between capitalist liberal democracy as the only model of modernity, and radical political Islam of the al-Qaeda type seen as a regressive social formation, was based on a false separation of connected intellectual histories. Pointing out the narrow, hubristic post-Cold War discourse of the free market as the defining feature of modernity,

Gray pours scorn on the kind of reading Rushdie advances in his post-9/11 essays and fiction: 'No cliché is more stupefying than that which describes Al Qaeda as a throwback to medieval times. It is [says Gray] a by-product of globalisation'.[9] Islamist terrorism, like globalized commerce, observes no national boundaries, and relies on the same technological networks as liberal capitalism. Moreover, the utopian dimension of radical Islamism is shaped at least as much by western positivist thinking—which spawned other revolutionary movements aggressively propounding their distinct views of the good society, such as Marxism and Fascism—as by any traditions within Islam. Even if radical Islam peddles a view of itself as antithetical to post-Enlightenment modernity, its twentieth-century founding fathers, such as Sayyid Qutb and Abdullah Azam (Osama Bin Laden's mentor), still drew on tactics like political violence by a revolutionary vanguard, which owed more to those products of the Enlightenment and its aftermath like Bolshevism or European anarchism than to any Quranic model. Gray observes, 'The Romantic belief that the world can be reshaped by an act of will is as much part of the modern world as the Enlightenment ideal of a universal civilization based on reason. The one arose as a reaction against the other. Both are myths'.[10] The 'doctrine of redemption in the guise of a theory of history'[11] is common to the Christian tradition and to those other progressivist agendas (including, one might add, the kind of radical secularism espoused in our time by celebrity atheists such as Sam Harris, Christopher Hitchens and Richard Dawkins, where the Promised Land is a kind of post-Darwinian New Atlantis of scientific knowledge).[12] The radical Islamist paradise is of a more conventional stripe, but each of them offers its utopias nonetheless. As Gray concludes, 'what passes for secular belief in the West is a mutation of religious faith'.[13] Even so, these bifurcations—the secular-as-modern versus religion as a comforting but corruptible form of superstition, and the reality of personal emotional motivation versus the veneer of collectivist political rhetoric—everywhere mark *Shalimar the Clown*.

The struggle between secular humanism and theocratic absolutism is delineated most fully in the scene, near the middle of the book, when Shalimar undergoes initiation at an ISI-sponsored Islamist training camp, somewhere in Pakistan. At this point, the seeds of division sown by agitators such as Maulana Bulbul Fakh, the foul-breathed iron man of fundamentalist certainties, have begun to sprout in the valley. When the Maulana reappears in the training camp he appears to have grown in stature along with the appeal of his uncompromising doctrine, and his robotic qualities are underlined by the fact that he seems to be made entirely of metal. He is equipped with a remorseless argument that sets him at odds with the novel's clearly dramatized values of tolerance and conviviality. In a sermon designed to stir feelings of self-abnegating zeal among the assembled militants, he proclaims a religion not of love but of war and a submersion of the ego to crush the infidel:

Ideology was primary. The infidel, obsessed with possessions and wealth, did not grasp this, and believed that men were primarily motivated by social and material self-interest . . . The true warrior was not primarily motivated by worldly desires, but by what he believed to be true. Economics was not primary. Ideology was primary. (265)

And, even more tellingly:

'The infidel believes in the immutability of the soul . . . But we believe that all living things can be transformed in the service of the truth. The infidel says that a man's character will decide his fate; we say a man's fate will forge his character anew. The infidel holds that the picture of the world he draws is a picture we must all recognise. We say his picture means nothing to us, for we live in a different world. The infidel speaks of universal truth. We know that the universe is an illusion and that truth lies behind the illusion, where the infidel cannot see. The infidel believes the world is his. But we shall drive him from his redoubts and cast him into darkness and live in Paradise and rejoice as he plunges into the fire.' (267)

Of course, the values of humanism to which the Maulana takes exception here are precisely those of the novel form in which character is taken to have a relationship to destiny, whether direct or in the form of a struggle against restrictive social conventions. Shalimar is one of the few in the audience not directly moved by the preacher's demand for obliteration of the ego, for the simple reason that he is more interested in learning the techniques of combat to assist him in taking revenge on the man who cuckolded him. Throughout this section, the Maulana's portentous announcements are undercut by Shalimar's antiphonal response that redraws the aims of self-denial in the service of a very personal quest. As a trained performer he can act the part of the zealot with the rest, but in reality the demands of his bruised ego are always paramount.

Here is the essence of Rushdie's difficulty in dealing effectively with the collectivist motivations of religious fanaticism in the resolutely individualist form of the novel. The political, to have any purchase on the reader, must always resolve itself into the personal. Yet, his conviction that terrorist action is really underpinned by personal injustice runs deeper than this. In an essay reflecting on the 9/11 attacks, Rushdie refuses to excuse mass murder on the pretext of striking back against US government policies. However, he does so by an intriguing but unexplored shift of focus away from the proclaimed political motivations behind the attacks, and from the idea of Islamist terrorism as a manifestation of a collective will at odds with the heterogeneous freedoms of the West. He says: 'individuals are responsible for their actions . . . The terrorist *wraps himself in the world's grievances to cloak his true motives.*

Whatever the killers were trying to achieve, it seems improbable that building a better world was part of it'.[14] The essay moves on, however, without exploring what these 'true motives' might be. Are they to do with local factors? Upbringing? A sense of emasculation? Or repressed sexual impulses?[15] We are not told. Perhaps Rushdie himself is not clear or, more likely, recognizes the mixed motives that animate all human action. What is significant, though, is that it cannot really be something as intangible as religious faith, no matter how warped, that leads people to kill and sacrifice themselves.

Similarly, radical political Islam must show its true colours via a symbolic association with other, more familiar totalitarianisms. Thus, the metallic Malauna Bulbul Fakh, with his harsh 'rust-covered' voice is symbolically linked to those other faceless 'metal men' of violence from earlier in the book, the Nazis. And just as the Maulana has declared the primacy of 'ideology', so later another advocate of the jihadi cause refers to 'our international' (276), for all the world as if he was a member of some mid-twentieth-century Communist regime. The effect of these more subtle, but nonetheless significant, historical conflations is to position the insurgents as irrevocably 'Other' to the liberal humanistic values the novel espouses, since we all know where political (and religious) extremism leads. The narrative technique effectively tells us nothing about the real motivations that might prompt someone to join these groups and, in performing its sly historical elision, adds little to our understanding of contemporary 'clashes of civilisations' either. In short, it does not encourage us to interrogate the discourse of what has become known as the war on terror; it merely confirms its totalizing rightness.

Yet Rushdie does offer a substitute to fill the void in his characters caused by their depoliticization. The shift from the political to the personal traced in Shalimar's journey is in fact common to almost all the main characters. It resolves itself through the problems they have in ridding themselves of the burdens of their pasts. More or less all the main protagonists appear to be suffering from some kind of nostalgic melancholia: a melancholia that is shared by the narrative voice as it goes about lamenting the loss of the paradise of Kashmir to the forces of violence and hate.

In his classic treatise on 'Mourning and Melancholia', Freud distinguishes between the healthy process of mourning and the emotional paralysis of melancholia as responses to the experience of loss. He describes how, in melancholia, the loss of a love object is accompanied by the patient's inability to let go: something that results in the incorporation of the lost object into the very structure of the ego:

> Reality-testing has revealed that the beloved object no longer exists and demands that the libido as a whole sever its bonds with that object. An understandable tendency arises to counter this—it may be generally observed that people are reluctant to abandon a libido position, even if a substitute is already beckoning. This tendency can become so intense

that it leads to a person turning away from reality and holding on to the object through a hallucinatory wish psychosis.[16]

The melancholic refuses the loss of the love object and instead internalizes it as a way of retaining and resuscitating it, as Judith Butler puts it: 'not only because the loss is painful, but because the ambivalence felt toward the object requires that the object be retained until differences are settled'.[17]

In their revision of Freud's theory, Nicolas Abraham and Maria Torok develop this idea of the internalization or 'incorporation' of the lost love object. They say, 'Grief that cannot be expressed builds a secret vault within the subject. In this crypt reposes—alive, reconstituted from the memories of words, images and feelings—the objective counterpart of the loss, as a complete person with his own topography'. They describe this process elsewhere as 'endocryptic identification'.[18]

Shalimar the Clown is full of instances of love objects that return as spectral, internalized presences to haunt those who once held them dear. Boonyi's mother Pamposh, who died in childbirth, reappears in a dream to sanction her daughter's sexual independence. Other cases of psychic connection to those in one's past include passages in which Shalimar and his unfaithful wife have a telepathic conversation as he returns to wreak his revenge on her; Kashmira begins to hear in her head the voice of Shalimar as they slowly circle each other ahead of their final encounter; she also feels the presence of her now-dead mother Boonyi drawing her back to India to discover her fate; and—perhaps most tellingly—Kashmira is effectively 'haunted' by thoughts of the loving if distant father she has witnessed being brutally slain on the street in front of her.

Moreover, there are several kinds of death (including death-in-life) characters undergo, and numerous crypt spaces too. When she attempts to return to Pachigam after news of her affair with Max has broken, Boonyi finds that she has been declared dead in her absence, having brought disgrace on the community, and is forced to live in an old shack away from the rest of the population, tended only by her childhood friend Zoon Misri, a rape victim who is likewise considered contaminated and therefore 'dead' to erstwhile friends and family. Another crypt space is the hut in which Zoon's attackers take refuge before disappearing, presumed dead but in fact effecting an escape to join those who will later return to bring real death to Pachigam.

Throughout the novel there is a strong sense that the becalmed atmosphere of rural Kashmir is a false idyll that can only temporarily survive against the surrounding turmoil of post-Partition power politics. Several characters hold out for a vision of a harmonious, non-communal Kashmir, long after events have rendered that view obsolete. Boonyi's father, the local teacher, who has a fondness for Romantic literature, laments the breakdown of Hindu-Muslim relations. The local *sardar*, Harbans Singh, a fellow Romantic, passes on to his son Yuvraj a belief that we can learn from the natural world and should rejoice in 'what can be held in the eye, the memory, the mind' (358). After the decimation of Pachigam, Yuvraj continues to tend his father's garden, creating an enchanted space away from the furies of communalism: a space where Kashmira is temporarily lulled into passivity and torpor on her visit like some modern-day lotus eater. Thus, Kashmir itself becomes a kind of crypt space in the novel.

Abraham and Torok also write of the 'phantom' formed by shameful secrets, often those of a previous generation, which can lead to psychic disturbance. Such secrets may be unwittingly transmitted from parent to child. Somewhat controversially they propose that, 'the phantom is a formation in the dynamic unconscious that is found there not because of the subject's own repression but on account of a direct empathy with the unconscious or the rejected psychic matter of a paternal object'.[19] In societal terms, Boonyi pays the price for inheriting her mother's copious sexual appetites. In turn, her daughter Kashmira carries the need to discover the truth about her mother's fate, but is also weighed down by the sins of her father. After his heroic exploits in World War II, Max goes on to be a fairly shameless advocate of American strategic interests the world over. Something of a mixture of Henry Kissinger and J. K. Galbraith, Max uses his reserves of personal charm to win friends in India, whilst all the time prioritizing his own, and his adopted country's, interests. As more of Max's dubious dealings with the world—and with her own mother—become known to Kashmira, she begins to discover something of the source of her own emotional coldness and adolescent psychological difficulties. The trauma of the discovery begins the break-up of her worldview:

> Was she, in mourning her butchered parent, crying out (*she had not wept*) for a guilty man? . . . The words *right* and *wrong* began to crumble, to lose meaning . . . Max, this stranger . . . part arms dealer, part Kingmaker, part terrorist himself . . . Max, her unknown father, the invisible robotic servant of his adopted country's overweening amoral might. (335–336, emphasis added)

On a first reading it seems that Kashmira is haunted, her life blighted, by the actions of the murdering Shalimar. However, on closer inspection it could be that the real phantom haunting her is the original sinner, Max, who took her mother away from her rightful husband and began the tragic cycle of events. As such it could be that the arrow unleashed from Kashmira's bow on the last page and aimed at the heart of Shalimar may miss its true target after all. At the end, with the arrow suspended mid-flight, we are still uncertain whether the discoveries she has made will allow Kashmira to lay her ghosts and move forward into the future.

For Abraham and Torok it is, in particular, the loss of connection with the maternal body—that process which, according to Lacan, brings the subject into being as an independent entity—that leads to the compensatory acquisition of language. One of the characteristics of melancholia is the failure of this displacement. Sufferers will avoid certain topics and there arise lacunae in speech. Abraham and Torok say: 'It is because the mouth cannot articulate certain words, cannot utter certain phrases . . . that in fantasy one will take into the mouth the unspeakable, the thing itself'.[20] Incorporation is therefore profoundly anti-linguistic. In the novel too emotional or literal inarticulacy is also a feature of some figures. Shalimar is always more at home with actions than with words. He proves a devoted but tongue-tied suitor for Boonyi early on, and it is significant that both he and Boonyi have talents that take the form of bodily motion, rather than words: Shalimar as a tightrope walker and Boonyi as a dancer.

Moreover, this inability to articulate is reproduced at the level of the narrative voice too. At several points, Rushdie's narrator produces a breathless torrent of words, hesitates or edits himself—particularly as he describes the break-up of Pachigam's ancient way of life. The characteristic Rushdiean multiclausal sentence is used to describe the ashamed and equivocal attempts of a village elder to explain the new rule, imposed by militants, preventing Hindus from watching the community's only television: 'having regard to the gravity of the regional situation, and having weighed the available options, and only for the time being, and in this dangerous climate, and until things blow over . . . ' (285). In registering its incredulous horror at the displacement of the *pandits*, the narrative resolves into a single long sentence, without punctuation, each part of which ends with the question, 'Why was that?' (297). And finally, the narrating voice makes several false starts and eventually gives up altogether when attempting to articulate the atrocities that see Pachigam effectively wiped off the map. It asks repeatedly who was responsible—'Who burned that orchard . . . Who made those men disappear . . . Who poisoned the paddies . . . Who raped that woman'—before breaking down, seemingly verbally defeated by the enormity of events:

> What happened that day in Pachigam need not be set down here in full detail, because brutality is brutality and excess is excess and that's all there is to it. There are things that must be looked at indirectly because they would blind you if you looked them in the face, like the fire of the sun. So, to repeat: there was no Pachigam any more. Pachigam was destroyed. Imagine it for yourself.
>
> Second attempt: The village of Pachigam still existed on maps of Kashmir, but that day it ceased to exist anywhere else, except in memory.
>
> Third and final attempt: The beautiful village of Pachigam still exists. (309)

The turn in these efforts is significant: from outrage, to banality to fantasy. There are no words to describe these events because they are in excess of language. What goes up in flames with the houses and fields is a particular vision of Kashmir as a harmonious cross-communal paradise, one shared by the narrator and, one feels, the author too. It is a vision that Rushdie has clung to ever since Tai the Boatman rowed slowly across the misty Dal lake on the opening pages of *Midnight's Children*. But it is just that: a fantasy. Echoes of Milton's *Paradise Lost* sprinkle the text of *Shalimar*, and Pachigam before the Fall is for long stretches a paradise on earth, brimming over with nature's plenty and the fruit of human kindness. Yet, this is a phantasmal construct into which Rushdie is tapping, and one with a particular lineage. On one level, Kashmir early in the novel is like the Alhambra at the end of *The Moor's Last Sigh*, an ecumenical pre-lapsarian space where the best of all worlds can meet. However, Florian Stadtler quotes Mridu Rai's observation that this idea, summed up in the term 'Kashmiriyat', is the product of a particular revisionist take on a valley that was always marked by some degree of communal tension. Rai's point is worth quoting at length:

> Since the 1930s the term has increasingly come to be understood as a reflection of a peerless tradition of regional nationalism, to stand above petty religious rivalries and founded on the historical survival of what is perceived as a more salient legacy of cultural harmony. However, Kashmiriyat so defined was an idealised 'remembering' of one of several shifting meanings of 'being Kashmiri': it was not only summoned but also circulated in very specific political and historical moments. Until [the first part of the twentieth century] . . . the religious nature of the Dogra-Hindu state of Jammu and Kashmir had set into motion a competition channelled along religious lines for the symbolic, political and economic resources of the state among communities also defined religiously. Yet present-day votaries of a 'secular' Indian nationalism would have us believe that this was an aberration of the grander traditions of religious neutrality that were a hallmark of a Kashmiriyat handed down from the ancient past.[21]

Perhaps all pastoral pathos is the product of Freud's hallucinatory wish psychosis. Yet in the case of *Shalimar the Clown*, Rushdie's text seems to have incorporated a lost love object—the fantasy of a Kashmir cleansed of religious difference—at the expense of an attachment to the much more politically fraught realities of that contested province. Politics is a messy and unwelcome intrusion into the business of everyday life, of rubbing along together. The political kills off the personal—or at least the fantasy of the primacy of face-to-face relations—but the text memorializes this earlier, more innocent way of life, going as far as to make the fate of Pachigam and its cast of characters the structuring principle in its exploration of world politics.

As the English novel moved away from its origins in the Puritan spiritual autobiography, religious morality came increasingly to be replaced by a morality based on a post-Romantic diluted pantheism coupled with social ethics—a move that can be followed through the works of the Brontes, George Eliot and D. H. Lawrence. At the same time the proselytizing spirit, as personified by actively religious characters, changed from a guarantor of right judgement to a specimen of self-interested hypocrisy. Rushdie writes at the end of this tradition, at a time when the work of secularization might have been thought to be complete, were it not for the puzzling resurgence of religious identity claims in the modern world. His view of secularism is commensurate with his understanding of the polyphonic humanism of the novel form. The small boy who declared his atheism to that indulgent grandfather is now, to borrow a phrase from Yeats, 'a sixty-year-old smiling public man'[22] who finds himself faced once more with an old foe. His battles with it form the subject matter of *The Moor's Last Sigh*, in the guise of Hindu nationalism, as well as *Shalimar the Clown*, with its Islamic clerical caricatures. In both cases, characters that claim our sympathy reject the orthodox path presented to them. This is, in part, a testament to Rushdie's questioning spirit. Yet the form of this rejection bears the hallmarks of his deeper inability to believe in belief.

Notes

1. Johan Hari, 'Salman Rushdie: His Life, his Work and his Religion', *Independent*, 13 October 2006.
2. Salman Rushdie, *Shalimar the Clown* (London: Vintage, 2006). All page numbers refer to this edition.
3. See Victoria Schofield, *Kashmir in Conflict: India, Pakistan and the Unfinished War* (London and New York: I. B. Taurus, 2000).
4. Salman Rushdie, *Step Across This Line: Collected Non-Fiction, 1992–2002* (London: Vintage, 2003), 306.
5. Frederic Jameson, 'Third World Literature in the Era of Multinational Capitalism', *Social Text* 15 (Fall 1986): 69.
6. Rushdie quoted in Florian Stadtler, 'Terror, Globalization and the Individual in Salman Rushdie's *Shalimar the Clown*', *Journal of Postcolonial Writing* 45.2 (2009): 193.
7. Rushdie, *Step Across This Line*, 394 (emphasis added).
8. Ibid., 396.
9. John Gray, *Al Qaeda and What it Means to be Modern* (London: Faber and Faber, 2003), 1.
10. Ibid., 25.
11. Ibid., 105.
12. See Sam Harris, *The End of Faith: Religion, Terror, and the Future of Reason* (New York: W. W. Norton, 2004); Christopher Hitchens, *God is not Great: The Case Against Religion* (London: Atlantic Books, 2007); Richard Dawkins, *The God Delusion* (New York: Random House, 2006)
13. Gray, *Al Qaeda*, 116.
14. Rushdie, *Step Across This Line*, 392–393 (emphasis added).

15. Each of these possibilities has been suggested by non-Muslim writers trying to come to terms with a mindset they find alien and baffling. See Martin Amis, *The Second Plane: September 2001–2007* (London: Jonathan Cape, 2008); John Updike, *Terrorist* (London: Penguin, 2007); and Sebastian Faulks, *A Week in December* (London: Vintage, 2010).

16. Sigmund Freud, 'Mourning and Melancholia', in *On Murder, Mourning and Melancholia* (London: Penguin, 2005), 204. For a consideration of the impact of mourning and melancholia in literary texts, and on international conflicts, see Patricia Rae, ed., *Modernism and Mourning* (Lewisburg: Bucknell University Press, 2007).

17. Judith Butler, *Gender Trouble: Feminism and the Subversion of Identity*, 2nd edn. (London: Routledge, 1999), 79.

18. Nicolas Abraham and Maria Torok, 'Introjection-Incorporation: Mourning *or* Melancholia', in Serge Lebovici and Daniel Widlocher, eds, *Psychoanalysis in France* (New York: International Universities Press, 1980), 8; and Nicolas Abraham and Maria Torok, *The Shell and the Kernel: Renewals of Psychoanalysis*, Vol. 1, ed. and trans. Nicholas T. Rand (Chicago and London: University of Chicago Press, 1994). Derrida says of endocryptic identification that it 'seals the loss of the object but marks the refusal to mourn'; see Jacques Derrida, '"Fors": The Anguish Words of Nicolas Abraham and Maria Torok', in Nicolas Abraham and Maria Torok, eds, *The Wolf Man's Magic Word: A Cryptonomy* (Minnesota: University of Minnesota Press, 1986).

19. Abraham and Torok, *Shell*, 181.

20. Lebovici and Widlocher, *Psychoanalysis*, 6.

21. Mridu Rai, *Hindu Rulers, Muslim Subjects: Islam, Rights and the History of Kashmir* (Delhi: Permanent Black, 2004), 224; see also Stadtler, 'Terror', 199.

22. W. B. Yeats, 'Among School Children', in Richard J. Finneran, ed., *The Collected Poems of W. B. Yeats* (Basingstoke: Macmillan, 1983), 215–217.

Contributors

Rehana Ahmed is Lecturer in English Studies at Teesside University where she teaches modern and contemporary literature. She is the editor of *Walking a Tightrope: New Writing from Asian Britain* (Young Picador, 2004), the co-editor of *South Asian Resistances in Britain, 1858–1947* (Continuum, 2011) and the author of a range of articles on British Asian literature, culture and history. Her primary interest is in South Asian British Muslim fiction, and she is currently writing a monograph on this subject which will be published by Manchester University Press.

Kristy Butler was raised in Monument, Colorado, and is currently a doctoral candidate at Mary Immaculate College, University of Limerick, in Limerick, Ireland, where she also received her MA in Modern English Literature in 2010. Her thesis is entitled 'War of the Words: Invasion, Colonization and the Political Gothic', and her research interests include intertextuality, cultural theory and Gothic studies.

Claire Chambers is Senior Lecturer at Leeds Metropolitan University, where she teaches contemporary writing in English from South Asia, the Arab world and their diasporas. She is the author of *British Muslim Fictions: Interviews with Contemporary Writers*. Next she will write a monograph entitled *Literary Representations of British Muslims, 1966–Present*. Both texts in this two-book series are published by Palgrave Macmillan, and supported by funding from the British Academy and Arts and Humanities Research Council. She has also published widely in such journals as *Postcolonial Text* and *Contemporary Women's Writing*, and is co-editor of the *Journal of Commonwealth Literature*.

Anna Hartnell is Lecturer in Contemporary Literature at Birkbeck, University of London, where she convenes the MA in Contemporary Literature and Culture. Her research has focused primarily on contemporary literary and cultural constructions of 'America', and has been particularly concerned with the ways in which the national narrative is articulated in relation to race and religion, as well as its intersections with postcoloniality and globalization. She is the author of *Rewriting Exodus: American Futures from Du Bois to Obama* (Pluto, 2011).

Salah D. Hassan is Associate Professor in the Department of English and core faculty in the Muslim Studies Program at Michigan State University. His research projects have recently been oriented around the representation of Arabs and Muslims in the media and also projects of self-representation. He is co-coordinator of the project Islam, Muslims and Journalism Education (IMAJE), co-curated RASHID & ROSETTA, an international online art exhibit on the theme of the Rosetta Stone, and is the co-producer of the documentary film *The Death of an Imam*. He is completing a book manuscript tentatively titled *Palestine in Theory*.

Anshuman A. Mondal is Reader in English at Brunel University. He is the author of *Nationalism and Post-Colonial Identity: Culture and Ideology in India and Egypt* (RoutledgeCurzon, 2003), *Amitav Ghosh* (Manchester University Press, 2007) and *Young British Muslim Voices* (Greenwood, 2008). He has published widely on Muslim-related issues, including 'Multiculturalism and Islam: Some Thoughts on a Difficult Relationship', *Moving Worlds: A Journal of Transcultural Writings* 8.1 (2008) and several pieces of journalism in the current-affairs magazine *Prospect* and the *Guardian*'s Comment is Free. He is currently writing a book on Muslim-related freedom of speech controversies.

Lindsey Moore is Lecturer in English Literature at Lancaster University. Her research focuses on Arab women's writing and visual media, and on postcolonial women's writing more broadly. Her publications include the monograph *Arab, Muslim, Woman: Voice and Vision in Postcolonial Literature and Film* (Routledge, 2008); special issues of the *Journal of Commonwealth Literature* ('Glocal Diasporas') and *Postcolonial Text* ('Glocal Imaginaries'); and several articles on Arab writing. She was Principal Investigator on the AHRC-funded project 'Islamism in Arab Fiction and Film, 1947 to the Present' (2009–2010).

Bart Moore-Gilbert is Professor of Postcolonial Studies and English at Goldsmiths, University of London. He is the author of *Kipling and 'Orientalism'* (1986), *Postcolonial Theory: Contexts, Practices, Politics* (1997), *Hanif Kureishi* (2001) and *Postcolonial Life-Writing: Culture, Politics and Self-Representation* (2009). He has also written numerous articles and chapters in books on colonial and postcolonial literature and theory. He is currently writing a monograph on Palestine and postcolonialism.

Peter Morey is Reader in English at the University of East London. He is the author of numerous essays and chapters on postcolonial literature, as well as the books, *Fictions of India: Narrative and Power* (2000) and *Rohinton Mistry* (2004). He was co-editor of, and contributor to *Alternative Indias: Writing, Nation and Communalism* (2006). More recently he has been Principal Investigator for the AHRC-funded Framing Muslims International Research Network, has co-edited a special issue of the journal *Interventions* on the representation of Muslims, and (with Amina Yaqin) is the author of *Framing Muslims: Stereotyping and Representation after 9/11* (2011).

Stephen Morton is Senior Lecturer in English in the Faculty of Humanities at the University of Southampton. His publications include *Gayatri Spivak: Ethics, Subjectivity and the Critique of Postcolonial Reason* (Polity, 2007), *Salman Rushdie: Fictions of Postcolonial Modernity* (Palgrave Macmillan, 2008), *Gayatri Chakravorty Spivak* (Routledge, 2003), *Terror and the Postcolonial*, co-edited with Elleke Boehmer (Blackwell, 2009), *Foucault in an Age of Terror*, co-edited with Stephen Bygrave (Palgrave, 2008), and articles in *Textual Practice*, *Parallax*, *Interventions*, *Wasafiri*, *Public Culture* and *New Formations*.

Ruvani Ranasinha is Senior Lecturer in Postcolonial Literature at King's College London. She is the author of *Hanif Kureishi* (Northcote House in association with The British Council, 2002) and *South Asian Writers in Twentieth-Century Britain: Culture in Translation* (Oxford University Press, 2007). She has published widely on the cultural representation of diasporic Muslim identity, most recently in the volume *Thinking Through Islamophobia*, edited by Salman Sayyid and Abdoolkarim Vakil (Hurst, 2011). She is the lead editor of *South Asians and the Shaping of Britain, 1870–1950: A Sourcebook* (with Rehana Ahmed, Florian Stadtler and Sumita Mukherjee; Manchester University Press, forthcoming).

Sara Upstone is Principal Lecturer in English Literature at Kingston University, London, where she specializes in contemporary British and postcolonial literature. She is the author of two books, *Spatial Politics in the Postcolonial Novel* (Ashgate, 2009) and *British Asian Fiction: Twenty-First-Century Voices* (Manchester University Press, 2010). She is currently researching the role of literary form and genre in contemporary Black British writing.

Amina Yaqin is Senior Lecturer in Urdu and Postcolonial Studies and Chair of the Centre for the Study of Pakistan at the School of Oriental and African Studies (University of London). She has recently co-authored (with Peter Morey) *Framing Muslims: Stereotyping and Representation after 9/11* (Harvard University Press, 2011) and co-edited a special issue of *Interventions* entitled, 'Muslims in the Frame', 12.2 (July 2010). She is currently working on her next project, entitled *Imagining Pakistan*.

Index